THE FIRST LADY
OF WORLD WAR II

THE
FIRST LADY
OF
WORLD WAR II

Eleanor Roosevelt's
Daring Journey to the
Frontlines and Back

SHANNON McKENNA SCHMIDT

Copyright © 2023, 2024 by Shannon McKenna Schmidt
Cover and internal design © 2024 by Sourcebooks
Cover design by Ploy Siripant
Cover and internal images © Bettmann/Contributor/Getty
Images, WorldPhotos/Alamy, pics five/Shutterstock.com
Internal design by Ashley Holstrom/Sourcebooks

Published by Sourcebooks
P.O. Box 4410, Naperville, Illinois 60567–4410
(630) 961-3900
sourcebooks.com

Cataloging-in-Publication Data is on file with the Library of Congress.

Printed and bound in the United States of America.
SB 10 9 8 7 6 5 4 3 2 1

To travelers and trailblazers, and to all those who follow in the paths Eleanor paved.

CONTENTS

Prologue   ix

PART I: THE SOUTH PACIFIC

Chapter 1: The Nearest Thing to Heaven   1
New York to San Francisco

Chapter 2: Rise Above These Fears   17
San Francisco to Honolulu

Chapter 3: Island of Forgotten Men   29
Christmas Island

Chapter 4: Pacific Flight 321   45
Penrhyn Island, Bora Bora, Aitutaki, Tutuila, and Viti Levu

Chapter 5: No Place for You, Ma'am   67
New Caledonia

PART II: NEW ZEALAND AND AUSTRALIA

Chapter 6: News to Us   85
Auckland, New Zealand

Chapter 7: A Modern Crusader   99
Wellington, New Zealand

Chapter 8: More Than All the Guns, Planes, and Tanks 115
Rotorua, New Zealand

Chapter 9: Like Mushrooms in the Jungle   127
    Auckland, New Zealand

Chapter 10: No Frail Flower   133
    Canberra and Melbourne, Australia

Chapter 11: Womanpower   151
    Melbourne and Sydney, Australia

Chapter 12: The Heroism and the Horror   167
    Rockhampton, Townsville, Mackay, Cairns,
    and Brisbane, Australia

PART III: GUADALCANAL

Chapter 13: Morale Wins Wars   191
    New Caledonia, Efate, and Espiritu Santo

Chapter 14: Rest in Peace   203
    Guadalcanal

Chapter 15: The Real Tragedy   217
    Espiritu Santo, Wallis Island, Christmas Island,
    and Honolulu

Epilogue   235

Acknowledgments   241
Source Notes   243
Notes   255
Index   305
About the Author   317

PROLOGUE

Seated in the dark, freezing bomb bay of a heavily gunned U.S. Navy bomber, First Lady Eleanor Roosevelt finally arrived on Guadalcanal in the South Pacific in 1943. The island had been hard-won by American-led forces earlier that year, wrested from Japan's control after a grueling six-month fight. Eleanor determinedly stepped from the plane, ready to witness the wreckage of war. She emerged into the sunlight, enveloped in the tropical heat, to find a place of extremes—thick mud in the rainy season, and now the climate so dry that the bluish-gray hue of her Red Cross uniform was soon obscured by clinging dust. Operating on little sleep, she had less than twenty-four hours to honor the fallen and to experience what servicemen's lives were like as they held guard in this strange, dangerous world where war had taken them.

Eleanor had waged a determined personal campaign to visit Guadalcanal, surmounting the resistance of U.S. military commanders and of the commander in chief, who feared for her safety. Japanese soldiers were rumored to be hiding out on the far side of the island, and it was still a target of enemy air attacks.

By the time Eleanor reached Guadalcanal, she had already

traveled more than seventeen thousand miles during an arduous five-week tour of the Pacific theater. Now, a further test of endurance awaited the fifty-eight-year-old First Lady on the battle-scarred island.

———

When Franklin D. Roosevelt won the presidential election in 1932, Eleanor was well established as a writer, educator, traveler, and political advocate. Although she supported her husband's desire to be president, she was fearful of having her identity absorbed into the customary role of First Lady. Traditionally First Ladies were discreet figures in the presidential background, overseeing social functions and taking no active part in public life. She dreaded becoming "a prisoner in the White House, with nothing to do except stand in line and receive visitors and preside over official dinners." So concerned was she about losing her independence, she considered divorcing Franklin rather than become First Lady.

"I had watched Mrs. Theodore Roosevelt and had seen what it meant to be the wife of a president, and I cannot say that I was pleased at the prospect," Eleanor admitted.

Instead she tossed tradition aside as the nation, "unaccustomed to First Ladies darting about, watched her with mingled admiration and alarm." Gas station attendants on the road between New York and Washington, DC, kept an eye out for her famous blue roadster, while a man in Maine refused to believe she was the president's wife because she drove her own car. A couple from Atlanta telegrammed the president, demanding "MR. PRESIDENT WOULD YOU PLEASE SUGGEST THAT MRS. ROOSEVELT CONFINE HER DUTIES MORE TO THE WHITE HOUSE."

But it was outside the White House where Eleanor decided that she could best help her husband, by being his "listening post." It was vital, she believed, for politicians, and especially the president, to keep in touch with public opinion, "the moving force in a democracy." In the self-made role, which fueled her strong sense of social responsibility and satisfied her wanderlust, Eleanor ceaselessly crisscrossed the country giving speeches and inspecting New Deal initiatives. She visited factories, schools, hospitals, homesteads, and migrant camps. Everywhere she asked people what they thought and what they needed, information that aided the president and his policy advisers. "I want to know the whole country," she said, "not a little part of it."

And she meant it. In May 1935, Americans opened their newspapers to find out their First Lady had explored a coal mine. Beneath the hills in rural Ohio, she descended two and a half miles through subterranean passageways. Wearing a large gray coat over her dress and a lighted cap atop her head, she rode in the front car of an electric-powered train used to transport coal from the depths of the mine to the surface. A longtime advocate for the rights of coal miners and other workers, she seized this chance to learn about their livelihood firsthand and exercise her firm belief that in order "to understand people and their problems she must understand their work and environment." Eleanor spent an hour and a half underground. She saw how coal was mined, entering a chamber where minutes earlier coal had been blasted from the walls, and discussed wages and working conditions with hundreds of miners.

Dubbed a "reporter at large for the White House," Eleanor sometimes traveled at her husband's request. The year after taking office, he sent her on a precedent-breaking trip to the Caribbean, primarily to investigate labor and living conditions in Puerto Rico. She was already on record as the first president's wife to travel by air, and this flying trip over water enhanced her reputation as fearless and unconventional. The next month, she was featured on the cover of a general interest magazine as "America's Most Traveled First Lady." During her inaugural year, Eleanor logged a remarkable forty thousand miles, a feat she averaged annually over the next decade. A reporter who accompanied the First Lady to Puerto Rico noted in the corresponding magazine article, "More than any woman who ever lived in the White House she has succeeded in being herself despite its taboos."

"You know my Missus gets around a lot," Franklin boasted in a cabinet meeting. "She's got great talent with people."

But America is not always accepting of First Ladies who do not conform to type, and Eleanor sharply divided public opinion. "Mrs. Franklin D. Roosevelt probably is the target of more adverse criticism and the object of more praise than any other woman in American history," concluded the *New York Times* on the results of a Gallup poll conducted shortly after she returned from Great Britain during World War II. The criticism most frequently given by poll respondents was that she was "too much in the public eye" and that "she ought to stay at home, where a wife belongs." With about equal frequency came approval of the fact that "she has a personality of her own" and that she "doesn't allow herself just to sit at home and do nothing."

In October 1942, Eleanor traveled to Great Britain, another landmark occasion. No other First Lady before her had journeyed abroad on her own *or* flown across the Atlantic, where German planes and submarines now stalked the skies and seas. She secretly flew in a fixed-wing seaplane to an airport on the coast of Ireland, using the assumed name "Mrs. Smith."

Eleanor surfaced at London's Paddington Station, where a red carpet was rolled out for her arrival, and on hand to greet her were King George VI and Queen Elizabeth and a throng of reporters and curious onlookers. Eleanor spent nearly a month in Great Britain, seeing how women were contributing to the country's war effort and visiting the U.S. troops stationed there. Prime Minister Winston Churchill was duly impressed with the way she charmed and bolstered the British people, telling her afterward, "You certainly have left golden footprints behind you." Eleanor's tour through Great Britain was hailed as "an event of great historic importance" and "the most unconventional and dramatic act of an unconventional and dramatic career."

Less than a year later, Eleanor was poised to top even that undertaking. While ascending together in the cage-style, wood-paneled elevator in the family quarters at the White House, Franklin said to her, "I think it would be well if you were to go to Australia, New Zealand, and the Pacific Islands."

Eleanor immediately responded, "When?"

———

In times of crisis, whether personal or professional, Eleanor's solution had always been to work harder and to push herself more. A journey to the Pacific theater, where the United States and other Allied nations had been at war with Japan since the bombing of Pearl Harbor nearly two years earlier, would come at a great personal sacrifice, demanding more of her than even the trip to Great Britain. It required fortitude and courage, exactly the kind of wartime task she craved. She would log some 25,000 miles, a distance roughly equal to the Earth's circumference. She would be on the road longer than ever before, traveling farther and at a faster pace, covering more ground, enduring more discomforts, and facing danger.

Eleanor insisted that her itinerary include the island of Guadalcanal, where Allied forces had successfully launched the first major offensive against the Japanese earlier that year and which was still in the enemy's sights. To her and to many other Americans who closely followed news of the harrowing, arduous fight, Guadalcanal was "a symbol of the war in the southwest Pacific" and represented the immense suffering and sacrifices being made by "our boys."

Despite Eleanor's desire to make the trip, she prepared for the top secret mission with a heavy mind and heart. She was continually a lightning rod for criticism, and that summer in 1943, the personal attacks on her were particularly virulent. In late June, racial tensions in Detroit had escalated into a two-day riot that left thirty-four people dead, the majority of them Black. Although Eleanor had warned of increasing hostilities, driven by a sharp population increase as people flocked north for defense industry jobs in a segregated city with inadequate housing and other shortages, critics in both the north and the south laid blame on her. Eleanor was accused of stirring discord by advocating civil rights and practicing social equality at the White House. Her actions contributed to "the growing impudence and insolence of [Detroit's] Negro population," proclaimed one Mississippi newspaper, adding, "Blood on your hands, Mrs. Roosevelt!" Concerned that the political fallout was damaging to the president, some government officials thought that Eleanor's leaving the country for the Pacific could help defuse the situation.

In addition, Eleanor's travels were a constant source of critique for her detractors. Two weeks before her scheduled departure in mid-August, a major newspaper ran a story about the copious letters the Office of Defense Transportation received from disgruntled citizens protesting the First Lady's other travels. Many of the correspondents asserted that they would "stay at home when Mrs. Roosevelt does," defying the government office's guidelines for essential travel only due to space limitations on trains and a gasoline shortage.

However, Eleanor and the White House believed the trip could help reinvigorate the home front and revive the strong sense of national unity that existed in the dark, shocking days after Pearl Harbor. In Eleanor's view, people were overly optimistic about the war, which was turning in the Allies' favor in both Europe and the Pacific. The tide of the war had turned in large part because of the

United States' rapid, steady turnout of planes, ships, and armaments. But this momentum could be lost, as Americans at home were becoming dangerously complacent. Any slackening in production risked the war's outcome and the lives of the men on distant battle-fields, fighting to keep war off the country's doorstep.

Most American civilians were far removed from the realities of conflict. Shielded by the government from even seeing graphic photos of fallen servicemen, they were losing sight of the bigger picture, sadly falling back on historic battle lines within the country. A month before the riots in Detroit, twenty-five thousand white workers at a city plant that manufactured engines for bombers and PT boats staged an unauthorized, weeklong walkout to protest the promotion of three Black employees. Elsewhere, nearly two thousand strikes over labor and management issues, along with racial disputes, took place in the first half of the year at coal mines, shipyards, textile mills, and factories across the nation, impacting the flow of critically needed war supplies to the troops. Eleanor's journey to the South Pacific would link the fighting front and the home front, reminding the letter writers, the strikers, and others that the stakes were high and victory far from certain.

As Eleanor knew from her tour of Great Britain, traveling through the Pacific theater would cost her deeply, both physically and mentally. Viewing firsthand the destructiveness of war and the exorbitant human cost it exacted is difficult for even the most decorated soldiers and battle-hardened generals. Still, she was compelled to undertake the journey, driven by an enormous sense of responsibility, particularly toward the young generation being sent into battle, and by an ever-present spirit of adventure. "They say I shall be uncomfortable at times on this trip, and it does not worry me at all," said Eleanor. "If our boys can stand it for months and in some cases it has already been almost two years, I think that I shall be much too interested to notice any discomfort."

MONGOLIA
MANCHUKUO
(KURIL IS.)
(Jap.)
GOBI OR SHAMO
(DESERT)
Hsinking
Harbin
Vladivostok
HOKKAIDO
GREAT KHINGAN M.
Mukden
Hakodate
Ominato
INNER
MONGOLIA
Peiping
Dairen
(Jap.)
CHOSEN
Keijo
HONSHU
Tientsin
Hwang
Sian
Tsingtao
Keishu
Kyoto
Tokyo
Ho
Yokohama
Lanchow
YELLOW
Sasebo
Kobe
Osaka
CHINA
Nanking Nagasaki
KYUSHU
Chungking
Sea
Shanghai
Yangtze Kiang
Changsha
Hankow
RYUKYU IS.
OGASAWARA JIMA
(Jap.)
Foochow
Kunming
Canton
TAIWAN
(FORMOSA)
(Jap.)
HONG KONG (Br.)
Kwangchowan (Fr.)
Hanoi
Aparri
LUZON
MARIANAS IS.
(Jap. Mand.)
FRENCH
THAILAND
(SIAM)
Bangkok
Manila
PHILIPPINE
IS.
(Legaspi)
GUAM
(U.S.A.)
INDOCHINA
Saigon
(U.S.A.)
PALAU IS.
YAP
Gulf of
Siam
Davao
MINDANAO
CAROLINE ISLANDS
TRUK IS.
(Jap. Mand.)
PONAPE
MALAY
STATES
(Br.)
BR. N. BORNEO
Brunei
(Br.)
Sandakan
Singapore
SARAWAK
(Br.)
Kuching
HALMAHERA
SUMATRA
(Neth.)
Palembang
BORNEO
(Neth.)
CELEBES
(Neth.)
AMBOINA
BISMARCK ARCH.
NEW IRELAND
TERR. OF NEW GUINEA
(Aust) Mand.)
Rabaul
BOUGAINVILLE
SOLOM
YSABEL I.
MALAITA
NETHERLANDS INDIES
NEW GUINEA
PAPUA
(Neth.)
TER
OF PAPUA
(Aust.)
NEW
BRITAIN
Lae
Buna
GUADALCANAL
Batavia
JAVA
(Neth.)
Java Sea
Soerabaja
COCOS IS.
(Br.)
CHRISTMAS
I.
SUNDA IS.
TIMOR
(Neth.)
Arafura Sea
Port
Moresby
NDIAN
Darwin
Gulf of
Carpentaria
Coral Sea
NEW
Broome
Daly Waters
Townsville
NORTH WEST CAPE
GREAT
Alice Springs
EASTERN
Noumea
OCEAN
AUSTRALIA
DESERT
Lake Eyre
Brisbane
LORD HOWE
(Aust.)
Fremantle
Perth
Darling R.
DIVIDING R.
Sydney
CAPE LEEUWIN
Great
Australian Bight
Adelaide
Murray R.
Canberra
Melbourne
Tasman Se
Bass Strait
TASMANIA
Hobart

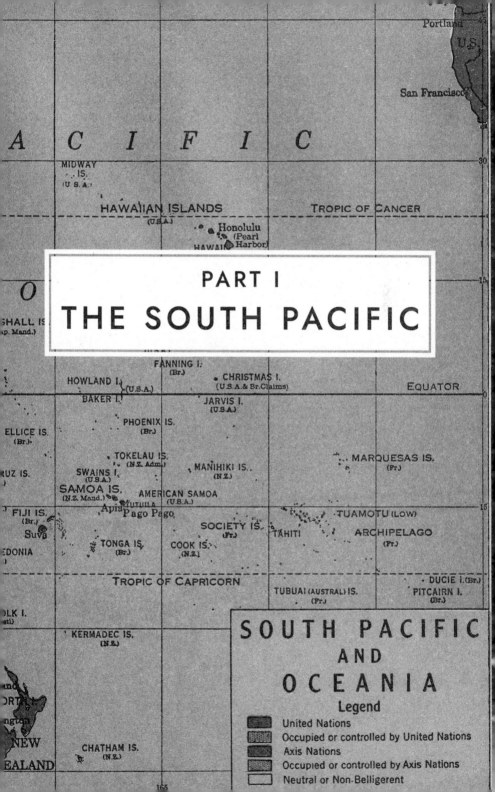

Portland
U.S.
San Francisco

A C I F I C

30

MIDWAY
IS.
(U.S.A.)

HAWAIIAN ISLANDS
(U.S.A.)

TROPIC OF CANCER

Honolulu
(Pearl
Harbor)
HAWAII

15

O

SHALL IS.
p. Mand.)

PART I
THE SOUTH PACIFIC

FANNING I.
(Br.)

HOWLAND I.
(U.S.A.)

CHRISTMAS I.
(U.S.A. & Br.Claims)

EQUATOR

0

BAKER I.

JARVIS I.
(U.S.A.)

ELLICE IS.
(Br.)

PHOENIX IS.
(Br.)

UZ IS.

TOKELAU IS.
(N.Z. Adm.)

MARQUESAS IS.
(Fr.)

SWAINS I.
(U.S.A.)

MANIHIKI IS.
(N.Z.)

SAMOA IS.
(N.Z. Mand.)

Tutuila
AMERICAN SAMOA
(U.S.A.)

15

FIJI IS.
(Br.)

Apia
Pago Pago

TUAMOTU (LOW)

Suva

SOCIETY IS.
(Fr.)

TAHITI

ARCHIPELAGO
(Fr.)

EDONIA

TONGA IS.
(Br.)

COOK IS.
(N.Z.)

TROPIC OF CAPRICORN

DUCIE I.(Br.)

TUBUAI (AUSTRAL) IS.
(Fr.)

PITCAIRN I.
(Br.)

LK I.
tl)

SOUTH PACIFIC
AND
OCEANIA

KERMADEC IS.
(N.Z.)

Legend

nd
ORTH
ngton
NEW
EALAND

CHATHAM IS.
(N.Z.)

165

CHAPTER 1

THE NEAREST THING
TO HEAVEN

"Eleanor Roosevelt [is] America's most unusual woman. She is free of the inhibitions which have relegated wives of previous presidents to mere social and decorative roles. She does what she wants to do and finds time to do it."

—*DAILY TELEGRAPH*, SYDNEY, AUSTRALIA, AUGUST 28, 1943

New York to San Francisco, August 16–17

In August 1943, Eleanor Roosevelt set out from her home in Hyde Park, New York, to begin the long journey to the Pacific theater, striving to keep intact the secret that she was on the move. Although she held regular press conferences while at the White House and detailed her activities in a six-day-a-week, syndicated newspaper column, "My Day," the media was eager to make headlines out of her personal life. When she moved apartments in New York City the year before, journalists and cameramen staked out both the old and new residences and doggedly followed her as she motored downtown. No detail was too small to escape notice, from the kind of car she was driving (a friend's maroon convertible, with several paintings stowed in the back seat) to the first item to emerge from the moving van (a barrel labeled "glass").

Eleanor aired her annoyance about the trivial interest in her personal life. "With all the world news that there is to read, with things of real importance happening, things which may mean that the people of the United States have much to worry about in the near future…certain things seemed to me a little ludicrous yesterday," she admonished in "My Day" after the move. "When I am in New York City, except for official functions, I feel that I am an unofficial person leading a private life."

Despite Eleanor's reproach, the press was persistent. The month before she left for the Pacific, reporters tracked her down at a lakeside ranch in the Nevada mountains. She had joined a friend who was in short-term residence there to obtain a speedy divorce, spending her time hiking, horseback riding, and taking sunrise and moonlight strolls. Eleanor's relaxing getaway, a rare occurrence for her, was interrupted when she was forced to give a press conference and set the record straight after rumors began circulating that her daughter, Anna, was the one seeking a divorce.

Under such intense scrutiny, Eleanor couldn't easily begin her trek to the Pacific unnoticed. As she flew cross-country from New York City to San Francisco for the first leg of the trip, she diverted the media's attention by revealing another secret. "I can now say that the [British] Prime Minister and his daughter, with the other members of his party…were at Hyde Park with us for the past few days," she divulged in "My Day." Winston

Churchill's visit was both a working get-together with President Roosevelt and a brief respite before the two world leaders attended a military conference in Quebec.

For the next ten days, prewritten "My Day" columns listed Eleanor's location as Hyde Park, a short train ride north of New York City. There was some speculation in newsrooms as to why she didn't accompany the president to Quebec, but no reporters delved any deeper. With the press none the wiser, she was in the air and on her way to the Pacific theater.

———

Eleanor first took to the skies in 1929, when she flew twice in a single day. While the First Lady of New York State, she was asked to christen a research plane, a "flying laboratory" owned by an aeronautical instrument company. She accepted the invitation on one condition: no flight, no christening. After pouring a bottle of ginger ale over the glistening propeller of the six-passenger plane, which she named the *Governor*, she went for a twenty-minute ride over Albany while Franklin remained below. Eleanor accepted a second invitation to fly to New York City later that afternoon, although the plane was grounded halfway due to an electrical storm and she proceeded by train.

By this time, the public's enthusiasm for the "flying machine" had been building for a decade, fueled by stunt pilots called "barnstormers," who thrilled with aerial acrobatics, and by speed-setting air races that attracted bigger crowds than baseball games. Then there were daring aviators like Charles Lindbergh, who vaulted from obscurity as a U.S. Air Mail pilot after he completed the first solo, nonstop flight across the Atlantic, and Amelia Earhart, the first woman to accomplish the feat.

As civil aviation expanded, most of those same eager spectators kept their feet firmly planted on the ground. For such an "air-minded" nation, enthralled by the airplane's speed and modernity, few people, even those who could afford the ticket prices, were willing to risk going aloft themselves. Conjecture had established that only the bravest and most athletic people were fit to fly. Although planes had proven to be a relatively safe and reliable mode of transportation, the experience was far from comfortable for travelers. Since airliners were not pressurized, they flew at low altitudes, making them susceptible to battering by the elements, and a plane could drop hundreds of feet in minutes if hit by turbulence. Air sickness was common, and cabin crews often had to speak through megaphones to be heard above the din of the engine and the howling winds.

In 1932, Franklin Roosevelt arrived in dramatic fashion in Chicago to accept the Democratic presidential nomination—by airplane. Traditionally a candidate waited weeks for a formal notification, building in ample travel time to their destination by slower means, and did not address the convention in person. That Franklin showed up there the very next day, accompanied by Eleanor and two of their sons after a nine-hour flight from Albany, made front-page news. Using the technologically advanced transport signaled that a dynamic, forward-thinking new leadership was taking command. The gesture also gave denial to whispers that Franklin's physical condition—he was partially paralyzed due to adult-onset polio—made him unfit for the presidency and that he would be unable to accomplish the duties of the office.

To boost flying, especially among women, who made up only a small percentage of air travelers in the early days, Eleanor allowed her name and likeness to be used in airline industry promotions. A 1939 advertisement featured a color photograph, taken by her son, showing her seated on an airplane next to a curtained window. Wearing a floral-print dress, she appeared relaxed, smiling, with knitting needles in hand and a skein of yard resting in her lap. A tag line declared her the "First Lady of the Land, First Lady of the Air." The ad noted the number of miles she had traveled by plane in the last several years alone— one hundred thousand, today the equivalent of thirty-three cross-country trips—and encouraged others to follow suit and experience "the great boon of wings." Eleanor was often asked if she objected to her children's flying. She tartly replied that they flew frequently, mainly for business and sometimes for pleasure, and that as adults, the decision was theirs to make and not hers.

For Eleanor, traveling by plane was a practicality, a faster means of traversing the country than going by train. Plus it appealed to her adventurous spirit. "If you have never flown you cannot realize what a sense of freedom you have, up above the clouds, beyond the reach of telephone or telegram," she wrote in a magazine article. "Flying is the nearest thing to heaven most of us are likely to experience during our mortal lives." So enthusiastic was Eleanor about flying that she seriously considered becoming a pilot. Two weeks after Franklin was elected president in November 1932, with Eleanor incoming as First Lady, she met Amelia Earhart. When introducing the flying ace at a lecture, Eleanor expressed her admiration, saying, "She has done so many things which I have always wanted to do." Amelia offered to take her on as a pupil and arranged the physical exam needed for a student pilot permit, which Eleanor passed. But she gave up on the lofty goal after Franklin asked her to hold off for his sake and not add to his worries. It was one of the few restrictions he requested of her, and although it disappointed her, she respected his wishes.

While not a pilot herself, Eleanor routinely flew as a passenger and sometimes had occasion to take the controls. After she boarded a friend's small plane in the Hudson Valley, the pilot allowed her to fly the aircraft for a while, following the Hudson River south toward New York City, an experience that gave her "a real sense of exhilaration."

One evening, Eleanor and Amelia skipped out on a White House dinner party, still clad in formal attire, and headed to a nearby airfield. Several reporters were invited along on the flight to Baltimore and back as "the First Lady of the Land and the first woman to fly the [Atlantic Ocean] went skylarking together tonight in a big Condor plane." The outing was arranged to promote the Amateur Air Pilots Association and to help prove to the public that flying was safe. "It does mark an epoch, doesn't it," Eleanor remarked, "when a girl in evening dress and slippers can pilot a plane at night." She rode partway in the cockpit, enchanted by the view. "It was lovely," she recalled. "Out there in front with no obstructions to the view one could see everything and it felt like being on the top of the world."

Eleanor took her first cross-country air trip shortly after officially becoming First Lady in 1933, traveling from Washington, DC, to Los Angeles to visit one of her sons. At the time, transcontinental flights were a test in endurance, taking about twenty hours and involving at least two stops for refueling. On that journey, she was joined by the publisher of the *Fort Worth Star Telegram*, who accompanied her from Texas to the West Coast. "Her rapid air tour," he reported, "twice spanning the continent, was a physical feat calculated to take the 'bounce' out of a transport pilot. But Mrs. Roosevelt came through smiling, having for those who greeted her at every last stop the same vivid graciousness."

Eleanor's adventurous undertaking so impressed cowboy turned entertainer Will Rogers, then the highest paid actor in Hollywood and an enthusiastic supporter of air travel, that he praised her as the new heroine of aviation. "Here is what she really takes the medal for: Out at every stop, day or night, standing for photographs by the hour, being interviewed, talking over the radio, no sleep," he wrote in a letter printed in the *New York Times*. "And yet they say she never showed one sign of weariness or annoyance of any kind. No maid, no secretary—just the first lady of the land on a paid ticket on a regular passenger plane."

———

Ten years later, with the nation at war, Eleanor couldn't avoid being seen entirely while traveling from New York to San Francisco. There was no aircraft available for the First Lady's private use. A bomber converted into a transport plane, named *Guess Where 2*, was designated for the president and outfitted with beds, tables, chairs, and other amenities, but it was sidelined before he ever flew in it due to safety concerns. The *Guess Where 2* was sometimes used by other government officials, and in the summer of 1943, it was ferrying the "Flying Senators," five lawmakers, including James Mead of New York, on a global inspection tour. Even if it were available, Eleanor likely would not have used it anyway. Doing so would invite more criticism of her travels, plus she enjoyed the camaraderie of flying with the public.

After the United States entered World War II, even with all available military planes in operation, there were still shortages for transporting supplies and shifting personnel. As a solution, commercial airlines were asked to work with the military. Civilians were permitted to fly but were subject to strict regulations. They could be bumped from a flight at any time prior to takeoff if someone with a higher priority status claimed the seat, even if it meant they were stranded during a refueling stop.

While heading to San Francisco, Eleanor chatted with an Oregon-based businessman, a representative of pea and bean growers, about the farming industry during a stopover in

Cleveland. At a second stop in Elko, Nevada, the next morning, she talked with a sailor on his way to the Pacific Northwest to report for duty. By this time, her presence on a flight was a common enough occurrence and unlikely to raise suspicion. But if pressed about why she was traveling to California, Eleanor had a ready response that would conceal her true purpose: She was attending a friend's wedding.

Once again, the media missed its chance for a scoop on the First Lady's whereabouts. The day before her arrival in San Francisco, newspapers announced the forthcoming nuptials of ballroom dancer Mayris Chaney and her fiancé, bandleader Hershey Martin. The couple had obtained a marriage license and planned to exchange vows that same week, it was reported, along with the noteworthy fact that the bride was a close friend of Eleanor Roosevelt.

The wedding, arranged to take place while Eleanor was in town, was held at the home of Dr. Margaret Chung, the first American woman of Chinese descent to become a physician. A well-known local personality, Dr. Chung counted among her patients and acquaintances movie stars, politicians, and military leaders. Prior to the United States' official involvement in World War II, she recruited American pilots, known as the Flying Tigers, to join the air force in China, an ally in the Pacific. Once the country went to war, she used her vast network of connections to help pass legislation establishing the WAVES, the U.S. Navy Women's Reserve. Most famously, she created a surrogate family by "adopting" more than one thousand American servicemen, primarily pilots, who affectionately referred to her as "Mom Chung." (Like Eleanor, she was an aviation enthusiast, and she learned to fly a plane.) When asked where her sons were serving, Dr. Chung replied, "They are wherever men are flying and fighting for freedom." From across the world, her sons sent her items that she displayed in a specially designated room in her home: battle-scarred mementos like the control column from a German plane shot down over the English Channel and a Japanese flag captured on Guadalcanal.

Wartime San Francisco was electric with activity. Defense industry employment drew people from across the country in numbers not seen since the Gold Rush a century earlier. Shipyard workers produced vessels at rapid speeds, the sounds of rivet guns and hammer presses echoing day and night. Mom Chung's sons and other uniformed men were everywhere, some serving on the bases and forts ringing the San Francisco Bay and others passing through on their way to duty in the Pacific.

The entire city was transformed into a heavily guarded fortress. Fighter planes screeched across the sky. Patrols guarded bridgeheads, beaches, tunnels, and railroad crossings. Searchlights swept the darkened bay, on alert for an enemy approach, and children were taught to recognize the shapes of Japanese planes. Antiaircraft guns were positioned in the hills overlooking the Golden Gate, a strait leading into the Pacific Ocean and the only way in or out of the bay. Lines of ships, laden with troops and supplies, sailed beneath the iconic reddish-orange bridge bound for the Pacific theater.

Driving across the Golden Gate Bridge after dark, car headlights dimmed by law, Eleanor's destination was Hamilton Army Airfield north of San Francisco. She was dressed in a white collared blouse, a knee-length, grayish-blue skirt, and a matching single-breasted jacket bearing the American Red Cross emblem on the upper left sleeve. An Australian newspaper later described her appearance and attire in detail, down to the color of her eyes, which "are blue, with a smoky tinge, exactly matching the uniform of the American Red Cross which she is wearing throughout her tour."

As soon as the Pacific trip was a possibility, Eleanor met with Norman Davis, chairman of the American Red Cross, and offered to inspect the organization's facilities while she was there. "I hoped in this way to show that I was doing a serious job and not just running around the war area causing trouble," she said. Having planned to send someone to inspect American Red Cross work in the region, Davis readily took Eleanor up on her offer, appointing her a special delegate and providing her with a letter of credentials. He suggested that she wear the organization's uniform and requested that she make a report to him on her return.

Founded by Clara Barton in 1881, the American Red Cross offers help and support during times of disaster and armed conflict. A copyist at a government office in Washington, DC, at the start of the Civil War, Barton gave up her desk duties to transport food, medical supplies, and other provisions to the battlefields, where she nursed and comforted the sick and wounded. Later, while traveling in Europe, she learned about the Red Cross, an international humanitarian organization established in Switzerland, and she volunteered her services when the Franco-Prussian War broke out. Witnessing what the Red Cross was able to facilitate on a massive scale—supplies from across Europe ready for the field and nurses trained for duty—she was aghast that the United States had declined to join the organization in 1864, while the Civil War was underway, thinking of the needless suffering that could have been avoided if such a system had been implemented.

"It is hard to believe that at any time the Red Cross did not exist. How could we feel we were fulfilling our obligations to sick and wounded human beings when this organization was not in existence?" Eleanor asked in "My Day." She was a longtime member and supporter of the Red Cross. During World

War I, she had volunteered in Washington, DC, helping to run a canteen for servicemen at Union Station and overseeing a recreation room at the Naval Hospital.

By wearing the Red Cross uniform while traveling in the Pacific, Eleanor explained, "I would feel easier visiting hospitals and meeting servicemen," for whom the insignia was a familiar and reassuring sight. She knew the trip would inevitably be "attacked as a political gesture," she told her friend Joseph Lash. "I am so uncertain whether or not I am doing the right thing that I will start with a heavy heart." Donning the organization's attire and assuming the task of inspecting its facilities armored Eleanor with an additional layer of validity for being in the Pacific.

Plus, by forgoing all civilian clothing and wearing only the uniforms—seersucker for the tropics and wool for the colder climes in New Zealand and Australia—she reduced the number of items she brought. Adhering to the transport plane's strict luggage limit was especially challenging when it included toting a cumbersome manual typewriter, which she used to write "My Day," wiring the typed copy from the Pacific to her editor in New York.

Eleanor was a practical and self-sufficient traveler, skills honed during hundreds of thousands of miles on the road. Not long before leaving for the Pacific, she spent time with Madame Chiang Kai-shek, the First Lady of China. After a stay at the White House, Madame Chiang embarked on a cross-country train trip to the West Coast and back again, speaking to audiences about the importance of U.S. support for China in the war against Japan. Much to Madame Chiang's amazement, Eleanor and her secretary and traveling companion, Malvina "Tommy" Thompson, packed their own bags, answered their own phones and mail, and declined a security detail. "Tommy and I had taken practically the same trip, following in her footsteps, a few days behind her," recalled Eleanor. "What mystified Madame Chiang was how it was possible for us to travel alone while she had forty people, yet never enough to do the things she needed to have done."

Now, in San Francisco, Eleanor's hands were nearly bare, stripped of adornment except for a gold wedding band. She left her Tiffany diamond engagement ring and other jewelry with Tommy for safekeeping, something she had never done before embarking on her many other trips. "I realize that anything can happen to us at any time, but it gave me a queer feeling, especially as she did not leave them home when she went to Great Britain," Tommy told a friend. Although Eleanor was a seasoned traveler, she was trepidatious enough about the Pacific trip to leave instructions with Tommy on what to do with her jewelry if she didn't return.

Aviation tragedies, even personal ones, never diminished Eleanor's enthusiasm for flying. Two years after Will Rogers penned his laudatory letter about her, he perished on impact when a small plane in which he was traveling with aviator Wiley Post crashed in a lagoon in northern Alaska. Then, in 1937, Eleanor anxiously scanned newspapers for word of Amelia Earhart, who along with her navigator vanished in the South Pacific while on an around-the-world record-setting quest. When plotting her course, Amelia selected tiny Howland Island for a necessary refueling stop as she crossed the Pacific Ocean. (She successfully entreated President Roosevelt to have a runway built there.) The island was two miles long and half a mile wide, and she knew that "such a small spot in the Pacific" would be difficult to see from the air. Contemplating crossing the broad ocean expanse concerned Amelia. "I shall be glad when we have the hazards of its navigation behind us," she admitted.

As days passed with no word of the missing pair, Eleanor understood that her friend must have met a grim fate. "Much as I hate to acknowledge defeat, I think we will have to accept what seems now a certainty that she is added to the list of people who have lost their lives in the interest of adventure and science," Eleanor wrote in "My Day." "She would have it so, I know, and would not regret going."

Navy ships and planes scoured the ocean for signs of Amelia, covering more than 260,000 square miles in the most extensive search mission ever undertaken by the United States. Finally, more than two weeks after the aviator disappeared, an official order was issued: "All search for Earhart terminated."

———

Even with highly experienced pilots, traveling by air through the Pacific for an extended period of time came with risks. The first transoceanic leg of Eleanor's trip alone, from San Francisco to Honolulu, Hawaii, crossed more than two thousand miles of ocean. Some flights never even made it out to sea. In June 1942, a plane taking off from Hamilton Field developed motor trouble. While swinging around to make an emergency landing, it crashed into a hillside, immediately bursting into flames and killing all fourteen men on board. The plane was a four-engine LB-30, the same type of aircraft Eleanor boarded at Hamilton Field that August. She traveled in this plane throughout her trip to the Pacific and back except for instances that necessitated using smaller or more secure aircraft.

The LB-30 was the name given to B-24 bomber exports for Great Britain and France, although the latter country fell to Germany before receiving the requested aircraft. After entering World War II, the United States kept a number of LB-30s, using some as bombers and converting others into acutely needed transport planes. To speed up the production process for the transports, rather than start from scratch, the military modified designs for heavy bombers. Armaments and bombing equipment were eliminated to lighten the load for cargo. A floor was installed through the bomb bay, windows and a door were cut into the sides of the plane, and seats could be added or removed as required.

Eleanor's flight was conducted by the Air Transport Command, a unit formed by the War Department to ferry combat planes to the fighting fronts and to shift aircrews and other high-priority personnel. They also delivered mail and urgently needed materials, such as airplane and radio parts, and for a couple of generals, cigars and wool for uniforms. By mid-1943, the Air Transport Command operated more than ninety thousand miles of routes throughout the world and had an accident rate of one per two hundred planes.

There were inherent safety issues when turning tactical planes into transport aircraft. "An evil bastard contraption" was how one pilot bluntly described another B-24 bomber-to-transport conversion. "It was a ground-loving bitch, and with heavy loads it rolled, snorted, and porpoised interminably before asserting its questionable right to fly," he grumbled. "The failure of any one of the four engines on take-off was an extremely serious affair, a part of which was due to its hasty conversion from bomber to transport." Crews complained about a host of hazards with the fuel system, the engines, and cockpit accessories. Leaking fuel tanks were common and midair fires an ever-lurking danger.

In early 1943, a converted bomber crashed into the ocean while making a final approach at Canton Island, a stop on Eleanor's itinerary. Three months before she set out for the Pacific, another one crashed minutes after takeoff in Mackay, Australia, a rest leave area for servicemen and a place she was also scheduled to visit. All but one of the forty-one troops on board perished. News of the disastrous flight, the worst crash involving a transport aircraft in the southwest Pacific during the war, was kept under wraps by the military to safeguard morale. Also kept under wraps was an incident at the Auckland, New Zealand, airport a mere month before Eleanor arrived, when a transport taking Japanese diplomats and their families to be exchanged for Allied prisoners of war crashed in the nearby hills shortly after takeoff.

Typically, Tommy traveled with the First Lady, as she had when Eleanor visited Great Britain the year before. This time, Eleanor hoped to avoid some of the criticism that resulted from that trip "by taking up as little room as possible." She journeyed to Honolulu, as she did throughout the trip, on a regular transport flight, sharing space with supplies and sacks of mail.

The only concession was a small bed installed so that Eleanor had a place to rest, and instead it was most often used for storage. The plane's six-man crew was captained by Roy Pickering, a former barnstormer and commercial airline pilot who began flying as a teenager. Another crew being transferred to Honolulu was also aboard the flight from San Francisco. One told the First Lady he attended college near Hyde Park, and another, in high school at the time, went to meet her at a speech she gave in Oklahoma.

Compared to the commercial airliners Eleanor routinely flew in, the transport plane was bare bones. The space was rustic, with exposed metal, loud and rumbling, and the temperature was frigid. She added a removable, scarlet-colored flannel lining to her Red Cross–issued overcoat and slept in it for warmth. Eleanor was incredibly tolerant of the discomforts of travel, whether overnighting in airplane seats or standing on crowded trains. Instead she was usually swept up in the excitement, especially during a journey as momentous as this one.

As Eleanor awaited takeoff at the San Francisco–area airfield, she was beset by mixed emotions. A wave of loneliness washed over her, knowing she would be cut off from her loved ones for weeks. And yet it was also an undeniably dramatic moment, nearing midnight as the city faded in the distance and the plane headed out over the vast, dark expanse of the Pacific Ocean.

CHAPTER 2

RISE ABOVE
THESE FEARS

"You don't want to go to war... I don't want to go to war. But war may come to us."

**—ELEANOR ROOSEVELT, ADDRESSING
A PACIFIST YOUTH GROUP, 1940**

San Francisco to Honolulu, August 17–18

Throughout the 1930s, with conflicts brewing in Europe and the Pacific, President Roosevelt began building up the country's armed forces. His edict to strengthen the navy in particular stemmed from his anxiety about Japan, whose leadership viewed the United States—which had economic interests and a military presence in the Pacific—as the impediment to its domination of the region. He believed war with Japan was likely inevitable, and in 1940, he ordered the U.S. Pacific Fleet moved to Hawaii. That move, on top of decades of reinforcing the military presence at Pearl Harbor and the adjoining areas in Honolulu, created a formidable center of sea and air power.

"Hawaii is today about as impregnable a fortress as human ingenuity can make it," Samuel W. King, the territory's delegate in the U.S. House of Representatives, asserted in a speech on May 29, 1941.

In addition to touting Hawaii's attributes as a defensive outpost, King painted a vivid picture of the exotic destination. He described "a beautiful land of great mountains, deep valleys, and high plateaus—of beaches and coves and rugged cliffs. Above all, it is a green land—hillsides and valleys and coastal plains alike verdure covered all the year 'round. It is a grand place to play, to loaf, or to work." Matson Lines put Hawaii on the tourist map in the 1920s and '30s, cruising adventurers from San Francisco across the Pacific Ocean, followed in 1936 by Pan American with its faster and thrilling seaplane flights. Despite rising political tensions in the region, the Hawaii Tourist Bureau continued to promote America's "Paradise of the Pacific" throughout 1941. December issues of *Good Housekeeping*, *National Geographic*, and other popular magazines, carrying enticing color advertisements encouraging travel to "enchanting" Hawaii, were on newsstands when Pearl Harbor was bombed on the morning of Sunday, December 7.

An attack by Japan in the Pacific came as no surprise to the U.S. government. Secretly intercepted cables written by Japanese diplomats and cracked by code breakers indicated an attack was coming, although where and when was never specified. Diplomatic talks between the two countries were strained but still ongoing up until the time of the devastating strike on Pearl Harbor. President Roosevelt's personal message to Japanese emperor Hirohito the day before, appealing for peace, went unanswered. In a gross miscalculation, military strategists mistakenly believed that a convoy of aircraft carriers could not cross the vast distance to Hawaii undetected and that Japan would initially strike somewhere closer to their home country.

The president formally responded to the bombing of Pearl Harbor on December 8, delivering an afternoon speech—including the now-famous phrase "a date which will live in infamy"—before a joint session of Congress. But Eleanor was actually the first public figure to address the nation after the tragic event. Sunday evening, the same day the attack took place, her weekly radio show, *Over Our Coffee Cups*, was scheduled to broadcast. The First Lady went on the air as planned, giving an update on what was happening behind the scenes in Washington and offering an encouraging message to the American people. Despite "a clutch of fear at your heart," she said, "I hope that the certainty of what we have to meet will make you rise above these fears." She ended the amended introduction by advising listeners that solidarity as a nation was paramount to conquering the threat facing the country. "I feel as though I was standing upon a rock," she said, "and that rock is my faith in my fellow citizens."

Four days later, Germany and Italy declared war on the United States, drawing the country into a two-ocean conflict, with most of Europe already fallen to the Nazis.

———

"Look at your map," President Roosevelt instructed during a radio address to the nation two and a half months after Pearl Harbor. "Follow with me in the references which I shall make to the world-encircling battle lines of this war."

In movie theaters, cafés, kitchens, and living rooms across the United States, some 61.3 million people, nearly 80 percent of the adult population, tuned in to hear the president's talk—part update on the progress of the war and part geography lesson—as he emphasized the conflict's vast scope. "It is warfare in terms of every continent, every island, every sea, every air lane in the world," he told listeners. "We must all understand and face the hard fact that our job now is to fight at distances which extend all the way around the globe."

Eleanor listened to Franklin's address—which was broadcast to the world by short-wave radio in a variety of languages—during a Democratic National Committee dinner at a Washington, DC, hotel, a map spread out on the table in front of her. The president's suggestion that people have a world map or a globe handy while he spoke ignited a buying frenzy. Consumers turned out in droves at retailers like New York City map publisher C. S. Hammond & Co., which stayed open well past its afternoon closing time. Employees darkened the windows and locked the front door several times throughout the day, but resolute map seekers would not be deterred. By nightfall, the shop had sold out of its regular stock plus an additional two thousand copies of a new atlas retrieved from a warehouse and brought by taxi to the store.

That evening, President Roosevelt delivered on his self-imposed promise to be forthright with listeners. Despite some successful strikes by the U.S. Navy against enemy holdings in the Pacific, Japan still firmly had the upper hand. Ultimately, though, the president reassured his audience, "We are daily increasing our strength. Soon, we and not our enemies will have the offensive; we, not they, will win the final battles; and we, not they, will make the final peace."

At the time of the president's talk, the world was in chaos. Nazi forces had marauded across Europe for more than two years and were moving into North Africa. The Japanese had invaded China, had bombed northern Australia, and were striking hard and fast to lay claim to territories across the Pacific. Great Britain surrendered its colony Singapore to the Japanese in what Churchill called "the worst disaster and largest capitulation in British history." General Douglas MacArthur would soon flee the Philippines, with some seventy thousand American and Filipino prisoners of war enduring the Bataan Death March shortly after.

The Atlantic and Pacific oceans, vast buffers that once gave the United States a sense of security, had become "endless battlefields on which we are constantly being challenged by our enemies." Along the United States' Eastern Seaboard, Hitler's U-boats wreaked havoc, targeting oil tankers, merchant vessels, and cargo-passenger ships. Smoke and fire were often visible from the shoreline as the torpedoed ships sank into watery graves. And on the night President Roosevelt asked Americans to consult their maps, residents of southern California heard only half of his speech. A blackout was ordered in the region after a Japanese submarine surfaced off the coast and shelled an oil field near Santa Barbara.

For the next six months, American forces continued to be on the defensive in the Pacific, notwithstanding some crucial success disrupting the enemy's momentum at Midway, the Coral Sea, and other battles. Then a shift began.

Reconnaissance planes spotted an airfield under construction by the Japanese on Guadalcanal, the largest of the Solomon Islands in the South Pacific and roughly eleven hundred miles from Australia. Thwarting Japan's plans to establish a base on Guadalcanal was imperative to keep them from severing communication lines and blocking supply routes to Australia and New Zealand. And if the island was successfully taken, the United States could use it to launch its own operations, beginning a long drive across the Pacific and eventually reaching Tokyo.

In August 1942, Operation Watchtower, the first major Allied offensive against Japan, got underway as forces stealthily approached Guadalcanal. The U.S. Marines landed on the island and swiftly accomplished their primary objective, taking control of the airfield. Nearby, two smaller islands were rapidly seized from the Japanese. Details were scant in the early days of the Solomon Islands campaign, but optimism ran high as newspaper headlines trumpeted the welcome news: "America on the Offensive."

Eleanor and the rest of the nation tracked the progress of the struggle for Guadalcanal, where troops fought on a hellish battlefield. What "looked like a tropical paradise on first arrival," recalled a marine corps surgeon, was a landscape that proved as perilous as enemy weapons. Amid oppressive heat and humidity and near-constant rain, in dense, dark jungles teeming with disease-bearing insects and in valleys with razor-sharp grass, troops withstood relentless enemy bombardments and savage hand-to-hand fighting.

Two months into the fight, President Roosevelt instructed the Joint Chiefs of Staff "to make sure that every possible weapon gets into that area to hold Guadalcanal." He had cause for concern. The initial jubilation surrounding Operation Watchtower waned in the days and weeks that followed as land and sea forces suffered serious setbacks, including one of the worst defeats in U.S. Navy history, which occurred when the Japanese staged a surprise night surface engagement. In one hour, four ships were lost and more than one thousand men perished.

Pessimism was taking root among some military commanders and began seeping into the home front. The navy was too timid, claimed the media, frozen with inaction by the fear of losing more ships. The headlines were blunt: "Jungle Island Becomes the Heart of Great Battle for the Pacific." Morale

was dipping, especially among the marines, who had been fighting continuously for two months on Guadalcanal with scant
supplies and no reinforcements. A change in command in the
region was needed.

Elation abounded across the Pacific fleet and on the home
front when Admiral William F. Halsey was tapped to immediately take charge as commander of the South Pacific Area and
South Pacific Forces. "We got the news: the Old Man had been
made COMSOPAC. I'll never forget it!" said an air combat
officer on Guadalcanal after hearing the news. "One minute we
were too limp with malaria to crawl out of our foxholes; the next,
we were running around whooping like kids."

The American public was already familiar with Admiral
"Bull" Halsey and what he could accomplish. In the bleak,
uncertain days after Pearl Harbor, as fear seared the nation,
military leaders in the Pacific were ordered to "undertake some
aggressive action for effect on general morale." The intent was
to fill headlines with stories of American feats, not Japanese. In
early 1942, in sailed Admiral Halsey, executing the first offensive strikes of the war, successfully targeting enemy installations
in the Marshall and Gilbert Islands with hit-and-run air and
sea raids. "We had been whipped in the attack that opened the
war and had been on the defensive ever since," Halsey later said
of the strikes. "Now the offensive spirit was reestablished; officers and men were bushy-tailed again. So, presently, was the
American public. At last we had been able to answer their row-
eling question, 'Where is the Navy?'"

Known as "a rough, tough fighting man," quick to praise and
to blame when warranted, Halsey was "the sort of a leader men
will follow right to hell and back." His optimism, confidence,
and daring—with the experience and acumen to back it up—
endeared him to the men in his command, inspiring their loyalty

and earning their respect. The admiral's strategy for winning the war was "attacking and not retreating; fighting aggressively instead of defensively." His aggressive stance also appealed to American civilians, who found in "Knock-'em Down Halsey" a wartime hero who gave them hope. "I like your seagoing looks and the manner in which you fight," an admirer wrote to the sixty-one-year-old admiral. Solidly built with a weather-beaten face defined by a heavy jaw and piercing blue eyes, Halsey looked rugged, ready for a brawl, like a man who would follow through on his tough talk.

With the Solomons campaign at grave risk of unraveling, Admiral Halsey took over the "Navy's toughest command." Immediately, he devised a plan to reinforce the marines on Guadalcanal and to break Japanese dominance of the sea, stopping the enemy's steady flow of replacement troops from reaching the island.

As the fighting continued into 1943, the public's desire for information kept pace. On New Year's Day, reporter Richard Tregaskis, one of two journalists to witness the marines' invasion of the island, published *Guadalcanal Diary*, which became an instant bestseller. The book offered readers a firsthand account of the action in the swamps, jungles, and hills on ground the Japanese called "Death Island."

News outlets continued to report daily on the progress of the fighting on Guadalcanal. Correspondents dodged bombs and bullets to send dispatches from the front lines. *Time* featured on its cover Major General Alexander Vandegrift, commander of the marine ground forces. *Life* published letters Vandegrift sent to his wife, penned every few days amid the combat on Guadalcanal and published while the action was ongoing.

"Some of my men were lost. They were such fine men, these boys. Even though we get ten Japs to one, that is still too high a price," he wrote the day there was an increase in enemy bombing attacks. On another occasion, Vandegrift lost twenty-eight men. The boys were restless when nothing was going on, he relayed, "but when there is a job to do, they fight like young demons." At the same time, the navy was dueling on the surrounding seas, while a combination of army, navy, and marine airpower roared overhead, "doing a superb job and licking hell" out of the enemy. "When you see these boys go up and know what they are doing, it makes you proud to have them with you."

Finally, in February, after six months of unfathomable hardship and death, it was announced, "Foe Quits Island." By the time the clashes concluded, the Solomon Islands campaign had claimed the lives of some seventy-one hundred Allied servicemen.

———

Eleanor met many of the men wounded on Guadalcanal during visits to West Coast hospitals. Hearing their harrowing stories heightened her determination to visit there on her trip to the Pacific theater. But she faced a daunting obstacle in adding the island to her itinerary: her husband, the president. Although ground combat had ceased, Guadalcanal was still on the front lines and enduring enemy bombardment. Just two months before Eleanor's departure for the Pacific, Japan made an aggressive, ill-fated night raid to reclaim Guadalcanal, losing ninety-four planes in the attempt. Franklin was in favor of her making the trip but understandably reluctant to have her put directly in harm's way. She bluntly informed her husband that it would be difficult for her to continue visiting the wounded if, "when I was to be in the Pacific area anyway, I were not permitted to visit the places where these men had left their health or received their injuries."

The couple's son James, who helped lead a raid on Makin Island during the Solomons campaign, rallied on his mother's behalf to help convince Franklin that a visit there was viable. And Eleanor learned that two friends, Joseph Lash and Cecil Peterson, were stationed on Guadalcanal with the army air forces, giving a stop there even greater significance. "So you too join the ranks of those who will remember the Island you are now on," Eleanor wrote to Joe. "I only hope they let me go there."

Eleanor stood her ground, believing it was essential that she get to Guadalcanal. She persuaded Franklin to leave the final decision to the commanders on the ground. When she left Hyde Park, setting out for the Pacific, tucked in her luggage were letters from the president addressed to the commanding officers in the region stating that he was willing to have her go to Guadalcanal "if it did not interfere with the conduct of the war."

———

As Eleanor prepared to leave Hyde Park, a flurry of activity was taking place six thousand miles away. On Bora Bora and other islands strung across the South Seas, U.S. Navy officers arrived by air hand-delivering instructions marked "super secret." The high-security couriers came bearing orders from Admiral Halsey, who directed each outpost to get ready to receive an army transport plane carrying a "most distinguished United States female passenger."

Arrangements for receiving and accommodating the passenger needed to be handled with the utmost secrecy, warned the admiral, and information was limited to those who absolutely needed to know. Airtight provisions for security and safety were to be made using all available resources not employed in military operations. Halsey forbade the use of the passenger's name in print and issued a stern warning after two Red Cross directors violated the instructions. "Intercept any such further messages," he commanded. Halsey was taking no chances with the First

Lady's safety while she was in the Pacific theater or risking any leaks about where she was headed.

As Eleanor's plane neared Hawaii, she watched the sky color into a brilliant red, the sun rising shortly before touchdown. Eager to point out the sights to the First Lady, a young pilot had her switch seats for a better look as Pearl Harbor came into view. Located on the southern end of the island of Oahu, the harbor was called *wai momi*, or "pearl waters," by the Hawaiians for the pearl oysters that once grew there.

Large and landlocked, with only a slender entrance opening into the Pacific, Pearl Harbor was thought to be ideal for sheltering a fleet of ships, one of the features that attracted the notice of early naval officers visiting Hawaii. Nothing but ocean lay between there and the West Coast of the United States, which had sought to control access to Hawaii by making it a territory in 1900, rather than risk being exposed to attack should another country lay claim to it.

When Eleanor landed in Honolulu, her whereabouts were still under wraps. "My stop was very hush hush and they tried to let no one see me, so I felt very important, mysterious, and unreal," she wrote in a diary she kept while in the Pacific, addressed to Tommy and shared in installments with the president. Immediately after arriving at Hickam Field, headquarters of the Hawaiian Air Force and adjacent to the naval base at Pearl Harbor, Eleanor was spirited by car to a general's home for a breakfast gathering attended by local senior officers in a garden abloom with brightly colored tropical flowers.

Then came a close call that had the navy brass on edge. Several people in attendance asked Eleanor to autograph their "short snorters." Paper currency taped together end to end, short snorters were held and signed by those who had made transoceanic flights. (The name was a slang term for a less-than-full drink.) A mess boy assisting with waitstaff duties who had no short snorter offered up his liberty pass for Eleanor to sign. A tense day ensued when commanding officers realized the autograph seeker had departed right after breakfast on an eight-hour recreation leave. Had he been picked up by the shore patrol, whose primary task was ensuring that servicemen on liberty didn't become too rowdy, and asked to show his pass, news about the First Lady's presence in the Pacific would have been impossible to hide.

After a brief stopover in Honolulu and still incognito, Eleanor was back in the air, heading deeper into a theater of war unlike any other in history—one where fighting took place across great distances on water and in places with harsh, unfamiliar surroundings. As *Life* magazine illustrated to its readers with an aerial view of a globe, the Pacific Ocean sprawls across nearly half the planet, transforming the area into "the vastest single battlefield over which man has ever fought."

CHAPTER 3
ISLAND OF FORGOTTEN MEN

"When you think of your boys out there, remember that for most of them, for the first time in their lives, they are living a Robinson Crusoe life."
—ELEANOR ROOSEVELT, SPEECH TO ROTARY CLUB OF NEW YORK, JANUARY 6, 1944

Christmas Island, August 18–20

Rumors were swirling thick and fast among the servicemen stationed on Christmas Island. Increased patrols and other heightened security measures led to speculation that someone significant was coming to their Pacific outpost. Guesses ranged from a troupe of chorus girls to politician Wendell Willkie, whose book *One World*, recounting his globe-spanning tour meeting with Allied heads of state, soldiers, and citizens, was currently on bestseller lists. Despite anticipating a VIP arrival, "onlookers were first amazed and then astounded" when First

Lady Eleanor Roosevelt emerged from the plane that landed on the white coral runway.

On a world map, like those President Roosevelt asked listeners to have on hand during his radio address in the early days of the war, Christmas Island is a speck in an ocean larger than all the world's land surfaces put together. "I wondered how we ever picked up such a tiny dot, and why the first wave which came along did not wash it away," Eleanor observed. Despite its diminutive size, in the war of "vast distances" the president described in his speech, Christmas Island was a critical link in the chain of island bases connecting the United States with Australia. The coral atoll, some thirty-two miles long and seventeen miles wide, was a refueling stop for aircraft after leaving Honolulu.

As diplomatic relations between the United States and Japan deteriorated, the War Department sought to strengthen its military presence in the Pacific beyond Hawaii and designated the Philippines a top priority. The island nation, a U.S. territory that came under its control after the Spanish-American War in 1898, was nearer to Japan, and it was thought that a buildup of airpower there might serve as a deterrent to war. To achieve this show of might, heavy bombers needed to be flown to the Philippines as soon as they rolled off assembly lines.

With a bomber's long cruising range and ample fuel supply, the fastest and most economical way to move them from place to place was to fly them where they needed to go. (Fighter planes, on the other hand, had a short range and were crated and shipped to the front.) The existing air route from the United States to the Philippines was too risky, since it traversed Japanese-held territory. Seeking a safer alternative, the War Department tasked scouts with identifying islands geographically suited to be used as bases for a path through the South

Pacific. This new route would help ensure a continual flow of equipment and supplies, bring in flight crews and ground personnel, and aid in safeguarding communication lines.

Military and civilian engineers were clearing and grading runways on Christmas Island when they received word that Pearl Harbor had been bombed (followed ten hours later by a crippling attack in the Philippines). Panic ensued on the primarily defenseless island, where a small number of troops were equipped only with rifles and a few machine guns. Rumors that a Japanese submarine was spotted on the edge of a large lagoon that opened to the sea stoked fears even further, and civilian workers clamored for passage off the island. Instead it was locked down, subject to radio silence by War Department decree, and construction crews were ordered to toil around the clock.

By the end of January, one of two runways on Christmas Island was completed and inaugurated the next day when a flight of B-17 bombers landed for refueling. Several weeks later, nearly two centuries after English navigator Captain James Cook sighted the island on Christmas Eve, the SS *President Johnson*, once a mail carrier and then a luxury liner, steamed in from the United States. Along with an army task force of some two thousand men, the ship came bearing thousands of tons of supplies—construction and communication equipment, food and medicine, jeeps and tanks, and fuel and ammunition. "There is nothing there. Everything they eat, everything they wear, every place that they live has to be brought in from the U.S.," explained a naval officer. "There is no such thing as living off the country in the South Pacific, unless you live on coconuts alone."

Most Americans serving overseas during World War II had never been beyond the country's borders prior to entering the military. Fantasies conjured by glamorized book and film versions of a tropical paradise conflicted with the realities of life in the South Seas. "American fighting men in the Pacific live in a strange world," *Life* magazine informed its readers. "On these coral islands they find climate, vegetation and hidden dangers which are strangely different from the temperate, urban civilization at home." Military field guides attempted to guard servicemen against expecting a Hollywood backdrop, telling them, "Some things are as you expected—coral reefs and coconut palms, green jungles and natives whose clothing doesn't cost much." But some things would not be found, for they never existed "outside the imagination of novelists and movie directors. Others the movies never showed—including diseases, smells, and bites." On Christmas Island, even the youngest servicemen told Eleanor that they felt the effects of the climate and lacked energy in the middle of the day. Overall, "Christmas is a healthy place," she reported to Franklin. "I did not feel the heat as there is a breeze most of the time, but you perspire walking around all the time during the day."

The South Pacific islands "are beautiful, there's no denying that," declared a navy lieutenant. "I've seen nothing more poetically beautiful than palm trees silhouetted against a tropical sunset, and the nearest thing to fairyland is the underwater panorama of brilliantly colored coral and fish on the floor of a Pacific bay. But don't let the beauty fool you." His chief complaint was the heat, sometimes so intense that "the sun seems just a few feet over your head instead of astronomical millions." Another gripe was that "thousands of soldiers, sailors and marines have made a diligent search of all the islands under our control without finding Dorothy Lamour." A sultry, dark-haired beauty, Lamour was an actress famous for her portrayals of South Seas heroines clad in her trademark silk sarong.

Further dispelling any idyllic notions were the signs of war everywhere. On Christmas Island, waves washed up against barbed wire strung along miles of beaches. Machine-gun pits were dug in the sand, observation towers rose, shores were patrolled, and a pursuit squadron scouted for the enemy from the air. Troops were constantly on watch but saw little action. Staving off boredom and loneliness and keeping up morale and interest in the work being done were constant challenges. The president specifically asked Eleanor to visit these islands, where servicemen often felt marginalized and distant from the fighting. "Under those circumstances it is hard to feel you are making a vital contribution to the war and it makes all your personal sacrifices harder to bear," she noted.

Here on Christmas Island, their world was restricted to a tiny area occupied solely by male service personnel and a small number of local islanders. A flat expanse, barely rising above sea level, the atoll was surrounded by blue-green water melding into a seemingly endless horizon. Adding to the sense of remoteness, once stationed in the Pacific, servicemen were there indefinitely. Cargo space was prioritized for bringing supplies into the region and for taking the wounded stateside, limiting furloughs home.

Lodgings were canvas tents and huts with waist-high walls camouflaged among groves of coconut trees. One officer turned over his rustic quarters to Eleanor for two nights. "I think the idea that a lady was going to occupy them had not crossed his mind," she wrote in her diary. "He hurriedly re-arranged things and told me how I could have some privacy if I desired, by letting down certain window coverings which ordinarily were left up for the sake of more air." At a handmade table and chairs, with a string-pulled light overhead, she placed her typewriter. Frequent supply shortages and chronic delays inspired ingenuity and resourcefulness among the servicemen, from making their own furniture out of crates and boxes to improvising missing machines parts.

Next Eleanor conquered the vagaries of the "vastly complicated" bathroom plumbing. "I could take a shower and did have running water in a basin and a toilet, all of which I considered great luxury out here," she reported. She didn't mention that it was cold showers only. Whether lodging in a palace or a spartan cabin, Eleanor was enormously adaptable to her surroundings. And she had roughed it before. During summer visits to Theodore Roosevelt's home in Oyster Bay, New York, "Uncle Ted" had taken Eleanor and her cousins on camping trips. Those outings "taught us many valuable lessons," said Eleanor. "The chief one was to remember that camping was a good way to find out people's characters. Those who were selfish showed it very soon, in that they wanted the best bed or the best food and did not want to do their share of the work."

Years later, when Franklin's physical limitations due to polio prohibited him from participating in the outdoor activities he had enjoyed with his older children, Eleanor took on the rugged role. Determined that their two youngest sons would have similar experiences, she set out to become "more of an all-around person than I had ever been before." She learned to ice skate, overcame a long-standing fear of water to master swimming, and took lessons to improve her driving so she could safely go on road trips with the boys. As always, Eleanor's independence and intrepidness didn't sit well with everyone. While journeying through the Adirondack Mountains to the Roosevelt family vacation home on Campobello Island in Canada, she traveled in a seven-passenger Buick with two female friends and several youngsters, including her sons, camping along the way. When no public camping sites were available, Eleanor asked permission to pitch their tents on farmland. "Where are your husbands?" one man demanded to know. "Mine is not with me, and the others do not have husbands," she replied. "I don't want women of that kind," the farmer stated. Eleanor piled her entourage back into the Buick and found somewhere more welcoming to spend the night.

That evening on Christmas Island, Eleanor arrived in time for the much-anticipated entertainment, seeing Betty Grable on-screen. A favorite pinup girl of the armed forces, Grable starred in two feature films that year, the musicals *Coney Island* and *Sweet Rosie O'Grady*, which along with other Hollywood fare were shown on bases and aboard ships in battlefront areas from Iceland to the South Seas. As part of its patriotic war efforts, movie studios shipped, free of charge, new feature films every week to military exchanges throughout the world. The coveted pictures were transported to the troops, even in the most remote reaches, "by plane, boat, trucks, jeep or anything that moves."

Movie sales soared during World War II, with home-front cinemas drawing some ninety million viewers each week. In San Francisco, Detroit, and other places where factories turned out armaments twenty-four hours a day, movies were shown around the clock to accommodate workers regardless of their schedule. For those on the fighting fronts, movies were more than a relaxing diversion after a long factory shift. They were a remedy for battle fatigue and a connection to home. "Training films help to win the war, and entertainment films help morale tremendously," an army major pointed out. "Pictures are the foremost recreation for our troops, and next to mail from home, they are looked forward to by our boys more than anything else."

Improvised movie theaters were mainstays on military bases and often constructed within days of capturing enemy territory. In the tropics, theaters ranged from simple outdoor setups, the darkened jungle skyline as a backdrop, to more elaborate, permanent structures. Some were created simply by stringing a screen between two palm trees, while others had specially made projection booths and thatched stands to hold the screen and shield it from rain. Even a sheet of target cloth tacked to a wall could serve as a movie screen. Seating was often benches made from palm trees, as on Christmas Island, or empty gas barrels or large wire reels turned on end. Hand-lettered signs cheekily welcomed viewers to the Roxy or the Playhouse. "Saw a wonderful show last night. *Sweet Rosie O'Grady*, with Betty Grable," an airman wrote to his fiancée. "We are doing plenty O.K. as far as the cinemas are concerned. I hope it keeps up as it's the best form of relaxation that I know of." Even when tropical showers came down in torrents, if the movie equipment was protected, the men turned up their raincoat collars and sat through the show.

A War Department field manual cautioned, "Rarely is it advisable to close places of entertainment because of the effect on morale and the fact that the men tend to congregate in other places." Pre-movie time and reel-changing breaks were social periods during which attendees would smoke, chat, and "mill about waving and shouting, gossiping and indulging in horseplay." The traditional social nicety of keeping quiet in a theater was upended in these unusual movie-viewing surroundings, as troops admonished on-screen villains and shouted warnings to heroes and heroines. "Here every spectator has a fighting man's right to sound off," said a marine corps officer.

The night Eleanor joined the troops on Christmas Island, they were on their best behavior. "It is to the eternal credit of all the men at the show that throughout the performance not a squawk was heard—a very unusual occurrence." They didn't know that, earlier in the evening, she had barely managed to avoid an outburst during an unsettling incident. Before going to the movie, she returned to her quarters for a handkerchief. Switching on the light in the cabin revealed, to her horror, that

the entire floor was covered with what looked like large red bee-
tles. "I might have screamed if I had not been the only woman
on the Island, and I knew a feminine scream would attract a
good deal of attention," Eleanor admitted to Tommy. Instead
she stamped her feet, the bugs skittering through the cracks
in the floor. After a hasty inspection of her bags and the bed
showed no additional invaders, she retrieved her handkerchief
and calmly continued on to the movie, keeping quiet about the
insect encounter. "I hope no one ever knew how terrified I was
for a few minutes," Eleanor wrote in her diary early the next
morning, logging an entry before setting out for the day.

Even "My Day" readers, who were well aware of Eleanor's
consistently whirlwind schedules, would have been impressed
with what she accomplished on Christmas Island. She undertook
an intensive, marathon inspection, setting the rigorous pace she
would keep throughout the trip. (She had worn out reporters—
and the soles of her shoes—in England the year before. "Mrs.
Roosevelt Finally Gets Tired; Shock to Reporters" announced a
newspaper headline. She stuffed the failing footwear with paper,
refusing to buy new shoes or have repairs done so as not to take
anything away from the strictly rationed British.)

Eleanor's first stop that day on Christmas Island was the
station hospital, a small but functional facility in an abandoned
coconut plantation building. With generators powering the
lights and the X-ray machines, everything from routine dental
work to lifesaving surgeries was performed. A large tent adjacent
to the main medical building accommodated bed patients, the
first of hundreds of sick wards Eleanor walked over the next five
weeks. She made a practice of going bed to bed, asking each man
his name and his hometown and offering sympathetic concern
or a jovial remark.

Fulfilling her pre-trip commitment to Norman Davis,

Eleanor looked over the facilities run by the American Red Cross. During World War II, the organization provided a vast support network for service personnel around the world. One of its monumental tasks was addressing the mental and emotional well-being of the troops—helping to combat boredom and loneliness and keep spirits raised. In cities in New Zealand and Australia, where troops were stationed and others came while on leave from the battle areas, spacious clubs—as well as rest homes for those recuperating from injury or illness—offered an array of amenities along with restaurants and soda fountains, entertainment venues, and overnight accommodations. On the islands, thatched-roof huts housed more modest facilities, while nearer the battle areas, a field director would simply pitch a tent to use as an office.

Thomas S. Montgomery, a Red Cross field director on Guadalcanal, arrived while the fight for the island was still underway, bringing 4,000 books, 2,000 sewing kits, 2,500 toothbrushes, 40,000 sheets of stationery, 15,000 envelopes, 5,000 packs of gum, 1,000 decks of cards, and much more. His short-wave radio drew a crowd, and so did sing-alongs around the piano he had crated and sneaked aboard a ship. He had a coconut grove cleared for a baseball diamond and an unused building turned into a basketball court where tournaments took place in between bombing raids. Three times a week, Montgomery loaded a jeep and drove as far as he could before making his way on foot to frontline foxholes. There he doled out candy, popcorn and, especially popular, chewing tobacco, since the glow of a cigarette in the dark could give away a position to the enemy.

Along with comfort items like candy, chewing gum, and tobacco, the Red Cross supplied necessities. Hospital patients, often brought in from the battlefield without a single possession, were provided with shaving equipment, toothpaste and toothbrush, soap, and other items. "It is strange how values change—money means little for these men who have no way of spending it," explained a Red Cross medical-social worker in the South Pacific. "But a comb or a razor blade rank with the gifts of the Magi."

One of the most important services Red Cross workers rendered was offering counseling and guidance on personal problems. They were a link between servicemen and their families, relaying messages and appeals for assistance on domestic matters to local stateside chapters. "It is not a glamorous job to follow up on a family problem," said Eleanor, "but it makes a world of difference to the soldier so far away from home." And could perhaps save his life, since soldiers anxious about issues at home might be distracted on the battlefield.

Red Cross workers were endlessly versatile, running movie machines, repairing electric generators, planting gardens, serving as card game referees, giving haircuts, and hunting down supplies. They crafted entertainment programs for the able-bodied and for hospital patients, along with therapeutic activities for those recovering from injuries. Recreation rooms were stocked with books and magazines, letter-writing supplies, playing cards and board games, musical instruments, and portable phonographs. They devised activities specific to different locations and utilized materials at hand. On Christmas Island, the Red Cross director, a Texan named Arthur Cunningham, successfully encouraged an interest in shell carving and jewelry making with mother-of-pearl, taught to the troops by local craftsmen, and organized weekly deep-sea fishing expeditions. "One of the boys was a boatbuilder, so the boys built their own boat," Eleanor reported. "These fishing trips are good sport and they sometimes provide the only fresh food that comes to that island if the meat boat from Honolulu or New Zealand happens to be late."

Eleanor's tour of Christmas Island continued as she "saw

everything the men were doing," from the infantry and artillery headquarters to the mechanized laundry room (a luxury since in some places, washing clothes was done by hand with a bucket and scrub brush, and on the fighting fronts, in rivers and streams). She greeted staffers at the radio station and newspaper office and shook hands with the payroll clerks who, even in the midst of war, paid wages and performed other necessary administrative work. At the Special Service Office, Eleanor inquired what was most needed by the men. Whenever she asked the question on the island, the answer was always the same: fishing tackle. She later put out a call in "My Day," entreating readers to send spare fishing gear to the Red Cross for distribution among the troops.

Not wasting a single minute, Eleanor boarded a jeep for an excursion to the other side of the island, accompanied by several officers and enlisted men, who joined the group at her request. The box-shaped vehicle, doorless and with a removable cloth roof, was a product of war. In 1940, the War Department called for bids on a lightweight, all-terrain vehicle that could be standardized for use across the armed forces. In record time, the jeep was developed and turned out in large numbers. The compact car, which could be shipped as ready-to-assemble kits or stacked several high for shipping, was found on all war fronts, carrying officers and men about their daily duties, transporting the wounded, hauling artillery and supplies, and mounted with machine guns when needed. Beloved for its versatility and dependability, the jeep's main drawback was delivering an uncomfortable, teeth-jarring ride on hard seats prone to causing painful cysts at the base of the tailbone. A reporter who took a two-hundred-mile ride in the new "peculiar looking vehicle" likened it to a bucking bronco. Or, as the article headline proclaimed, the jeep was "Reminiscent of Teddy Roosevelt: It's Rough Rider."

There was no direct way for Eleanor's group to reach their destination on the far side of Christmas Island. A forty-mile trip wound around a large inner lagoon, studded with islets and coral flats, water hues ranging from seafoam and emerald green to mineral-colored red. Along the way, they stopped at various points, "lonely little camps" where boys were stationed on watch. "In one place they were struggling with their outdoor fire and the quite evidently new and difficult task of making gravy for their pork chops," recalled Eleanor. "I'm certain now every boy should learn to cook and live out in the open." Arthur Cunningham, the Red Cross director, who "knew all the boys by name," swapped out records among the various outposts. Listening to music on a phonograph "was their only recreation, and the machines ran morning, noon and night." The journey ended at the wistfully named Paris, a rest camp for men who had been on the island more than three months. The slice of land between the ocean and the lagoon hardly looked any different from the rest of the island, but during a several-day stay, at least "the absence of routine must be a relief."

Everywhere Eleanor went on the island, GIs were eager to hear about what was happening on the home front. They asked after the president, with one soldier reminiscing about seeing him in Narragansett, Rhode Island, several years earlier while the commander in chief was inspecting naval facilities. What did Broadway look like without its bright lights? asked a New Yorker. The famous theater district and the surrounding area in Times Square were required to go dark after it was discovered- that its intense illumination outlined ships against the shore, making them visible to enemies at sea. The most dangerous spot Eleanor had been in the war, she told a soldier, was riding in a taxi in a New York City blackout.

One thing most soldiers, sailors, and marines stationed

overseas shared was a voracious hunger for news from home. Mail shipments could be sporadic, often weeks or months late. Current magazines and newspapers were scarce, and any hometown papers, from New York City to rural North Dakota, were read and reread until they fell apart. When newcomers arrived at a base, the grapevine kicked into overdrive, spreading who they were and where they were from, and they were sought out and besieged for stateside stories.

Loneliness was a constant, unshakable companion of soldiers on foreign duty, wrote Lieutenant General Robert Eichelberger, who was stationed in the Pacific, in a postwar memoir. "A good many million Americans who went overseas probably share my reminiscent wonderment at how quickly the soldier feels himself estranged from his native land." After a year's absence, he found himself writing to his wife "as though America were in another world." Heightening the feeling of isolation, servicemen couldn't reveal to their loved ones exactly where they were, since military censors forbade mentions of specific locales in correspondence. The censors were often heavy-handed with other information as well. A young woman wrote to the director of the U.S. Office of Censorship complaining that when she opened mail from her soldier boyfriend, she found a cut-up letter and a note from the censor. "Your soldier still loves you," it said, "but he talks too much."

After returning home from the Pacific, Eleanor received letters from people asking if she could reveal exactly where she encountered one of their loved ones. A woman from Washington State had a brother who wrote home saying he had seen the First Lady on September 14, his birthday, and that "her presence was like a gift from home." Since her sibling was not allowed to reveal place names, the woman wanted to know if Eleanor could ease her mind by telling her the locale she visited on that date.

Tommy responded on Eleanor's behalf, gently explaining that the First Lady too was bound by censorship rules.

For the GIs on Christmas Island, Eleanor's visit broke the monotony and set the place abuzz. "She seemed to represent to the average soldier in this far away outpost, the folks back home, and everything we hold so dear," wrote a soldier in a troop-produced publication. "We think she did a lot to buck up our morale and put new life in our daily routine." They were charmed by her graciousness and her interest in them and dazzled to have a celebrity in their midst. She posed for pictures and signed autographs and short snorters by the hundreds. While some of the men on Christmas Island were hoping a troupe of chorus girls would turn up, most were gratified to instead have a visit from such a maternal figure. "She reminded one more of some boy's mother back home, than the wife of the President of the United States—and we all loved it," continued the correspondent. Eleanor was so friendly and down to earth that the GIs had a hard time reconciling their surprise visitor as the same person who had entertained kings, queens, and other world leaders and government elite.

Eleanor began her trip to the Pacific with some anxiety about whether the troops would find her being there "agreeable or just a bore." To the soldiers on Christmas Island—isolated, lonely, homesick, marooned for an indefinite length of time— her appearance made a tremendous impact. "Her kindness and consideration brought this 'Island of Forgotten Men' very much back to life," reported a GI journalist. Declared another, "It takes great courage to do what Mrs. Roosevelt is now doing, and you have to hand it to her—she has what it takes."

CHAPTER 4

PACIFIC FLIGHT 321

*"The schedules are hard, but I hope I do a good job. Like
fighting the war this type of trip isn't worth doing
unless the job accomplished is good."*

**—ELEANOR ROOSEVELT IN A LETTER TO
JOSEPH P. LASH, SEPTEMBER 1943**

*Penrhyn Island, Bora Bora, Aitutaki, Tutuila,
and Viti Levu, August 20–25*

After Eleanor's whirlwind thirty-six hours on Christmas Island,
Pacific Flight 321 was airborne and bound for Bora Bora. The
aircraft traveled a route dubbed the "Milk Run," along which
transport planes carried mail, movies, magazines, and miscellaneous supplies to outlying bases. A milk run was a slang
term coined by flying crews to describe a routine mission or
one where minimal resistance from the enemy was anticipated.
As an airman put it, "When you did not get any holes in your

plane, it was called a milk run." But even a milk run could turn hazardous, which one bomber crew discovered after being surprised midair "by a bunch of very good Japanese fighter pilots," nearly running out of fuel before being able to disengage from the skirmish.

Nothing was guaranteed this close to the front lines. The First Lady's plane, should it be discovered, would make an enticing target for the enemy. As she headed toward Admiral Halsey's headquarters on the island of New Caledonia, he closely tracked her progress and received confirmation as she arrived at and departed each stop. Command on one island was chided after mistakenly relaying that she arrived there at 2:30 a.m. rather than in the afternoon, as it was more hazardous to utilize airstrips that were less well lit. "Cannot believe you would permit flight as important as this to depart [or] to arrive during night hours," his cable rebuked.

To help ensure Eleanor's safety, the military imposed a blackout on information about her tour of the island bases, using only the identifier Pacific Flight 321 in official dispatches. On her return from England, there were many high-level discussions about how to safely send her home. Her visit was so widely publicized that a commercial flight carried the risk of being tracked and shot down by the Germans. At that time of year, due to the weather, commercial planes flew to the United States by way of Portugal, Africa, and South America. As a solution, officials quietly placed her on board a military plane with ferry pilots who were returning to the United States after delivering a bomber. Now, as she traveled through the South Pacific, the White House continued to maintain its silence, releasing no statements as to her exact whereabouts.

Secrecy was sacrosanct during wartime. While military censors monitored what servicemen penned in letters home,

restrictions were also placed on the press. Newspapers, magazines, and radio stations all followed a code of practices issued
by the Office of Censorship. Reporters were essentially on an
honor system not to disclose, unless authorized, information
that could aid the enemy, such as aerial photographs, movements of troops or cargo, factory production figures, and the
specific amount of damage sustained during an adversary's
attacks. Eleanor's mention of the weather, an off-limits topic,
in "My Day" prompted a stern letter from the censors, after
which she informed readers, "From now on I shall not tell you
whether it rains or whether the sun shines where I happen to
be." Eighteen words in one of Eleanor's columns transmitted from England attracted the notice of government censors for referring to a secret place. Officials on both sides of
the Atlantic tried to contact her for input before altering the
column but "could not catch up with her—she moves too fast"
and went ahead and edited the copy.

While for domestic news organizations, censorship was
largely voluntary and readily adhered to by the media in war
reporting, censorship in combat zones was compulsory and
highly restrictive in the Pacific theater. Like all journalism
transmitted from the area, Eleanor's columns were reviewed by
military censors before being sent to her editor for publication.
For security reasons, just as servicemen couldn't reveal their
exact locations, she could not disclose details like the number
of troops stationed at bases. She selectively named in print the
islands she visited and when necessary omitted identifying geographic details.

"My Day" readers learned that her next destination, a several-
hour stopover on the way to Bora Bora, was a small island with
a large, sheltered lagoon, a common natural feature in the South
Seas. She didn't divulge that it was called Penrhyn Island or that

it is part of the Cook Islands, sighted by the British explorer in 1770 during his last, ill-fated voyage. One of fifteen atolls and islands spread across nearly eight hundred thousand square miles and at the time administered by New Zealand, Penrhyn is a narrow ring of coral, broken in places, allowing entrance to the ninety-mile lagoon it encircles.

On Penrhyn, a later addition to the air ferry and communications route, Eleanor reported that soldiers were "very busy building the whole station," less restless for home than servicemen who had been stationed overseas longer. Her presence piqued the curiosity of local islanders, who showered her with shell necklaces, grass skirts, and other handmade gifts. The appearance of a female foreigner was an uncommon and exciting occurrence, even if they didn't recognize her. Are you "General MacArthur's 'woman'," they wanted to know. The ranking U.S. Army officer on the island revealed to Eleanor that she was the first white woman he had seen since leaving the United States ten months earlier.

In contrast to flat coral atolls such as Penrhyn and Christmas, volcanic islands like Bora Bora rise far above the ocean's surface, verdant and lush. At the base of a jungle-covered mountain where sheer cliffs merged with the sea, "narrow fingers of land shot out, forming magnificent bays, while about the whole was thrown a coral ring of absolute perfection, dotted with small motus (islets) on which palms grew," rhapsodized James Michener in *Return to Paradise*. The lagoon "was a crystal blue, the beaches were dazzling white, and ever on the outer reef the spray leaped mountainously into the air. That was Bora Bora from aloft. When you stepped upon it the dream expanded."

Of the forty-nine islands Michener visited while in the navy, first as an aviation maintenance troubleshooter and then as a historical officer, he deemed Bora Bora the most beautiful—so exquisite that it seemed "to have been designed by some master artist." As part of French Polynesia, the island's political situation mirrored that of its governing country after France fell to Germany in June 1940. Division developed between supporters of Vichy France, which aligned with the Nazis, and those of the Free French, led by exiled president Charles de Gaulle, which fought the German occupation forces. Tensions on the island reached a near revolt before the Free French supporters prevailed and a pro-Allied government was established.

Bora Bora was largely unaffected by the outside world until war swept the globe. "Then in the dark days following Pearl Harbor the American Government, as a result of secret negotiations with loyalist French forces, invaded the island with bulldozers, juke boxes, airplanes, and lots of money." The once-tranquil Eden, with barely any roads and reachable only by boat, was transformed into a military stronghold and temporarily became home to thousands of U.S. Army and Navy personnel.

After the bombing of Pearl Harbor, the United States had an urgent need for an additional repair and supply base in the Pacific. A committee of military advisers was asked to identify an island between Panama and Samoa that was closer to the fighting while still offering some degree of safety from Japanese attack, particularly by submarine. On a large globe of the Pacific, they placed a string between the Panama Canal and Samoa to trace the route and narrowed down the search to several possibilities. Bora Bora won out when the Navy Hydrographic Office, which prepared and published maps, charts, and nautical books, supplied a chart of the island from the mid-1800s. Engravings on the chart depicted the island from different vantage points, one of which showed a substantial lagoon that could provide protected anchorage for large ships.

The navy immediately tapped two sources for more information. One was the editor of *National Geographic*, who was asked to compile everything the magazine had on Bora Bora. The other was a noncommissioned officer borrowed from the army who indicated familiarity with the island on his enlistment questionnaire. A geologist, he had spent two years there while researching a doctoral thesis and could comment on the suitability of the lagoon.

To familiarize themselves with the terrain, stateside engineers watched *Tabu*, a Hollywood movie shot on location in Bora Bora in the 1930s. They used the film footage to estimate the height of the hills so they could determine where to sink fuel tanks, which required camouflaging in the foliage, and the distance from there to the water to judge the necessary length of pipelines and hoses for refueling ships anchored offshore. From afar, they had to design the base layout and determine the necessary equipment for building an airfield, a hospital, living quarters, warehouses to stock ammunition, food, and other supplies, and facilities for fueling and repairing ships and planes, all of which was loaded onto cargo vessels and sent from the United States.

After landing at the airfield, Eleanor crossed the crystal-blue lagoon to the main island aboard a navy launcher. "There was no fanfare about Mrs. Roosevelt's arrival," an army correspondent reported. Which was how she preferred it. In the pre-trip dispatches with instructions from Admiral Halsey to island base commanders, he ordered by presidential directive, "Entertainment to be restricted to minimum but all installations and situations other than military plans will be made accessible to distinguished visitor on demand." Some acceded to the directive, while others actively worked to keep Eleanor from interacting with the troops. Instead they would have done well to heed an American reporter who advised in a London newspaper during her Great Britain visit, "The best thing to do with Eleanor is to go through the necessary formalities and then just turn her loose. She can be depended upon to see everything there is to see, meet everyone worth meeting."

The morning after her arrival on Bora Bora, Eleanor maneuvered her way into an advantageous setting for information gathering. Instead of breakfasting as expected in the officers' mess, she surprised down the ranks by eating with the enlisted men. Eleanor's sons, all four of whom were serving in various branches of the armed services, advised her to speak not only with officers like themselves but also with noncommissioned officers and enlisted men to find out the situation that really existed for personnel overseas. As she explained to "My Day" readers, there was "talk among the men which would never occur when officers were within earshot, and some talk among the officers which would perhaps not be as free if enlisted men were present."

Eleanor borrowed mess gear, a tin tray and cutlery assigned to each individual soldier, from an awestruck young man (who consecrated the dinnerware and vowed to spirit it away from the supply sergeant when the war was over). As she made her way down the chow line, the normally boisterous mess hall "was so quiet and civilized that she must have thought she had got into a girls' seminary by mistake," recalled an onlooker. "The GIs were all too flabbergasted to make any noise."

That morning at the breakfast table, the soldiers seated with the First Lady were tongue-tied—not an uncommon occurrence. A serviceman who met Eleanor on the island recalled in his hometown newspaper, "We were so overtaken by her splendid personality, that a great many of us blushed, as she came up and shook our hands, being introduced by our Commanding

Officer. Being formally introduced to the First Lady of the Land was so much of a shock to some that they were speechless the most part of that day."

Then one brave GI at the table spoke up and asked Eleanor if Franklin was going to run again for president. There was already speculation in political circles and in the media about whether Franklin would run in 1944, seeking an unprecedented fourth term. (A constitutional amendment ratified in 1951 limited presidents to two terms.) Although Eleanor didn't have an answer to the question, the ice was broken, and a lengthy conversation ensued about a topic uppermost in the majority of servicemen's minds: postwar jobs. To their queries on employment, she replied, "If we do our job at home, there will be jobs... when [you] return."

From the early days of the war, Eleanor advocated for legislation to support servicemen when they came home. The nation that sent them to war, she believed, had an obligation to plan ahead for their return and a moral imperative to not repeat past mistakes. She was determined that there be no recurrence of the post–World War I period when the country, weary of war and eager to move on, all but abandoned the men who fought, leaving them jobless and hungry.

In 1933, at an abandoned army barracks outside Washington, DC, Eleanor delivered an impromptu speech to a group of World War I veterans who gathered in the capital for the second year in a row asking for payment of promised postwar bonuses. The year before, when the "bonus army" first convened, then-President Hoover ordered federal troops to oust the veterans. Tanks rolled in, and the men and their families were tear gassed and their campsites burned. President Roosevelt was sympathetic to the veterans' plight but also opposed the bonuses. Instead he encouraged employment with the newly created Civilian Conservation Corps, which hired unmarried men, who lived in camps, to provide the manual labor for infrastructure and reforestation work. An adviser to the president took Eleanor on a surprise visit to speak with the fifteen hundred bonus army veterans. Eleanor waded through ankle-deep mud touring the camp and led a rendition of "There's a Long, Long Trail," a song popular during World War I. In the mess hall, men who were lined up for a meal greeted her with cheers and the clanging of tin plates.

Even though Eleanor had no news about the bonuses, the visit—and her sincerity—helped ease tensions between veterans and the government. "I have always had a deep interest in soldiers and never have forgotten the war days," she told the men. She described her wartime work in Washington, DC, in a Red Cross canteen and at hospitals visiting the wounded. "I want everyone who fought in the last war to have fair consideration. I hope we will never again have to ask of you that kind of service," she concluded. "I never want to see another war."

When war descended less than a decade later, Eleanor maintained her deep concern for the troops and their welfare. She continually communicated with servicemen, talking with them as she traveled the United States—in hospitals, aboard planes and trains, and at bases and servicemen's clubs from Seattle to Pensacola. While in England, she addressed GI complaints about late paychecks and, after Red Cross workers told her the men were developing blisters from wearing cotton socks, wrote to the man in charge, General Dwight D. Eisenhower, asking that they be issued more comfortable ones made of wool.

A young man Eleanor met at a Washington, DC, hospital was training to be a concert pianist until his hands were badly burned in battle. When he confided that practicing on the hospital's piano in front of the other patients made him self-conscious, she invited him to play at the White House, where there were three pianos and he could practice alone. "It took quite a bit of urging to make him agree, but finally he accepted the offer and came regularly," Eleanor said. Later he asked her to listen to him at the piano. "He played beautifully, and my heart ached for him because his hands would never permit him to play professionally. However he continued his musical studies and is now teaching music."

Eleanor responded personally to the copious letters she received from servicemen and their wives and parents, assisting with everything from having a soldier's poem published to securing funds from the Red Cross for a struggling family. She regularly forwarded notes to Secretary of War Henry Stimson and to General George Marshall, the army chief of staff. General Marshall assigned one, and later a second, member of his staff to handle Eleanor's correspondence, investigating complaints and taking necessary corrective action.

Shortly before traveling to the Pacific, Eleanor encouraged "My Day" readers to contact their congressional representatives regarding postwar matters for servicemen. The fall of Italian leader and Hitler ally Benito Mussolini several days earlier brought the possibility of peace in Europe ever closer. "Many people, who before would not discuss postwar activities because, first of all, the war must be won, now realize that the time has come to plan for peace." The questions she suggested asking their representatives included "What plans in my district have been made for the re-education of both workers and soldiers, those who need vocational training and those who wish to proceed with any type of academic or professional training?"

The same night, during a radio address, the president—to Eleanor's great satisfaction—addressed the topic. "I hope the men in the armed forces heard it," she wrote to Joe Lash.

Franklin promised listeners that plans were being made "for the return to civilian life of our gallant men and women in the armed services." He listed numerous benefits to which veterans should be entitled, among them mustering-out pay and higher education or trade training, and he had a pointed message for lawmakers. "I have assured our men in the armed forces that the American people would not let them down when the war is won," said the president. "May the Congress do its duty in this regard."

Before servicemen would be able to use any postwar benefits, the task at hand had to be completed. The flow of supplies had increased enormously since the start of the war, desperate days Admiral Halsey described as being symbolized by "a rusty nail and a frayed shoestring." The men were confident about beating Japan, but they confided in Eleanor their concerns over home front conditions. They questioned strikes and wondered about absenteeism in war plants, concluding that people on the home front didn't "know how big" their role was in the war. One man's proposed solution was to "send the strikers here and let us go home." Eleanor emphasized in post-trip reporting that the part played by troops in the Pacific was not a sideshow and reminded the public that there was only one way home for their loved ones: by winning the war.

———

"The President wanted me to say he appreciates the great work you are doing," the First Lady told an audience of soldiers and sailors assembled beneath the star-dusted night sky on Bora Bora, the four points of the Southern Cross glittering overhead.

"He said to tell you that you have done and are doing a wonderful job. He wants me to give you his deepest admiration and gratitude," Eleanor relayed. "Let me also express my gratitude and tell you that everyone back home misses you as much as you miss them and that we are living for that wonderful day when you will come back home."

The men responded to Eleanor's sincerity. "There is something about her, some rare quality of character or kindliness or mother-liness or good-will—call it charm if you will—that she was really striking," reported an army correspondent. "You felt instinctively that here was a woman who liked you. She was your friend. I don't mean to sound a bit maudlin or too sentimental, for after a good many years in the newspaper racket, I am not easily fooled, but the soldiers just naturally like Mrs. Roosevelt."

For servicemen who were lonesome and loath to admit it, Eleanor reminded them of home. The year before, while in London, she went from Buckingham Palace to a Red Cross club, "where the enlisted man is king." She mingled and chatted with servicemen, one of whom joined up at age seventeen and had three Nazi machine-gun slugs in his legs, and for a few hours they forgot their homesickness. "When a man's in foreign service a long way from his home and not too sure he'll ever see it again, he begins to think a little. He begins to feel proud when a great American woman takes his interest to heart," noted an army sergeant at the gathering.

Even those who professed to dislike the First Lady were often won over after meeting her or hearing her speak. "I have always been 'agin' [against] her until now, but she has the faculty of seeming as though she is not in the slightest hurry, that she came all the way out here just to talk to you and you and you," wrote a soldier in a letter home.

Others resented Eleanor's presence in the Pacific. "If they can get planes to bring Mr. Roosevelt's wife over here they can get boats to bring us back," groused a serviceman. When asked how he felt about being visited by the president's wife, another replied, "I'd rather be visited by my own."

Deployment overseas didn't mean leaving politics or prejudices at home. On Aitutaki, another of the Cook Islands and the site of a U.S. Army airfield, the colonel in charge, "a Massachusetts Republican, was snobby and not pleased to see me," Eleanor relayed in her diary. He announced to Eleanor that he opposed interracial marriage and was disturbed that some of his young officers wanted to marry local island women. He was concerned too that a spark would incite the white southerners under his command to start a feud with Black troops, who he admitted were doing very good work. Eleanor continued, "So he just prays Hell won't break loose."

For Black American soldiers, encountering racism was a sadly familiar occurrence. Even during the dire circumstances of wartime, racism was rampant, and the U.S. military—reflecting the country as a whole—remained segregated. Black servicemen primarily performed support roles and were not permitted to carry weapons or engage in combat.

In addition to having a condescending attitude, the snobby colonel committed the even worse offense of keeping Eleanor from some of the servicemen on the island. Less than half of the one thousand men were present when she gave an address. As she traveled through the Pacific, a pattern developed—military commanders stymied by the presence of a middle-aged American woman in their midst. On Penrhyn, the major who escorted her during her visit was polite but, she sensed, unsure what to do with her. The colonel in charge on Christmas Island, frosty at first, grew more friendly as he witnessed the gladness of the troops in having her there. At another stop, a general was coolly polite, telling her the marines were so scattered about the island that she could not meet many of them—but that she could dine with his officers. Other commanders she encountered were openly hostile, while the colonel on Aitutaki tried blatantly to scare her.

Spotted by Captain William Bligh in 1789, seventeen days before the mutiny on board the *Bounty*, Aitutaki consists of a triangular coral reef surrounding a large lagoon, out of which emerges a volcanic island. Standing at an island high point, steely-nerved Eleanor admired the scenery below despite a harrowing ride to get there. The colonel sped up an exceedingly steep jungle road with the First Lady as a passenger, heading for a radar station.

"I was amused, for I think the Colonel expected me to refuse to be driven up. If I survived, he expected me to prefer walking down," Eleanor wrote in her column. "He did not know my husband's love for building roads, and for being his own engineer. This sometimes results in a road which only my husband's car will climb when he, himself, is driving it!"

Eleanor was less lighthearted when relaying the story to Tommy, telling her, "I have never seen a steeper road…[and] was sure he took me to see if I would be afraid." Instead she refused to give the colonel the satisfaction of displaying any fear, drawing on her experiences riding with daredevil drivers like her brother Hall and the president. On the grounds of their Hyde Park estate, Franklin, who could no longer walk or horseback ride in the forests, employed a crew to construct roads, often crude and with steep grades and sharp turns, creating a network of some twenty miles in which he could drive his hand-controlled car. FDR's retreat, Top Cottage, was situated on a hill and reached via a narrow, winding road. Great Britain's Queen Elizabeth, visiting during the 1930s, took a wild ride with the president to attend a picnic at Top Cottage. Years later, she recalled holding on for dear life as Franklin "drove like a bat out of hell." When it came time to return to the main house, the queen refused to get in the car with him and rode back with the president's Secret Service detail.

Breaking with Bora Bora admirer James Michener, in Eleanor's view, the most scenically striking place she saw in the South Pacific was the island of Tutuila in American Samoa. Volcanic activity created a rugged terrain with tall, jagged, lushly green mountain peaks spanning the island's length. From a ship anchored offshore, "Tutuila looks like the Polynesian paradise about which one reads," wrote Ridgely Cummings, a journalist who joined the merchant marine during the war. Deep valleys descended to the coast, a fertile strip where banana, coconut, and other fruit trees flourished. Cleaving the island nearly in half was Pago Pago Harbor, dramatically picturesque and practical. With a narrow entrance easy to protect, deep water in a huge bay, and bounded by high ridges and hills, it was an ideal place for a military outpost.

In 1872, the United States negotiated with local chiefs to establish a small naval station at Pago Pago with refueling facilities and a communications center. Tutuila was later ceded to the United States along with four additional islands and two coral atolls that make up American Samoa, the only U.S. territory south of the equator. Another collection of Samoan islands lies farther to the west and at the time was administered by New Zealand.

In 1940, with war clouds brewing in the Pacific, the modest naval base was expanded and fortified. Thousands of U.S. Marines (*malinga* in the local language) were sent to reinforce the island, where defense was aided by two local guard units. Marines vastly outnumbered island residents, who maintained that for every coconut tree, there was a *malinga*.

Hot, humid, and wet year-round, Pago Pago had two

seasons according to servicemen stationed there since before
the war began: rainy and rainier, from gentle, rainbow-
brightened mists to sudden deluges. (A 1912 visit inspired
English writer W. Somerset Maugham to pen a short story
set in Pago Pago titled "Rain.") One challenge was that the
constant rain made the dirt roads difficult to navigate, especially with the military's heavy trucks, tanks, and tractors.
In grim jest, the marines nicknamed Tutuila "Alcatraz in
Technicolor," referring to the island prison in San Francisco
Bay. The younger marines, noted Cummings, "seemed high-
spirited and contented," while "among the older ones who had
volunteered to avoid the draft there was variation between
bored resignation and bitter resentment."

As a precaution, troops were required to carry full military
equipment with them and not to be separated at any time from
their rifle and ammunition by more than thirty feet. Tutuila
came under enemy fire in January 1942 when a submarine surfaced early one morning and shelled the naval station. Japanese
plans to launch Operation FS, the seizure of some Samoan
islands and others in the Fiji archipelago, were abandoned after
clashes with Allied forces at Midway and the Coral Sea resulted
in their heavy loss of ships. As the danger of Japanese attack
abated, Tutuila became a staging and support area for combat in
the Pacific, and marines prepped for battle at a jungle warfare
training center.

On Tutuila, Eleanor lodged in a four-bedroom guesthouse
in what seemed like the lap of luxury. For the first time during
the trip, there was hot and cold water and a comfortable mat-
tress to sleep on, she reported in "My Day." Acting as hostess
and staying with the First Lady was Lieutenant Edna R. Tilden,
a navy nurse from southern California. When the United States
entered World War II, there were nearly eight hundred nurses

on active duty with the Navy Nurse Corps, including Tilden, a number that increased to more than ten thousand by the war's end. Tilden found little glamour during an eighteen-month stretch of duty on Tutuila, only "rain, wind and dust, and always that intense tropical heat."

At a navy hospital, staff proudly pointed out to Eleanor that theirs was one of the only air-conditioned operating rooms in the islands—a perk appreciated by a prominent patient treated there the previous October. The same day Eleanor's arrival in London was announced in the press, another front-page headline proclaimed, "Rickenbacker Missing in Pacific on Flight Southwest of Hawaii." Captain Eddie Rickenbacker, a famous World War I fighter pilot, spent twenty-four days floating on a life raft in the ocean before being rescued. He was on his way to deliver a confidential verbal message from Secretary of War Stimson to General MacArthur in Australia when the converted bomber in which he was flying overshot a refueling stop on Canton Island, forcing the aircraft's pilot to ditch the plane in the water. The message Rickenbacker was tasked with delivering was likely a reprimand of MacArthur, who for some time had been lashing out at Washington, demanding additional war resources, sniping at the navy, and predicting disaster if the "Germany first" policy determined by Roosevelt and Churchill was not reversed in favor of prioritizing the Pacific. Rickenbacker kept his word never to reveal Stimson's message, which he delivered to MacArthur at his new headquarters in New Guinea after recuperating from his death-defying ordeal at sea.

Death constantly hovered in the Pacific war zone, like a tragedy that occurred while Eleanor was on Tutuila. "I heard one thing that troubles me," she wrote in her diary. "There is no wine or beer for the men so last night four men died from drinking distilled shellac." No one told her about the incident, but a photographer traveling in her party slept near enough to hear what went on when the still was found. An officer did tell Eleanor about a drink made by locals and given to U.S. troops. "It sends them berserk and he thought that was a factor which might bring trouble between his colored and white troops but none of the men had died of it. I think a better recreation program might help."

Recreational resources on Tutuila were lacking. "They have the most miserable Red Cross headquarters," Eleanor informed agency head Norman Davis in a nine-page report she submitted to him after the trip. Badly needed was a building for sailors who went ashore and had no place to sleep for the night. Air crews that were dropping in for a rest slept on cots without mattresses or pillows. There were no facilities, no place to write a letter or to play a game, and not even a single Victrola on the island. Equipment like phonographs and projectors deteriorated faster in the South Pacific humidity than in other climates. This might seem trivial to outsiders, Eleanor noted, but severely limited entertainment was a bigger factor than people at home realized.

The Red Cross "is doing a magnificent job" in the South and Southwest Pacific, "as far as it can be done with present supplies and personnel," Eleanor told Davis. But far more workers were needed in every field, especially for hospital work. She pointed out where the system worked well and where it didn't, offering suggestions for improving procedures and in the supply chain and noting where enlisted men had too little in comparison with officers.

Looking over places with a discerning eye was something Eleanor learned how to do from Franklin. While governor of New York State, he had asked Eleanor to accompany him on inspection tours of state-run facilities. He could drive around the grounds and survey a property's exterior, but since walking was difficult, he could not go inside "and get a real idea of how it was being run from the point of view of overcrowding, staff, food, and medical care," Eleanor explained. At first, her reports were "highly unsatisfactory" to Franklin, but he schooled her on how to notice if details corroborated what she was being told (for example, whether food cooking on the stove corresponded to the menu).

———

The "milk run" along which Eleanor was traveling culminated on Viti Levu, the main island of the Fiji archipelago, where she made stops at each of two U.S. bases located on opposite sides of the island. Officials in Fiji, the headquarters of the high commissioner of the British Western Pacific Territories, were notified of Eleanor's visit by Prime Minister Churchill.

While entertaining Churchill at Hyde Park prior to leaving for the Pacific, Eleanor rendered the usually loquacious prime minister temporarily speechless. During dinner one evening, she casually shared covert information with him: she was leaving the next day for a lengthy tour of the Pacific. Recovering from his surprise, Churchill turned to the president, a stern look on his face, and asked, "Did you say she was going alone?" Yes, answered Franklin. The First Lady was venturing solo for the first time on an extended trip, without a family member, a friend, or her personal secretary accompanying her, although precautions would be taken to ensure her safety. To Eleanor's chagrin, Churchill promised to notify his "people all along the line to look after her," meaning higher-ups in Australia, New Zealand, and British Crown territories in the South Pacific.

The prime minister's offer "was not reassuring" to Eleanor, who wanted to avoid formalities as much as possible. "I do not think Mr. Churchill understood Franklin's calm assurance that I was quite able to take care of myself," recalled independent-minded Eleanor. "I much preferred not having someone else to look after me."

While at Hyde Park, Churchill shared with Eleanor copies of letters taken from German prisoners of war captured in North Africa and recently declassified by British intelligence. In Fiji, as she did elsewhere, she read aloud excerpts from the letters, which showed despondency and a decline in morale on the part of Germany's soldiers and citizens. "Try to hold out, dear son; this year, too, will come to an end some day. When you can't do anything else, then permit yourself to be captured, because the main thing is to remain alive," counseled a mother. "Things just can't continue this way if the air raids are permitted to go on like this.... During the last few days I simply can't get hold of myself, I'm really close to despair.... Were we really born to lead such a horrible life?"

Eleanor shared the letters—which she thought might give courage to the men—during a daily morning conference where war information from every theater was reviewed. In the Pacific, ground fighting had ceased on New Georgia, while strides were made against enemy strongholds in New Guinea. Soviet troops reclaimed territory on the eastern front from the Nazis, and Allied planes conducted aerial offensives against key targets in German-occupied southern Italy. And of particular importance to Eleanor, Japanese forces were now "cleaned out" of the Aleutians, a U.S.-owned island chain some twelve hundred miles west of the Alaskan Peninsula, where her son James was serving.

As Eleanor island-hopped toward Admiral Halsey's head-quarters in Nouméa on New Caledonia, he awaited her arrival with anxiety and dread. "I could find no excuse for her entering my area and monopolizing planes, crews, and fuel that were needed for military purposes," he groused. Meanwhile, she anxiously awaited an answer to the question topmost in her mind: whether she would be going to Guadalcanal.

CHAPTER 5

NO PLACE FOR YOU, MA'AM

"We in America admire the quality of courage, the willingness to fight for the things that are believed in."
—ELEANOR ROOSEVELT, *AUCKLAND STAR*, SEPTEMBER 1, 1943

New Caledonia, August 25–27

"Guadalcanal is no place for you, ma'am!" Admiral Halsey tersely told the First Lady, unpersuaded by the president's letter of consent in his hand.

"I'm perfectly willing to take my chances," Eleanor responded. "I'll be entirely responsible for anything that happens to me."

"I'm not worried about the responsibility, and I'm not worried about the chances you'd take. I know you'd take them gladly," Halsey said. "What worries me is the battle going on in New Georgia at this very minute."

With aviation fuel in limited supply and all available fighter planes needed to conclude the New Georgia campaign, he didn't have a spare fighter escort to accompany her to Guadalcanal. Allowing her plane to go unescorted was unthinkable since Guadalcanal was still subject to enemy bombing raids.

The admiral's blunt declaration, swiftly delivered, was painfully disappointing news for Eleanor. Seeing the crestfallen look on her face, Halsey added that he would postpone his final decision until she returned to New Caledonia after traveling to New Zealand and Australia, depending on the status of the New Georgia campaign. "The situation may have clarified by then," he offered in consolation.

Admiral Halsey's vexation with Eleanor's presence in the Pacific had nothing to do with her personally. He had known her for years and truly liked and admired her. But according to him, one of an area commander's worst problems was having to accommodate the politicians, "special" correspondents, and "do-gooders" who believed their visit was a "morale factor" or that they were entitled to "see it from the inside." The First Lady he classed as a do-gooder and opposed her visit because he thought it was a political gesture. As with other VIP guests who came through the area, her being there took his focus away from the war and consumed resources. He also disliked the fact that representatives from the Australian government and from General MacArthur's staff insisted on coming to meet with Eleanor in Nouméa, which had no accommodations for them. Most egregiously, he had to don a necktie and "play the gracious, solicitous host." He had "no time for such folderol" and yet would have to make the time.

In addition to Halsey currently commanding the battle of New Georgia, word of Eleanor's impending arrival had coincided with personal woes. His son, an aviation supply officer on the carrier USS *Saratoga*, was returning to the ship after picking up spare parts from an island base when the plane in which he was flying crashed in the Pacific. When briefed on the situation, Halsey was adamant that the search be conducted according to regulations, just as it would for any downed serviceman. "My son is the same as every other son in the combat zone," he told his operations officer. "Look for him just as you'd look for anybody else." The crew of the plane, which veered off course and was forced to make a water landing, was missing for four harrowing days before being spotted by a search plane and rescued.

Halsey insisted that the search for his son follow regulations, but part of what landed him command of the South Pacific forces was his willingness "to throw the rule book away when unorthodox operations seem in order." His direct superior, Admiral Chester W. Nimitz, commander in chief of the U.S. Pacific Fleet, was irritated by the defeatist attitudes of his South Pacific commanders. He wanted someone optimistic. He wanted someone willing "to sail into hell itself if need be." He wanted "Bull" Halsey, as the media enthusiastically dubbed the daring admiral.

When Halsey received his new directive via a message in a sealed envelope marked "secret," he exclaimed, "Jesus Christ and General Jackson, this is the hottest potato they ever handed me!" He was eager to start swinging, and eight days later, he defeated the Japanese at the Battle of the Santa Cruz Islands. Within a month, he reversed the course of the Guadalcanal conflict and was promoted to full admiral.

An attraction to a life at sea was entrenched in Halsey, who was descended from a family of "seafarers and adventurers, big, violent men, impatient of the law, and prone to strong drink and strong language." He counted among his direct ancestors a pirate and a whaler. Staying on the right side of the law, he followed in his father's footsteps and attended the U.S. Naval Academy in Annapolis, Maryland. The school's yearbook branded the twenty-one-year-old Halsey "a real old salt."As a young sailor, he had a pet parrot as tart-tongued as he was and a tattoo of an anchor inked on his shoulder by a drunken crew member aboard ship. He was a career sailor and a veteran of World War I, during which he served as a destroyer commander, escorting convoys across the Atlantic. At age fifty-two, Halsey successfully competed with men thirty years his junior to become a naval aviator. He was assigned successive commands of carrier divisions during the late 1930s and early '40s, reaching the rank of vice admiral by 1940.

Halsey was at sea when the war began, commanding a task force ferrying marine fighter planes from Pearl Harbor to Wake Island, which was thought to be the likely target of a Japanese attack. He was due to arrive back in Honolulu at 7:30 a.m. on December 7, a half hour before the bombings began, but bad weather delayed his return. When his ship, the carrier USS *Enterprise*, sailed into Pearl Harbor that afternoon, the destruction and smoldering ruins were "enough to make me grit my teeth," he recalled. For him, the worst sight was the battleship USS *Utah*, sunk at her berth—the berth that his ship would have occupied if not for the delay. "Before we're through with 'em," Halsey swore, "the Japanese language will be spoken only in hell!"

While the United States rebuilt its fleet after the blow dealt at Pearl Harbor, Halsey directed the surprise attacks on Japanese-held islands in the Marshalls and Gilberts, the daring raids that made him a home-front hero. After the strikes, the task force evaded Japanese aircraft hunting for them by sailing in a squall back to Pearl Harbor. Two months later, Admiral Nimitz handed Halsey another risky assignment: commanding a task force that would bomb Japan on its own soil.

A hitch in the plan was that an aircraft carrier would need to sail dangerously close to Japan before launching naval planes, which had a limited flight range but could take off from the ship's deck. Bombers, larger and with greater fuel capacity, were land-based and required a minimum of twelve hundred feet of runway for takeoff. Spurred by President Roosevelt to find a way to strike Japan, military advisers came up with an audacious plan that had never before been tried. A crew of volunteer airmen was led by Colonel James Doolittle, a former speed racing pilot with an advanced degree in aeronautical engineering. They trained using medium-sized army bombers, learning how to force the lumbering planes to become airborne using just the 450 feet of a carrier deck.

On the day of the mission, all sixteen planes made it into the air, barely clearing the ocean's surface on takeoff, and subsequently dropped bombs on Tokyo and other Japanese cities. The "Doolittle raid" lightly damaged military and industrial targets but had an enormous impact on morale, buoying the American home front while embarrassing Japan and undermining its belief that its homeland was invincible to attack. In retaliation, the Japanese zeroed in on Midway Island, thinking the bombers launched from there. Having cracked Japanese codes, the United States knew an attack at Midway was coming and, after a five-day battle, dealt the Japanese navy a major defeat. The victory gave U.S. forces breathing room and time to prepare for offensive campaigns on Guadalcanal and elsewhere.

Admiral Halsey missed the action at Midway, sidelined for several months due to an illness before returning to duty. On board the *Enterprise*, Admiral Nimitz, after handing out medals at an awards ceremony, announced to the assembled sailors, "Boys, I've got a surprise for you. Bill Halsey's back!" The crew erupted into cheers, yelling, applauding, and whistling, a spontaneous and enthusiastic display of affection that brought tears to Halsey's eyes. Shortly after, he received orders to take command of the South Pacific forces. "Of all the admirals afloat in the Pacific," wrote a *New York Times* correspondent, "none [will] be more certain to inspire their loyalty and command their respect than Admiral Halsey."

Having Halsey in charge was fortunate for the naval forces fighting for Guadalcanal and especially for the marines trapped on the island with limited supplies. Unlike other commanders, he refused to accept that Guadalcanal could not be held. He traveled to the island battleground at first opportunity to assess the situation firsthand, something his predecessor never bothered to do. He slipped in inconspicuously with only two aides, riding around in a mud-spattered jeep, making for an area where the fighting was so recent that enemy corpses lay unburied. Halsey's visit to Guadalcanal gave a psychological boost to the men on the island. He spoke to reporters, heaping praise on the fighting forces persevering against heavy odds, the sound of artillery fire in the distance punctuating his talk.

———

Admiral Halsey was undoubtedly a heroic leader, but his belief that Eleanor was a "do-gooder" distraction hindered her mission in the Pacific. Adding to her burdens, she had to smooth over a diplomatic fracas soon after arriving on New Caledonia. She was intercepted on the island by Lieutenant General Robert Eichelberger, who was appointed by his boss, General MacArthur, to coordinate and oversee her tour of Australia. MacArthur had been ordered by the War Department to assume responsibility for Eleanor's visit, while the Australian government insisted that, as the president's wife—the American equivalent of a "queen"—she be their guest for the duration of her stay and that they be in charge of her itinerary. Eichelberger presented the dilemma to Eleanor, who offered a solution similar to what she had done in Great Britain. She would split the difference, first as the guest of Australia's governor-general in Canberra, the federal capital, and then place herself under Eichelberger's direction for the rest of her time in the country. Just as Admiral Halsey instructed the island base commanders to restrict entertainment to a minimum, Eleanor wanted the same throughout her tour. Her visit, though, was a momentous occasion for Australia's citizens and officials, who wanted to convey their esteem for her with red carpets and revelries as much as wartime circumstances would allow.

Eleanor expressed to Eichelberger her wish to spend the majority of her time seeing hospitals, troops, and Red Cross installations and meeting with women working in the defense industry. The simpler her reception in Australia, the better. She also made sure to clarify that the only attire she had to wear, even to formal functions, was her Red Cross uniform.

To Eichelberger, commanding a corps seemed easier than navigating the "booby traps and land mines of international diplomacy." His request that Eleanor send him a wire confirming that, after leaving Canberra, she wished to be under his direction was wise insurance, he found, when the Australian government renewed its persuasions to organize her eleven-day stay. Eichelberger brandished the telegram, intent on honoring Eleanor's wishes to keep the focus on the work she was there to do and not on herself.

On New Caledonia that night, Eleanor attended a dinner hosted by Admiral Halsey, gracefully concealing how devastated she was by the near-certain denial over visiting Guadalcanal. Instead she relayed her dismay to Tommy. "I doubt if I can get to Guadalcanal," she confided. "He sounds so doubtful that I am discouraged and really sorry that I came."

Eleanor's own morale was closely intertwined with going to Guadalcanal. Before the first bombs fell in the Pacific, the president gave a speech denouncing German aggression and reaffirming solidarity with democratic nations in the Americas and beyond. As Eleanor listened to her husband reassure and rally the nation, she thought about the call of duty that perpetually haunted her. "In my capacity of objective citizen, sitting in the gathering last night, I felt that I wanted to accept my responsibility and do my particular job whatever it might be to the extent of my ability," she wrote in "My Day." "I think that will be the answer of every individual citizen of the United States."

Eleanor had been denied what she most desired to do. When war broke out in Europe, she wanted to travel abroad to aid in Red Cross relief efforts for refugees displaced by the turmoil. But after German forces invaded Poland, they advanced westward through enemy lines so swiftly that it was deemed too dangerous for her to be in continental Europe. Her request was denied by the State Department due to the imminent possibility of a Hitler victory and the chance that she could be taken captive.

Instead, Eleanor's wish to contribute to the war effort in a meaningful way led to a milestone when she became the first presidential spouse to hold an official government post. In the mid-1930s, President Roosevelt—even while trying to maintain amity among European leaders, including direct appeals to

Hitler—had begun fortifying the country's defenses and build-ing up the military, believing that preparedness had an import-ant part in preserving peace. In May 1941, seven months before the United States officially entered World War II, he signed an executive order establishing the Office of Civilian Defense, which devised air-raid procedures, appointed aircraft spotters, supervised blackouts, and formed fire brigades in communities across the country in case of attack.

Eleanor joined the Office of Civilian Defense several months after its inception, focusing on coordinating civilian volunteers, particularly women and young people, and estab-lishing social services to enhance the program. Her elation at having a substantial wartime task—the gleam was back in her eye, noted Tommy—was short-lived. Five months into the posi-tion, she resigned. Even though she worked unpaid, her fears of becoming a lightning rod for criticism by Congress and the press were realized. Front-page stories and editorials pointed out "that the wife of any President cannot be looked upon as an individual by other people in the Government. She must always carry the reflection of influence or power beyond that of the usual government public servant. I hoped that this was not true, but I have found out that it was," Eleanor told "My Day" readers. "People can gradually be brought to understand that an individual, even if she is a President's wife, may have indepen-dent views and must be allowed the expression of an opinion. But actual participation in the work of the Government, we are not yet able to accept."

By the time Eleanor was compelled to quit her position at the Office of Civilian Defense in early 1942, the stakes had soared even higher with the bombing of Pearl Harbor and the United States' formal entry into the war. Once again, she con-templated how she could best serve and was unusually depressed and frustrated "at not having any specific work for the war," Tommy observed.

The question of responsibility continued to shadow Eleanor, the war never far from her thoughts. Although Franklin valued her opinion and benefited from the knowledge she gleaned from her various undertakings, she was not involved in the day-to-day running of the government or in war planning or strategy with him and his advisers. She was convinced that her association with the White House would prevent her "from doing any real job in World War II."

Then Eleanor's journey to Great Britain proved differently, offering her the chance to undertake an important task that was uniquely suited to her. The same was true of her tour to the Pacific, only this time she was determined to take it even further. If she didn't do something with an increased risk, she would feel she hadn't pushed herself enough or proven enough. The physical act of going to Guadalcanal reflected her emotional devastation about the war and was a way to show the fighting forces that she recognized the sacrifices they were making.

Eleanor especially felt a sense of obligation toward the young generation being sent into battle. Her personal determination to do as much as she could was constantly reinforced by the men she met. "These boys break your heart...they're so young & so tired," she wrote to a friend. "I take my hat off to this young generation & I hope we won't let them down." She was disturbed by the complacency with which older people seemed to accept sacrificing the youth to war and expecting them to bear the brunt of the fighting—young men who, if it were not for circumstances beyond their control, "would have their whole lives still before them."

After reading *They Were Expendable*, a novel based on the true-life account of a navy torpedo boat squadron that lost all but four of its more than sixty members in the Philippines in 1942, Eleanor expressed dismay. During the doomed battle for Bataan and Corregidor, thousands of U.S. and Filipino forces, with no reinforcements and inadequate supplies, were abandoned to the enemy. "There seems to be no excuse for ever considering human beings expendable," she wrote in her column. "If we ever again are guilty of leaving people without the best possible equipment in adequate amounts, in a world which requires such equipment, then somehow we should make it a prerequisite that the older people who are responsible are promptly sent out to die in these frontier battles. Why should the young always be expendable for the mistakes of the old?" She admitted feeling guilty since reading the book. "If ever again, I do not face the truth of a situation and do my best to make my fellow citizens face it too, I hope I get my proper punishment."

Moreover, not going to Guadalcanal went beyond Eleanor's fear of failure and a desire to pay tribute to the troops. She was concerned that she would be perceived as lacking courage. "I simply never will face another hospital at home for I will always feel that the men are thinking that I was afraid if I do not go." She considered traveling through Great Britain, which was relentlessly targeted by Hitler's sky-borne raiders, more dangerous than venturing to Guadalcanal. While Eleanor was speaking at a women's army training center near London, air-raid sirens sounded, followed by "nuisance raids," small-scale, sporadic bombing intended to keep the sirens sounding and put citizens on edge. Eleanor continued her speech without missing a beat, earning the admiration of the thousands of attendees who acquired their noncha-lance to the sirens after enduring them for several years. And hours after she visited the town of Canterbury in southeast

England, thirty German bombers strafed the city, reducing houses to rubble and killing civilians.

When Eleanor went to England, she asked Tommy if she wanted to accompany her. "I did not want to obligate her to take a trip that might entail some risk. She was entirely willing and gave as little thought to the possible danger as I did," Eleanor said. "It was not a sign of courage that I went ahead and did certain things which might have had some slight danger attached to them. It was simply that, like most human beings, I am not given to seeing myself disappear off the face of the earth. If it should happen, having no choice, I would, I hope, accept the inevitable philosophically."

Eleanor had courage in spades and didn't expend needless energy on being afraid. She referred to fear as "the great enemy" and had worked hard to vanquish it from her life, overcoming a childhood and early youth that "were one long battle against fear." She was afraid of the dark and of mice, afraid of displeasing people, and she had an acute fear of failure. In short, she was "afraid of practically everything," she said. "Painfully, step by step, I learned to stare down each of my fears, conquer it, attain the hard-earned courage to go on to the next."

Eleanor was resilient, largely tolerant of physical discomfort and hardship, but she was not invincible. After nearly two weeks traveling through the Pacific, she was feeling alone and alienated from her loved ones. In Great Britain, Tommy was with her, and she spent time with her son Elliott, who was stationed in England at the time. She also saw other family, friends, and acquaintances, including former classmates from the boarding school near London she attended as a teenager. On this trip, in addition to traveling without a close companion, mail took time to catch up with her, the same as it did for the troops, adding to a sense of isolation. "I am hungry for news of all at home," she told Tommy. "As I have no word from anyone, I wonder if they are keeping you informed of my whereabouts.... I feel a hundred years away as though I were moving in a different and totally unattached world. I don't like it much." Spending even limited time with her friend Joe, who was serving on Guadalcanal, would be "the one pleasant & happy personal thing." Likewise, she was thinking of Joe, a soldier far from home. "I am sorry as seeing all these masses of boys who seem pleased just to see me as a stranger makes me realize it might have meant something to [him]." She had promised Trude Pratt, Joe's fiancée and her close confidant, that she would try to see him and report back to her.

—

Eleanor buried her disappointment over Halsey's hard-line stance on Guadalcanal by continuing to keep a feverish pace. "When one isn't happy it is hard not to live at high speed," she told a friend.

Tacked on a wall in the MP's office on New Caledonia was a newspaper cartoon depicting a woman telling her husband that she thinks the First Lady has covered a few more miles than the president has. Eleanor had a sense of humor about seeing the prominently placed cartoon, telling "My Day" readers, "I'm quite sure the MPs thought I had covered them all in one day on New Caledonia." While there, she poured her energy into focusing on the troops: touring three hospitals, taking a boat ride to an officers' rest home and lunching there, making a speech at a service club, and addressing the 2nd Marine Raider Battalion, of which her son James had been the executive officer.

Eleanor's respect for the troops' sacrifices was deeply

personal for her. All four of her sons were in uniform, James with the marines, Elliott in the army air forces, and Franklin Jr. and John in the navy. "I imagine every mother felt as I did when I said good-by to the children during the war. I had a feeling that I might be saying good-by for the last time. It was a sort of precursor of what it would be like if your children were killed," she said. "Life had to go on and you had to do what was required of you, but something inside of you quietly died."

Neither she nor the president was privy to special information about their sons' whereabouts and activities. In mid-December 1941, Eleanor found out by reading the newspaper that Elliott had been assigned to an aviation unit, serving as navigator and observer in a reconnaissance squadron, and that he was headed to active duty. On the way to England, crossing the Atlantic, she saw a convoy of ships below—zigzagging to disguise its true course and confuse the enemy—and wondered if Franklin Jr. might be aboard one of the destroyers. Not long before she left for the Pacific, she telephoned the president, who began their conversation by saying, "Frankie is all right." Eleanor's heart sank as she asked what happened. The ship on which Franklin, Jr. served and other navy vessels were dive-bombed by enemy planes off the coast of Sicily. They fought off the attack but suffered damages and lost five men.

Eleanor sent a condolence note to a woman in Albany, New York, whose son died of wounds he sustained during the attack. "I know there is nothing I can say which would be of any consolation except that you can be proud your son was willing to give his utmost for his country," she wrote.

On New Caledonia, Eleanor's enormous efforts to engage with the troops did not go unnoticed by Admiral Halsey. Even in the short amount of time she was on the island, she impressed the rough-and-tough sailor, who admired "her har-dihood, both physical and mental." Although she detected a slight softening in his attitude, she left for New Zealand in low spirits, believing her request to visit Guadalcanal would be denied.

MONGOLIA MANCHUKUO (KURIL IS.)(Jap.)

BI OR SHAMO (DESERT) Hsinking Harbin HOKKAIDO

INNER MONGOLIA Mukden Vladivostok

GREAT KHINGAN MTS. Hakodate Ominato

anchow Sian Peiping Dairen (Jap.) CHOSEN Keijo HONSHU

Tientsin Keishu Tokyo Sea of Japan

Tsingtao Kyoto Yokohama

CHINA Ho Yellow Sea Sasebo Kobe Osaka

Chungking Hwang Nanking Nagasaki KYŪSHŌ JAPAN

Changsha Hankow Shanghai

Yangtze Kiang Foochow RYŪKYU IS. OGASAWARA JIMA (Jap.)

Kunming Canton TAIWAN (FORMOSA) (Jap.)

Hanoi HONG KONG (Br.) MARIANAS IS. (Jap. Mand.)

FRENCH Kwangchowan (Fr.) Aparri LUZON GUAM (U.S.A.)

THAILAND (SIAM) Manila PHILIPPINE IS. (U.S.A.)

Bangkok Legaspi PALAU IS. YAP

INDOCHINA Saigon Davao MINDANAO CAROLINE ISLANDS TRUK IS. PONAPE

G. of Siam South China Sea (Jap. Mand.)

MALAY STATES (Br.) BR.N.BORNEO Brunei (Br.) Sandakan HALMAHERA

gapore SARAWAK (Br.) Kuching BORNEO (Neth.)

SUMATRA CELEBES (Neth.) AMBOINA BISMARCK ARCH. NEW IRELAND

lembang NETHERLANDS INDIES NEW GUINEA TER. OF NEW GUINEA (Aust. Mand.) Rabaul BOUGAINVILLE SOLOMO

Java Sea (Neth.) NEW GUINEA NEW BRITAIN Lae YSABEL I. MALAITA

Batavia Soerabaja PAP Buna GUADALCANAL

JAVA TIMOR Arafura Sea Port Moresby

CHRISTMAS I. TIMOR (Neth.) NEW

COS IS. (Br.) Darwin Gulf of Carpentaria Coral Sea

INDIAN Broome Daly Waters Townsville EASTERN

NORTH WEST CAPE GREAT Alice Springs Nouméa

OCEAN AUSTRALIA DESERT Lake Eyre Brisbane LORD HOWE I. (Aust.)

Fremantle Perth Darling R. Sydney

CAPE LEEUWIN Great Australian Bight Adelaide Murray R. Canberra

Melbourne Bass Strait Tasman Se

TASMANIA Hobart

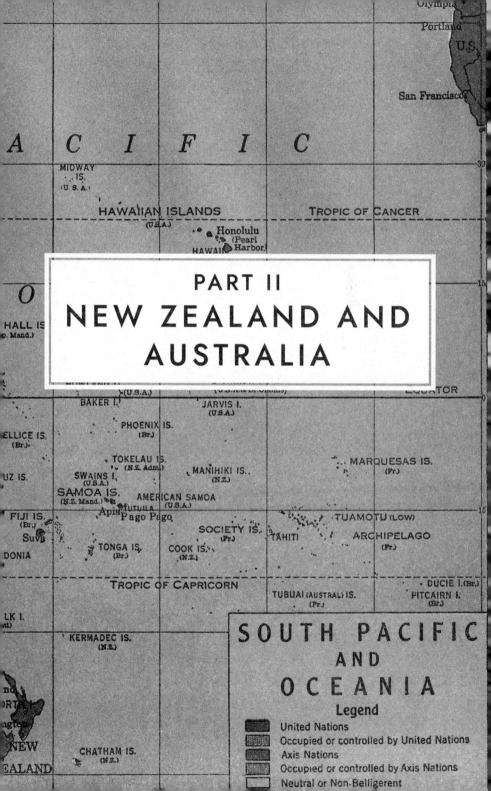

CHAPTER 6

NEWS TO US

"For the first time in history New Zealand yesterday welcomed as a guest to the Dominion the wife of a President of the United States—Mrs. Eleanor Roosevelt."

—NEW ZEALAND HERALD, AUGUST 28, 1943

Auckland, New Zealand, August 27

The switchboard at the White House began lighting up during the night of August 26, 1943, as reporters scrambled for the story once news broke that the First Lady was on the other side of the world in New Zealand. "It's news to us," a switchboard operator replied when informed of Eleanor's whereabouts and then refused to rouse anyone in the household for comment.

After Eleanor spent ten days secretly island-hopping across the South Pacific, her arrival at an air station in Auckland "had all the dramatic surprise quality associated with her tour last year to Britain." Service men and women who worked at the aerodrome waited on the tarmac, bursting into cheers as she exited the plane looking "as fresh and full of energy as if she had merely concluded a pleasant outing instead of a journey of thousands of miles."

Eleanor was greeted by a bevy of government bigwigs and their spouses, one of whom handed her a cascading bouquet of spring flowers. Minutes later, she was escorted to a battery of microphones on the steps of a building housing the officers' mess, where she stood poised and smiling. "I am very glad of this opportunity to come to New Zealand," she told listeners in a nationwide broadcast. "It is a great pleasure for me, and I want to bring my husband's greetings and to say I know he would like to be with me, but since he cannot I am glad I was able to come." She thanked women especially for the hospitality shown to American servicemen, who had been invited to stay in New Zealand homes, and expressed gratitude on behalf of their mothers and wives an ocean away. "We already feel," Eleanor concluded, "that we know you and that we are old friends. I hope to speak again before I go and when I know more about your country."

Until they heard the First Lady's voice, gentle and low, over the radio, New Zealanders had no idea she was on their shores. She was familiar to them through years of media coverage during her time in the White House. Her reputation as a crusader for social justice and women's rights preceded her, and they recognized and respected her unique role. "No other President's wife has exercised anything like the same power either in her own land or in the world without," declared a newspaper.

New Zealanders viewed Eleanor as a leading wartime figure, "a great fighter in the cause of the world's freedom." Plus, they were impressed that she had "the distinction of being perhaps the only woman at whom Hitler has persistently and hysterically screamed his denunciations." The führer accused her of "influencing her husband against the peaceful and self-effacing Germans, and that alone entitles her to the respect and regard of the rest of the world."

Warmly welcoming the First Lady was also a way of paying respect to President Roosevelt. His administration's progressive New Deal social and economic policies were regarded with favor in New Zealand, as was his prominent role in the battle against Axis aggression. The mayor of Auckland recalled the feeling of security and confidence inspired by the arrival of American forces in New Zealand earlier in the war. "It seems but yesterday," he later told Eleanor at a reception, "when to us it seemed that the end was almost at hand, and then suddenly the scene changed and we were joined in our struggle by the gallant men from your great continent. The very fact that we are able to extend our welcome today is due solely to the vast development of the defence forces in this part of the world, which to us augurs success to our joint efforts."

New Zealand was one of the first countries to take a stand in World War II. Along with Great Britain, France, and Australia, they declared war on Germany after the Nazis invaded Poland in September 1939. New Zealand and Australia, both independent, self-governing dominions within the British Commonwealth, pledged military and economic support in the fight against Hitler.

Although distant from the immediate danger zones, New Zealanders still feared attack or invasion of their small country, then with a population of just over 1.64 million (a fraction of the United States' 136 million inhabitants). Narrow and about one thousand miles long, New Zealand is made up of two main islands, the North Island and the South Island, and numerous smaller ones. Seasons are opposite those in the United States and the climate "topsy-turvy," Eleanor explained in "My Day"— milder weather in the north and colder as one heads south.

Mountains form a spine down the country, bordered by rolling farmland on the North Island and rising highest to the Southern Alps on the South Island. A marine corps photographic officer was on board a transport ship that cruised northward the length of the South Island. "Winter snows came right down to the water. Jagged peaks towered in perfect white from the deep blue sea into a cloudless sky," he recalled. "Hour after hour that glorious panorama glittered in the sun."

American service personnel were told in a *Meet New Zealand* guide prepared especially for them that combining Pennsylvania, Virginia, Maryland, Delaware, and Rhode Island would equal the area of New Zealand, with a population roughly that of Detroit, Michigan. The country's amazingly diverse landscape encompasses volcanic areas and hot springs, glaciers and fjords, forests and farmland, mountains and beaches. Thirteen hundred miles separate New Zealand from Australia, its closest neighbor, to the northwest across the Tasman Sea.

In the seas around New Zealand and Australia, German raiders lurked. Merchant vessels outfitted with concealed weaponry, the raiders laid mines and attacked passenger ships and freighters transporting food, raw materials, and other essential goods to the Allies. New Zealand, meanwhile, prepared its defenses by reinforcing harbors with explosives, establishing coastal air watch stations, and instituting a nighttime blackout. A home guard was created, composed of men not eligible for overseas duty (such as farmers, since food production was an essential service). The Women's War Service Auxiliary, through a volunteer registry, recruited women to aid in the war effort in jobs ranging from canteen and clerical work to fire fighting and transport driving.

Tensions in New Zealand heightened exponentially after the bombing of Pearl Harbor, particularly since most of the country's military was fighting with the British on distant battlefields. A New Zealand newspaper editorial laid blame for the country's vulnerable position on Prime Minister Churchill and on President Roosevelt. The editorial was in response to a speech delivered by Churchill in early 1942, during which he admitted that with Great Britain's focus on fighting Germany and Italy, there were insufficient means to protect its territories in the Pacific and the Far East—and yet they provoked Japan anyway. New Zealand and Australia were repeatedly assured that all was well and were allowed to keep sending troops. "The error lay in adopting a policy without first providing the means to meet the consequences."

In July 1941, Great Britain and the Dutch East Indies joined with the United States to impose financial and economic sanctions on Japan, which was faced with three choices—surrender, suffer economic strangulation, or fight. If Japan chose the third option, it would have to be done quickly before its dwindling resources were exhausted. "Mr. Churchill makes it plain that the Allies banked on Japan flinching. Instead, she called their bluff and found them unprepared," charged the editorial. "They had no right to accept such a palpable risk without adequate cover."

Two weeks after the editorial ran, Singapore fell, followed by bombings in the Australian coastal cities of Darwin and Broome. "The chief fear," the *New York Times* reported, "is that the foe will get a foothold in Northern Australia and then assault the northern industrial regions on the east coast." At the same time, the Japanese could begin a wide sweep to sever ties along the South Pacific route from the United States to Australia by seizing the line of islands that culminates with New Zealand.

After the fall of Singapore, New Zealand prime minister

Peter Fraser appealed to Churchill for assistance in strengthening his country's defenses. As he made clear in a cable to Churchill and in turn to President Roosevelt, "fear of our own personal fortunes" was not the driving force behind the appeal. Rather it was a firm belief that war in the Pacific would be long and hard and that the retention of Fiji and the successful defense of New Zealand were "absolutely essential." Among other concerns, should New Zealand fall to the enemy, Great Britain would lose 25 percent of its food supply, warned Walter Nash, the country's representative in Washington.

Behind the scenes, high-level negotiations illustrated the interconnectedness of a vast and complicated global war. Churchill was reluctant to relinquish New Zealand's troops, who had been trained to fight in the North African deserts. A more expedient and thriftier solution—and one that would not risk the delicately balanced situation in North Africa and the Middle East—was to have the United States send forces to New Zealand on the condition that the New Zealanders would remain where they were. President Roosevelt agreed to the request, notifying Prime Minister Fraser in March 1942, that "we are straining every effort" to send troops as soon as possible to New Zealand and to Australia.

Japan continued to wreak havoc, confident enough in its successes that an official threatened, "We shall take New Zealand. Neither America nor Britain can get out to her. If the New Zealanders are wise, they will not resist." Two days later, American forces arrived in the country, which, along with Australia, served as a base for U.S. military operations in the Pacific.

Beginning in mid-1942, over the next two years, some one hundred thousand American servicemen passed through New Zealand, staying anywhere from a few days or weeks to several months. They came to train for battle on Pacific islands, to be treated for combat injuries, and to rest and relax before heading back into the fight.

———

At the Auckland air station, inside the officers' mess, Eleanor shook hands with each reporter assembled in the billiard room for a press conference. After taking a seat in a cane lounge chair, she pleasantly answered a volley of questions about her trip and why she was making it, her interest in the Pacific democracies, and her wish to see the war work women were doing. Asked if she was tired, she laughingly disclaimed any feelings of fatigue. "I have had a very easy trip, and am not in the least tired," she said. "It has been smooth and very pleasant all the way."

When queried about the interest Americans had in New Zealand, Eleanor replied that before the Pacific war, there was comparatively little contact between residents of the two countries. "However," she added, "the boys have been writing home and saying what a nice country it is, how well the people entertain them, especially in their homes, and perhaps how they would like to come back here after the war is over to stay."

Female journalists in attendance particularly appreciated meeting a famous fellow "ink spiller." Even this far afield, the trailblazing press briefings Eleanor held at the White House were legendary. After Franklin took office in March 1933, she had announced that she would get together exclusively with newspaperwomen, who were not permitted at the president's press conferences. Eleanor's aim was twofold: to ensure they received space in print, since stories generated by the First Lady were newsworthy, and to communicate with the general public. Her goal was to make people more aware of White House activities and to encourage understanding of and engagement in the political process, especially among women.

Instituting women-only press conferences "represented a superb revolution," wrote a New Zealand correspondent. In doing it, "she kicked over an ancient prejudice." It was the belief of many editors that newspaper women were only fit to write about cookies and broken hearts and that women only wanted to read about those topics and nothing else. "The belief was ill-founded, but it was obstinate."

When the press conference at the airfield concluded, a fleet of motor cars whisked Eleanor and her government escorts to the Auckland train station, where a sizable crowd assembled to see her off. Eleanor boarded a plushily appointed viceregal carriage used by the governor-general, the personal representative of the British crown in New Zealand, who was accompanying her on the overnight journey to Wellington. Eleanor stood at the door of the carriage, bowing and smiling. She clasped hands with the nearest bystander, a woman who lived in close proximity to a U.S. military camp, thanking her for her kindness toward American servicemen. While the train inched forward along the track, Eleanor stood in the doorway and waved to the well-wishers on the station platform.

———

As Eleanor's train sped the length of the North Island toward Wellington, 430 miles to the south, stateside media outlets rushed to report on her dramatic doings. The initial reaction to the news of her whereabouts was astonishment: not that the peripatetic First Lady had surfaced in New Zealand but that the trip was such a well-kept secret.

Like most of Eleanor's undertakings, the revelation of her trip to the Pacific generated both support and scorn, much of it along political lines. Newspapers from coast to coast covered the trip, running daily reports on her overseas activities, and often stoked controversy with inflammatory editorials. Some acknowledged that Eleanor's visit would undoubtedly please the troops and raise morale, while others fell back on a familiar refrain—lamenting that the country did not have a more conventional First Lady. "KEEP HER AT HOME," screeched an Alabama paper. "The time has come for Federal officials to step in and call a halt upon the peregrinations of Eleanor Roosevelt."

Others praised her trailblazing ways. "Doing things that no other President's wife has done, [she] is true to herself, to her family and to the people of this country," noted one. "She has incredible energy and tremendous ambition to be useful." Another hard-hitting editorial took her critics to task, pointing out that "not all women are cast in the same mold" and that "they can have great value" in fields other than domesticity.

Eleanor was accused of using the trip as a ploy to generate material for her column and to drum up votes among servicemen should Franklin run in the next presidential election. ("The President is looking after the war—his wife is looking after the politics.") And the need for gasoline rationing was a favorite rant of those who slammed her "gadabouts." It wasn't immediately noted in news reports how she traveled to New Zealand or that she had visited Pacific islands along the way. Even after it was revealed that she did not fly on a private plane but rather on a regular Air Transport Command flight, some media outlets stuck to the false narrative.

Among the most vitriolic commenters was a longtime Roosevelt administration critic, the conservative columnist Westbrook Pegler, who often wielded his pen against the First Lady. He declared the trip a ruse for her to rendezvous with her friend Joseph Lash and a waste of taxpayer money (a deliberate oversight, since from the outset it was widely reported that Eleanor traveled at her own expense, including purchasing the Red Cross uniforms). "I say Mrs. Roosevelt had no right to fly to England or to the South Pacific," he blasted. "And I contend that she has exploited the office of the Presidency for a great private financial gain." (Another oversight since it was also reported that fees Eleanor earned from writing columns and articles about the Pacific trip were divided between the Red Cross and another aid organization.)

Coming to Eleanor's defense were the GI reporters on Christmas Island. With the information blackout surrounding her tour of the Pacific lifted, they were finally able to write about her visit in their troop-produced magazine *Pacific Times*. One article called out "a certain vitriolic columnist," dubbed "Pegbrook Westler," for making Eleanor a primary target of his "journalistic arrows." The president "was just a little too high for his brand of ridicule, and lesser dignitaries were deemed just common fodder for that type of attempted destruction. So, he settled on the wife of the President." And along with "columnist Sourpuss," other writers, political antagonists, and "all types of theatrical ham and just ordinary jerks" had heckled Eleanor in recent years.

"But today," continued the GI reporter, "an unstipulated number (military secret—remember?) of men at this station are in the happy position of being able to refute such evidence of poor taste and, generally speaking, of near-slander." After the First Lady's visit, whether they talked with her personally, attended one of her addresses, or heard about her secondhand, most agreed on three things: "(1) Mrs. Roosevelt is the possessor of a keen and inquiring mind; (2) She is genuinely interested in the well-being of the men in the service and can be expected to do everything in her power to maintain and further that well-being; (3) Above all, she is a GRACIOUS LADY!"

The *New York Herald Tribune* published side-by-side, contrasting letters from readers. "This last jaunt, to New Zealand—and I suppose Australia and heaven knows where else—is the last straw!" wrote "Disgusted Citizen" of Orange, New Jersey. The irate writer accused the First Lady of using her position to further her own interests and demanded a congressional investigation into her "activities." D. Allen of New Rochelle, New York, passionately lauded Eleanor, saying, "She has all the qualities the historians of the future and we of the present could hope for in the wife of the greatest President that ever lived. Aside from her grand sense of humor, she has sympathy and deep feeling. There seems to be nothing she can't appreciate, no matter who it happens to. She is certainly a natural for the White House, being able to mingle graciously with any one from any place and to talk interestingly on any topic. Her views are wholesome and hearty, for she's the most uninhibited personality in Washington. The fact that she is honest and straightforward enough to express her most refreshing opinions in the face of all sorts of nasty opposition is certainly admirable."

Others vented directly to the president. Mrs. Dane Sylvester, "a sailor's wife," griped that the gasoline usage could instead be utilized to bring mail to the troops. Another correspondent attacked the expense of the gas needed "to lug her all over hell's half-acre" before launching a petty personal attack: "She needn't kid us with any Moral building bunk as she is no glamor girl and Ginny Simms or Betty Grable would have pleased the boys more."

A serviceman's mother praised Eleanor's efforts and passed along a message from her son, who was serving "somewhere" in the Southwest Pacific: "There was a very important person here the other day and I was assigned to her personal guard. I wish I might tell all the folks back home the truly valuable work she is doing for our men over seas, and the good it is doing."

The American Red Cross received indignant letters saying the First Lady had no right to wear its uniform. Others accused them of playing politics by sponsoring her trip. Red Cross officials responded unequivocally to the allegations, reporting publicly that it did not pay Eleanor's expenses and that she contributed a large monthly check to the organization; she had every right to wear the uniform, having been an active canteen worker in the last war and honorary chairman of the National Committee on Volunteer Service in this one; and her visiting Red Cross installations in the Pacific was done with Norman Davis's encouragement. Although she didn't wear the organization's uniform in Great Britain, while there, she "surveyed virtually every Red Cross Club" as well as many isolated clubs at camps and air bases and recreational work at hospitals.

Eleanor was often asked if the criticism she routinely received troubled her or if it was hurtful or made her angry. She directly addressed the issue in an article, "How to Take Criticism," published in *Ladies' Home Journal*. A favorite talking point of her critics was that she "can have no sense of responsibility" since she was not elected to any office, an idea she countered. In the natural course of events, she came to know a great deal about the country and its people and circumstances. "Here is where criticism centers," she wrote. For instance, should the president's wife be interested in working conditions? "She has rare opportunities for knowing about them if she has eyes, ears and understanding. Should she be blind, deaf and dumb?"

Criticism is entirely permissible, Eleanor continued, hence the question: How much attention should a person pay to criticism? After all, no one enjoys being disliked. She could emulate a Dresden china figure, daintily placed on display, and avoid any unpleasantness. Or she could live as an independent citizen who uses opportunities for service in society and take the criticism that comes with it. "You're damned if you do and damned if you don't!" she stated. "If you run counter to others now and then, you have enemies; but life would become unbearable if you thought about it all the time, so you have to ignore the critics."

CHAPTER 7

A MODERN CRUSADER

"Mrs. R. literally took New Zealand by storm."
—MAJOR GEORGE DURNO, A PRESS OFFICER
ASSIGNED TO ACCOMPANY THE FIRST
LADY, IN A LETTER TO HER SECRETARY

Wellington, New Zealand, August 28–30

On a cold, cloudy day in mid-June 1942, the USS *Wakefield* sailed into Wellington Harbor with five thousand marines aboard. The weathered transport ship, which made it through bombings at Singapore four months earlier, on this voyage eluded numerous enemy submarines while traveling unescorted from Norfolk, Virginia, via the Panama Canal to New Zealand.

As the *Wakefield* came alongside the wharf in Wellington, a Royal New Zealand Air Force band struck up renditions of "The Stars and Stripes Forever" and the U.S. Marine Corps anthem. Servicemen crowded the ship's three tiers of decks for their first look at the country's scenic capital nestled between steeply rising hills and a wide, circular harbor on the southern end of the North Island. From an elevated vantage point, a Wellington resident witnessed the ship's arrival as he was digging an air-raid shelter in his backyard.

The men onboard the *Wakefield* were the first forces to arrive in Wellington after President Roosevelt's pledge to send troops to New Zealand (U.S. Army troops docked in Auckland two days earlier). They stayed for a month, lodging in military camps in the surrounding area, before shipping out to fight in the Solomon Islands, where the assault on Guadalcanal would soon begin.

Although no marching band greeted Eleanor on her arrival in Wellington, the largest battery of cameras ever assembled in the city set the train station ablaze with flashbulbs as photographers and cameramen commemorated the occasion. She exited the train carriage onto a red carpet, where she was welcomed by Prime Minister Fraser and members of the cabinet, the mayor, and senior officers of the U.S. and New Zealand militaries.

"Well, I'll be a so-and-so," exclaimed a U.S. Marine in amazement as Eleanor veered off the red carpet stretching through the station to approach him and two others, hand extended in greeting. A newspaper declared the encounter "the New Zealand counterpart of American miners looking up from their work on a coal face to see Mrs. Roosevelt coming towards them," referencing a popular 1933 cartoon satirizing the First Lady's habit of turning up in unexpected places (she took her famous trip into the mines two years after the cartoon ran).

Despite no official announcement about Eleanor's arrival time, word traveled faster than her train. On the drive to Government House, the governor-general's residence, a two-story, Tudor-inspired mansion where heads of state and other dignitaries were entertained, enthusiastic crowds gathered and waved as her car passed by.

Eleanor's arrival kicked off a three-day stay in Wellington, during which time she personified "the term 'American hustle.'" Her visit began with a round of official meet and greets, including a state reception at Parliament House, the main building of the governing body. In the basement of the grand, neoclassical edifice was the entrance to a bomb-resistant shelter, one of twenty-one shelters constructed on Parliament grounds due to fears of a Japanese attack.

"I hope when the time comes to build a world of peace we will again stand side by side, men and women, and try this time to lay a better foundation for peace than we did the last time," Eleanor told those assembled at Parliament House. "I am afraid that peace is not a thing that signatures on a piece of paper bring about. Peace, I think, has to be worked for day in and day out, just as we work to win the war."

The next morning, at Silverstream, a U.S. Navy hospital in the hills north of Wellington, patients greeted the First Lady, shouting, "We're glad you have come." Eleanor continued her practice of visiting wards by the dozen to speak with bedbound patients, significantly more of whom were being treated for malaria contracted in the Pacific than for combat injuries. The mosquitoes that transmitted malaria thrived in the damp, swampy environments where troops were fighting. "Disease was a surer and more deadly peril to us than enemy marksmanship," asserted Lieutenant General Eichelberger, who led the fight for Buna on the coast of Papua New Guinea. "We had to whip the Japanese before the malarial mosquito whipped us."

Eleanor understood the despondency of the malaria patients due to the lengthy amount of time they were held for treatment and observation, 120 days, and the uncertainty of the disease. Her son James was among the 60 to 65 percent of American troops serving in the Pacific to suffer from malaria, which attacks the red blood cells and the liver, causing fever, chills, nausea, and fatigue. While not typically fatal, the tenacious disease had long-lasting effects and could cause repeated attacks for weeks and months after someone contracted it. A Guadalcanal veteran Eleanor met the next year while awaiting a train near Hyde Park confided that he had experienced twenty-two recurrences of malaria.

At Silverstream, Eleanor joined some two hundred convalescing sailors and marines, nurses, and doctors in a concert and dance hall converted into a chapel for Sunday worship. The Episcopal service, conducted by a chaplain and navy captain using *A Prayer Book for Soldiers and Sailors*, included one of Eleanor's favorite Bible readings: Psalm 23, a verse emphasizing God's protection in the face of evil. The prayer book, containing an order of worship, the Holy Communion, prayers, psalms, Bible readings, and hymns, was published by the Army and Navy Commission of the Protestant Episcopal Church and sent as a gift to those in the armed forces.

After the service, Eleanor stepped onto the stage, delivering President Roosevelt's personal message of thanks to those present. "He said to tell you that every day he goes down to the Map Room in the White House and notes on the maps where you are and what you are doing," she said. "He can see exactly where every ship and every unit is fighting all over the world."

In the Map Room, a top-secret communications center in the White House, the president monitored military activities, received reports and coded messages, and communicated with other Allied leaders. Modeled on a similar setup in Churchill's underground bunker in London and a portable travel version, the Map Room (precursor to the modern-day White House Situation Room) was guarded around the clock and access highly restricted. Even the Secret Service was barred from entering. Maps of Europe, Africa, the Far East, and the Pacific were mounted on the walls, positioned low enough that the president could examine them while seated in his wheelchair. Different colored pins designated the locations and movements of Allied and Axis land, sea, and air forces.

Every few days, the president received from General George Marshall, the U.S. Army chief of staff, a summary of casualty figures as a reminder of the war's cost in lives. "It was done in a rather effective way, graphically and in colors, so it would be quite clear to him when he had only a moment or two to consider," said Marshall. "You get hardened to these things and you have to be very careful to keep them always in the forefront of your mind."

On a map of the United States in a lounge at a Red Cross club in the Hotel Cecil in Wellington, servicemen wrote their names and hometowns on pieces of paper and pinned them in the appropriate locales. The mural spanned an entire wall, so oversized that reaching the northern states required using the ladder kept handy for the purpose. "It was so fascinating to find guys from close to where you lived," said one marine. Eleanor commemorated her visit to the club by signing a slip of paper and adding it to the ones already pinned near Washington, DC.

A rest and recreation center for off-duty Allied servicemen, the Cecil Red Cross Club was a refuge from the spartan military camps where they bunked while in Wellington. Run by Red Cross workers and staffed by local volunteers, the club fostered connection among Americans and New Zealanders and was used equally by each country's troops. "We have found that we think the same thoughts and speak the same language," said Prime Minister Fraser at the club's opening ceremony, "and here we will be able to develop the good understanding that will never be lost."

For servicemen who roughed it on island battlefronts or spent weeks sequestered aboard a ship, the Cecil Red Cross Club was a wonderland rife with amenities. There was a soda fountain and a canteen serving "back-home food" like hamburgers, doughnuts, apple pie, coffee, and Coca-Cola. In the library, there were desks and writing supplies to pen a letter home. In a crafts room, newly opened the morning of Eleanor's visit, a dozen men were turning silver wire and plating into rings, bracelets, and identification discs. Adorning a wall in the crafts room was a scene from *Snow White and the Seven Dwarfs*, painted by a marine who in prewar days worked for the Walt Disney Company. A building adjacent to the main club was used for dancing and for playing billiards and Ping-Pong.

When preparations began for the Allied Services Club, also in Wellington, the impending arrival of U.S. forces was still a "dark State secret," William Perry, Minister of the Armed Forces and War Coordination, told a crowd during Eleanor's visit there. The creation of the club was intended as a gesture of friendship and cooperation. In addition, there was a more practical reason for the existence of service clubs. With New Zealand cities largely closed in the evenings and on Sundays, there was nowhere for off-duty servicemen to have a meal (the Allied Services Club served some six hundred pounds of steak on Sundays) or to go for entertainment. "You won't find subways, skyscrapers or night-life," U.S. troops were told in the *Meet New Zealand* guide.

What New Zealand lacked in nightlife, it made up for in hospitality. The Red Cross kept a list of people willing to host American servicemen, with one town alone offering five hundred homes. The specially created Home Hospitality Bureau, located next door to the Allied Services Club, invited servicemen to register and detailed their interests so they could be appropriately matched with host families. Even Prime Minister Fraser and his wife, Janet, invited American servicemen to join them for home-cooked meals and took them on outings.

For New Zealanders, nearly three years into the strain and anxieties of war, the "friendly invasion" of American servicemen was a reassuring yet disrupting occurrence. "There are difficulties inherent in settling en masse in another's country. Surface disputes are bound to crop up," Eleanor candidly relayed during a post-trip speech. Differing styles of the English language were spoken, driving took place on opposite sides of the road, and different monetary systems were used, all of which were explained to the new arrivals in the *Meet New Zealand* guide. A Wellington paper ran a humorous "News of the Day" item, good-naturedly poking fun at the foreigners while recounting an exchange between a hotel clerk and a U.S. serviceman who handed over an incorrect sum when asked for "two and six" as a deposit on a room key.

A cultural clash arose over romance in New Zealand and Australia. Dapperly dressed in better-tailored uniforms, American servicemen were solicitous and smooth-talking with the ladies, irking some local men. They were better paid and often flush with back pay accumulated while in combat, and the economic boom they sparked in certain sectors like flower shops, soda fountains, restaurants, and taxis escalated prices for residents. Goods already in short supply due to wartime constraints became ever scarcer due to American demand.

Largely, though, there was friendliness and mutual admiration between American troops and New Zealanders. Anyone who had a serviceman in the Pacific "ought to be extraordinarily proud," Eleanor told a stateside audience. "Not of what good fighters they are but of what wonderful diplomats. They have been the best ambassadors in New Zealand and Australia that we ever had."

The first marines who went to Guadalcanal sailed from New Zealand. When they later came out of the combat zone for rest and recuperation, New Zealanders were disappointed that instead of returning to their country, they were sent to Australia. "They went from here. They were our boys," Eleanor heard over and over. "We wanted them to come back."

New Zealanders invited servicemen into their homes for morning and afternoon tea, for weekend getaways, and for two- and three-week stays, often straight from hospitals. A woman in Gisborne, a port city on the North Island, went from expecting the one serviceman her daughter invited for Christmas to organizing a getaway for sixty patients from Silverstream. She arranged transportation for the entire group in a private rail car and secured lodgings for them with town residents. The men would often reciprocate their hosts' kindness by washing dishes and running errands. One woman appreciated the "frank friendliness, ready wit and appreciation" of her two houseguests, marines who had served on Guadalcanal. "I must say your city lads from Boston and Brooklyn, N.Y., gave us quiet country folks something to think of."

A couple named Mr. and Mrs. Sutton enjoyed looking after two young marines for several weeks at their home in a coastal town on the North Island. "It was just grand to feel that we could give them a little home life and little delicacies," Mr. Sutton told the Red Cross. When one of the marines had a recurrence of malaria, they recognized the signs and went to great lengths to nurse him back to health. "May I thank you for sending us two such splendid fellows," who "fitted into our home like our own family," Mr. Sutton said. "My wife has written asking you to send more lads from time to time."

—

During Eleanor's days in Wellington, from visiting a depot where volunteers packed parcels for prisoners of war to touring a laboratory using science and engineering to increase the effectiveness of defense production, she was not only seeing all she could but "being seen" as well. At a Ford factory, more than one hundred women paused their tasks and cheered "spontaneously and lustily" when she entered their workroom. The factory manufactured jeeps along with hand grenades, artillery fuses, mortar bombs, and other specialized war equipment. For the first time, women were employed at the factory and made up the majority of employees—"Girls who are doing a Man-sized Job," according to the company. Or as Eleanor described it, doing "dangerous work" and "doing it well, and with considerable skill."

Eleanor was so popular—charming audiences with her "effortless, womanly talks"—that even if she remained in Wellington another week, a newspaper declared, there would still be crowds at her functions. A civic reception held in her honor at a local theater drew interest from more people than the venue could possibly accommodate.

The civic reception was Eleanor's second night in a row filling the ample Majestic Theatre to capacity. The day before, she addressed a women-only audience. Long before the theater doors opened, women waited, four deep, in a line that extended down the street. Two thousand gained entry, while hundreds more waited outside hoping to catch a glimpse of her.

As Eleanor took the stage, the audience rose, their applause reaching a steady roar. She was escorted by Janet Fraser, a popular public figure admired for her longtime advocacy of health, education, and welfare issues, particularly for women and children. Mrs. Fraser was an adviser to her husband, the prime minister, and a leader in New Zealand's women's war effort. She was instrumental in the creation of the Women's War Service Auxiliary, which coordinated the activities of existing women's organizations so they could be used to best advantage, and served as its first president. Like Eleanor, she rallied and encouraged her countrywomen to contribute to winning the war. "The need for women to assist the war effort is greater than ever," she said during an appeal for auxiliary registrants after Pearl Harbor was bombed. "We must throw all our weight and all our enthusiasm into it, and I have confidence in the ability of our women to overcome any obstacles."

That evening, Eleanor delivered "a suggestive, thought-provoking message for the times," stressing the necessity for postwar cooperation among nations to avoid another devastating conflict in the future. Peace would be achieved not out of fear of a powerful tyrant but because people had enough to eat, shelter for their families, and employment that paid a decent living wage. With the end of the war in sight, now was the time to plan for the future. "It may cost many more young lives," she cautioned. "Many women may weep. But in the end the democracies will triumph and we will have another chance to strive to do better than we did before."

At the end of World War I, the United States retreated into isolationism and maintained contact with the rest of the world primarily through trade channels. "For too long a time we blinded ourselves," Eleanor said. "Finally, we reaped the bitter harvest and shared grimly in the economic depression which fell upon the world." This time, people should not rely solely on the work of their leaders at the peace table. "If democracy is to prove itself, the voice of the people must be more articulate," she continued. Every person must take full responsibility in making the leaders conscious of the wishes of the people, and seeing that built on the foundations of this war was "a progressive

economic and political building designed to straighten and pre-
serve peace."

The First Lady's "challenging address" was particularly apt
timing for New Zealanders and "worthy of close attention," suggested newspaper editorials. In less than a month, the country
would elect its new Parliament members to three-year terms, a
period that would presumably encompass the transition from
war to peace and the planning of the postwar order. Eleanor
was "keenly alert to the trend of feeling in public affairs," and
her conclusions carried authoritative weight. "Most timely it is,
therefore, to be reminded in the words of Mrs. Roosevelt, here re-
emphasized, that '*every person must take full responsibility in making
the leaders conscious of the wishes of the people.*' A General Election
is the one time in the constitutional life of a people when such
wishes may and *can* be expressed in unmistakable terms."

Standing onstage, silhouetted in a glow of light in the darkened theater, the First Lady seemed like "a modern Crusader,"
wrote a reporter watching her deliver the empowering speech.
Her weapons: microphone and typewriter.

———

"A woman's place [is] not in the public eye," Eleanor's high-
society grandmother, Mary Hall, once advised her. Had Eleanor
obeyed that command, had she adhered to the customs and conventions of what was expected from women in general and First
Ladies in particular, she would never have stood on that stage
or achieved so much else for which she is now admired. Instead,
the Majestic Theatre resounded with thousands of voices sing-
ing "She's a Jolly Good Fellow" in Eleanor's honor.

The journey that brought Eleanor to the stage in Wellington
began at age fifteen during the time she spent at the Allenswood
Academy, a girls' finishing school near London. She flourished

in the invigorating environment presided over by a headmistress, Mademoiselle Marie Souvestre, who mentored her. "Whatever I have become since," Eleanor later said, "had its seeds in those three years of contact with a liberal mind and strong personality."

When Eleanor sailed for England in 1899, she left behind a grim and unhappy childhood. She lost both her parents by the time she was nine and felt like an outsider during a neglected upbringing in her grandmother's gloomy household. She was painfully shy, fearful, and insecure about her looks. She was told no so often that she stopped asking for anything. From this somber setting, Eleanor went to the warm, welcoming atmosphere at Allenswood. She was well-liked and admired by her peers, and she thrived under the school's lively style of teaching. Independence and independent-minded thinking were encouraged, a revelation for Eleanor, whose society-conscious family found virtue in conformity. "Why was your mind given you but to think things out for yourself?" asked Mlle Souvestre.

After three years at Allenswood, to Eleanor's dismay, her grandmother ordered her back to New York, insisting she follow tradition and be formally introduced into society. She reluctantly made the rounds of parties, dinners, and dances and left early from the Assembly Ball where she was among the debutantes curtsying their way into the season. Navigating society was a demanding duty that nearly caused her to have a nervous collapse.

Eleanor decided that she would "not spend another year just doing the social rounds." She widened her interests, making new friends, taking German and literature classes, attending the opera and theater, and doing volunteer work, which helped develop the social consciousness that inspired so much of her later life. Two afternoons a week, she headed to a poverty-stricken, densely populated neighborhood on the Lower East

Side, a world away from the classy uptown section of the city where she lived. Eleanor volunteered at a settlement house, part of a progressive social movement providing medical care, education, and other community services, where she taught calisthenics and dancing to children. She also performed on-site inspections in garment factories and department stores for the National Consumers League, which sought to improve working conditions through advocacy and political lobbying.

When Eleanor's volunteer schedule conflicted with social gatherings, her godmother, "Cousin Susie," insisted she prioritize the festivities. Eleanor preferred to skip the parties, compelling Cousin Susie, who called her obstinate, to pity the man she might marry. The man Eleanor was to marry, Franklin Roosevelt, a university student, supported her work at the settlement house. She sometimes invited Franklin to meet her there, introducing him to a side of New York unfamiliar to him. As it did with Eleanor, seeing the tenement conditions had a powerful impact on Franklin, who "simply could not believe human beings lived that way."

However much fulfillment Eleanor derived from her work at the settlement house, she couldn't shake the firm grip of duty to her family and to her class and the expectations that came with it. "It would be difficult for anyone in these days to have any idea of the formality with which girls of my generation were trained," she reflected years later. And she had fallen in love. Eager to be "a part of the stream of life" and "to participate in every experience that might be the lot of a woman," she said yes when Franklin proposed.

When Franklin decided to forgo his law career to run for the New York State senate in 1910, "it never occurred" to Eleanor that she "had any part to play" in his political career. Her part "was to make the necessary household plans and to do this as easily as possible if he should be elected." After Franklin's victory, they relocated their young family to Albany, unusual for politicians at the time and a move that broke her away from her domineering mother-in-law. "For the first time I was going to live on my own," said Eleanor. "I had to stand on my own feet now and I wanted to be independent. I was beginning to realize that something within me craved to be an individual."

Eleanor initially took an interest in politics because "it was a wife's duty to be interested in whatever interested her husband." Beyond being a supportive spouse, she found the political atmosphere exhilarating. She regularly went to the State senate gallery to listen to debates and sat in on meetings Franklin held at the house. Although still somewhat shy and uncertain, she enjoyed meeting people and got to know everyone in town. She was popular, her thoughtfulness and kindness appreciated, which made friends and allies for Franklin.

Eleanor really came into her own after the United States entered World War I in April 1917. Living in Washington, DC, where Franklin was assistant secretary of the navy, she quit the capital's demanding social scene to address wartime needs. A prelude to her activities in the Pacific, she made regular visits to the Naval Hospital and helped run a Red Cross canteen for servicemen on their way to the front. In the railyards near Union Station, volunteers manned the tin-roof canteens, cold and drafty in the winter and sweltering in the summer, operating around the clock making coffee and sandwiches for upwards of fifteen thousand men each day. The Red Cross volunteers canvassed the idling trains, offering food and collecting letters and postcards to mail.

"I loved it. I simply ate it up," Eleanor said. "The war was my emancipation and my education." Moreover, she excelled at it. She put in the long hours that would become her calling card, doing everything from mopping floors to devising the accounting system.

Then the bottom dropped out of Eleanor's world. During the summer of 1918, as she labored in the canteen, Franklin traveled to Europe to inspect naval installations and meet with British and French officials. He returned home seriously ill with double pneumonia and was carried off the ship on a stretcher. While unpacking his bags, Eleanor came across love letters written to him by Lucy Mercer, her social secretary.

Devastated and feeling as if she had failed in her marriage, Eleanor offered Franklin a divorce on the condition that he first consider how it would affect their children. He declined the offer. The children's well-being was a concern and so were two other factors: he was advised that a divorce would end his political career, and his mother vowed to disinherit him if he scandalized the family by divorcing.

"I can forgive, but I cannot forget," said Eleanor. She and Franklin remained married and still cared for one another, although the romantic part of their relationship never resumed. "All my self-confidence is gone & I am on edge," Eleanor confided in her diary. A sense of failure and inferiority shattered her, although slowly she came to the realization that she would never achieve fulfillment through someone else.

Eleanor threw herself into her work and maintained a hectic pace of public activity. When World War I concluded, she turned her focus to the wounded at the Naval Hospital, where she visited daily and distributed cigarettes and flowers and offered kind, cheery words to the patients. A grateful mother wrote to thank her for the interest she took in her son. "He always loved to see you come in. You always brought a ray of sunshine with you, always had something to say to him."

When Franklin was nominated for the number two spot on the Democratic presidential ticket in 1920, he asked Eleanor to join him on a campaign train heading out west. She was the only woman on board, bewildered, lonely, and feeling as if she had nothing to do except listen to her husband give speech after speech with a rapt and adoring look on her face.

But an astute observer took notice of Eleanor. Franklin's political adviser, Louis Howe, believed she had a contribution to make to her husband's campaign with her sound judgment, organizational talent, and the way in which people responded to her natural warmth and courtesy. Louis began asking Eleanor for her input on Franklin's speeches and encouraged her to develop a cordial rapport with the reporters covering the campaign. She didn't think it was proper for her to speak with the media—the old influences rearing their heads—but Louis believed otherwise. As the train rumbled along, he explained the ways of the press and how to use them to advantage.

Later, as Franklin focused on his recovery after being stricken with polio, Louis turned to Eleanor to help keep the family name before the public so that her husband could run for future office. She continued working for the League of Women Voters, which had already recruited her for their board, and for the Democratic State Committee, networking and traveling around New York State doing voter outreach among women. By the time Franklin was elected governor, his stepping-stone to the presidency, Eleanor was a noted figure in state politics. To get to that point, which required giving the speeches necessary to raise the Roosevelt profile, she had to overcome her fear of public speaking. She had charisma but was still lacking confidence. With Louis's tutelage and encouragement, she refined her presentation and delivery, gradually becoming an effective and in-demand orator. It was the beginnings of a media presence so powerful that it brought her to the world stage and to the attention of the vaunted Axis propaganda machine.

CHAPTER 8

MORE THAN ALL THE GUNS, PLANES, AND TANKS

"We call upon the president and congress to declare war on Japan and racial prejudice in our country. Certainly we should be strong enough to whip them both."
—*PITTSBURGH COURIER*, DECEMBER 13, 1941

Rotorua, New Zealand, August 31

At the entrance to Whakarewarewa, a village in the Rotorua geothermal region on the North Island, Rangitīaria Dennan asked Eleanor if she could greet her as she did all distinguished guests. She then reached up on tiptoes, pressing her nose against that of the taller First Lady. The gesture, called the hongi, is a traditional Māori form of greeting akin to shaking hands. At the time, neither woman expected the firestorm the greeting would eventually cause. In fact, only a single cameraman captured the encounter. Caught off guard, the other press photographers in attendance pleaded with Rangi to repeat the gesture. She shook her head, saying, "I am sorry but we never do that twice, because to do so is bad luck."

The evening before, Jimmy Thompson, a local photographer, suggested to Rangi, a famous Māori guide and cultural ambassador, that she greet Eleanor with a hongi immediately after she arrived in the hopes he could score an exclusive image. Rangi refused to promise but told Jimmy she would leave open the possibility and that she would "see tomorrow." Until she came face-to-face with the First Lady, she didn't know whether the hongi would even happen. "But as soon as I saw her," said Rangi, "I realised she was the sort of person you could greet in the Maori manner without embarrassing or offending her."

Set amid steam vents, hot springs, and bubbling mud pots, Whakarewarewa was first occupied by the Māori, the original inhabitants of New Zealand, in 1325. Having played around the pools and steam vents as a child, Rangi "knew every nook and cranny" of the landscape, where she guided tourists of practically every nationality and rank. Whakarewarewa had "as much appeal" for royalty as for commoners, believed Rangi. "I think part of its pulling power is that it makes we poor humans feel so humble. Even kings and queens are made aware of their insignificance as they walk over steaming earth so thin that the terrible power beneath the crust can be felt through the soles of the feet."

Eleanor painted a vibrant picture of Whakarewarewa for her readers in "My Day." She recalled the "beautiful sight" when Pōhutu ("big splash"), the largest active geyser in the Southern Hemisphere, gave a mighty roar and sent columns of water leaping fifty feet into the air. She described the bubbling mud pools, mesmerizing with endlessly appearing shapes of flowers and figures.

The Māori utilized the colorful thermal landscape in their

daily lives, cooking over steam vents and in hot pools. "They feed 600 of our men at a time by using this outdoor kitchen," noted Eleanor. "The corn on the cob is cooked in a small pool which is well over boiling temperature." She learned greetings in the Māori language on the spot and exchanged them with women and children in the village. (She spoke several languages, including fluent French, and advised travelers to learn basic phrases as a courtesy in the countries they visited.)

Eleanor instantly liked Rangi, "a wonderful woman, brilliant and witty." As Rangi showed Eleanor and the others in her party around, she kept them entertained with wisecracks "that would have done credit to Bob Hope." In front of a large boiling mud pool, with blobs of mud being flung over the area like leaping frogs, Rangi stopped and glanced mischievously at the First Lady. With so much hot air emanating from the pool, Rangi suggested a name for it. "In America you would call it Congress Pool, uh?" Eleanor burst into laughter, agreeing, "And maybe we would."

Despite the moment of jocularity, World War II was "very much a reality at Whakarewarewa, with so many of our boys away," said Rangi. "Hardly a week would pass without someone receiving bad news—a boy killed, or wounded, or a P.O.W. Sometimes the news was good—a medal won, or a mention in dispatches."

American servicemen in New Zealand were invited on getaways to Rotorua, partly for relaxation and partly to foster cross-cultural understanding with the Māori. As they were told in the *Meet New Zealand* guide, "The Maori have fought for their rights, fought well and vigorously. Therefore, it is well to remember that the Maori today occupy a position in New Zealand society socially and politically equal to that of any pakeha or white New Zealander." Still, some U.S. troops were

uncomfortable with New Zealand's integrated society and insti-
gated skirmishes with Māori men. To defuse the situation and
build bridges, Māori leaders invited Americans to visit the various tribes and learn about their culture. From the first troop
landings in New Zealand, groups of several hundred servicemen
at a time were welcomed at Whakarewarewa, where they were
provided lodging, entertained with traditional song and dance,
and given tours of the terrain.

Meanwhile, Māori troops—all of whom enlisted
voluntarily—were fighting far from home. Part of the New
Zealand Army, they earned a formidable reputation while serving in Greece, Crete, North Africa, and Italy throughout the
war. Eleanor lauded their bravery during an evening reception at
a Māori meetinghouse, a wooden structure elaborately adorned
inside and out with carvings of ancestors, gods, and other figures. Three chiefs hailed her as "the queen of a great democracy"
and welcomed her on behalf of the Te Arawa confederation of
tribes and on behalf of all Māori.

"We in the United States know well what feats of valour
your men have performed in this war," said Eleanor.

When World War II began, Māori leaders asked the government to form an all-Māori battalion and insisted that soldiers be
given active duty. They would go as warriors, befitting their heritage, and not in support roles, as laborers and trench diggers, as
they had been in World War I. By this war's end, the 28th (Māori)
Battalion was one of the most celebrated and decorated units
in the country's forces, including the posthumous awarding of
the Victoria Cross to Second Lieutenant Te Moana-nui-a-Kiwa
Ngārimu, the first Māori soldier to receive the Commonwealth's
highest military honor. In Tunisia, he had led his men on an
attack, wiping out German machine-gun posts and holding a
key position through the night. Wounded in the shoulder and

the leg, Ngārimu refused to abandon his men and was killed early the next morning during an enemy counterattack.

That evening at the meetinghouse, H. Tai Mitchell, a renowned Māori leader, introduced Eleanor to Sergeant Haane Te Rauawa Manahi, who was decorated with a Distinguished Conduct Medal for his heroic actions in Tunisia. Hundreds of Italian and German troops were well entrenched at Takrouna, a steep, rocky outcrop rising nearly one thousand feet from a vast plain. After days of hand-to-hand fighting and under machine gun and mortar fire, Sergeant Manahi and a small band of soldiers scaled a sheer cliff face to reach the summit. Their daring deed was "the most gallant feat of arms I witnessed in the course of the war," declared a commanding officer.

"We think highly of men of courage who are willing to fight for the things they believe in," Eleanor told those assembled at the meetinghouse. "We are glad to be fighting side by side with you in this war for freedom."

During the reception, Eleanor was presented with a gift prized by the Māori, a greenstone tiki pendant. The hei tiki, a human image carved in stone or other material and worn around the neck, is emblematic of Māori culture, traditionally passed down as heirlooms and the most highly valued adornment fashioned from greenstone (pounamu). Wearing the pendant, which is believed to ward off misfortune, Eleanor concluded her speech, saying, "I am sure that this stone which I am wearing will take me back in safety to my home."

Eleanor's day in Rotorua—one of only three places in the country to host her—was newsworthy for focusing on New Zealanders rather than American servicemen. And as would be expected, the Māori "played a prominent part in the proceedings." When the First Lady arrived in New Zealand, H. Tai Mitchell's message of greeting to her on behalf of the Te Arawa confederation was personally delivered by none other than Prime Minister Fraser.

But Eleanor's stop here wasn't without controversy. News that she had received a traditional Māori greeting provided fodder for her stateside critics. "Why can she rub noses—as the papers state—with these people over there?" ranted a congressman from Michigan on the floor of the House of Representatives. "I do not know where the nose-rubbing custom originated, but they said she rubbed her nose against that of some Maorian woman."

Jimmy Thompson's photograph, published in *Look* magazine, ignited a media frenzy. Newspapers and magazines nationwide reported on the image and pondered its significance. The picture began to "cause a good bit of talk, particularly in the South, and the New Zealanders in Washington aren't any too happy about it, fearing that the picture will be misunderstood," wrote a newspaper columnist. Some media outlets were flippant, reprinting the photo with headlines such as "Nothing Like Good Nose Rub to Make Friends!" and "First Lady and Maori 'Kiss.'" Others were more disparaging, with one referring to Rangi as a "Maori squaw." Comedian Milton Berle joked about the photo, saying, "I hear the picture was arranged by the U.S. Nasal Training Station."

That a "simple hongi" caused such a commotion in the United States startled Rangi. Although there were "plenty of pakehas who do not want to mix with Maoris as their equals," she said, "generally speaking our two races get on better together than do any other white and coloured peoples anywhere else on earth."

While the extreme reaction to the hongi was unexpected, controversy over Eleanor's "race mixing" was hardly new. Throughout the 1930s and '40s, she had become one of the most outspoken advocates for civil rights, earning her the animosity of bigots. A high-profile scandal erupted when she resigned membership in the Daughters of the American Revolution, which refused to rent its Constitution Hall for a concert headlined by Marian Anderson, an acclaimed Black opera singer. "I am in complete disagreement with the attitude taken in refusing Constitution Hall to a great artist," Eleanor wrote in her resignation letter. "You had an opportunity to lead in an enlightened way and it seems to me that your organization has failed."

Even acts of basic human decency garnered outrage, such as when Eleanor poured a glass of water and walked across a stage to hand it to her friend, Mary McLeod Bethune, a leader in President Roosevelt's unofficial "Black cabinet," who had begun to cough while giving a speech. The same gesture that provoked racists spoke volumes to the Black community. "This is democracy in action," said a Black policeman who was in the audience.

"You would have to have lived in that era to know...what kind of an impact this had on the Negro population," said Pauli Murray, a writer and activist. "These kinds of symbolic gestures that Mrs. Roosevelt made were so significant to a group of people who were literally just coming out of the nadir, so to speak, of humiliation and degradation."

Eleanor was the first white Washington, DC, resident to join the local chapters of the National Association for the Advancement of Colored People (NAACP) and the National Urban League, and she attended the annual conventions of both organizations. She worked closely with Walter White, executive director of the NAACP, on anti-lynching legislation, for which he had been fighting for more than a decade, and pushed for a repeal of the poll tax.

In May 1943, with the poll tax up for a test vote in the House, Eleanor made a last-minute appeal for its abolition. Speaking during Harlem Week, an annual event highlighting Harlem's cultural life while also bringing attention to its ongoing economic and social issues, she said the repeal of the poll tax would be of benefit "not only for the colored people but for all people." In the same speech, she "called for equal justice before the law for all races, equality of opportunity, equality of employment and decent living conditions, and the privilege of all citizens to participate in government."

Eleanor's controversial stance on civil rights—augmented by the highly visible platform she had to amplify the cause— enraged her enemies. While she was in the South Pacific, Alabama governor Chauncey Sparks stated that he was planning to denounce her at the forthcoming Democratic National Convention while pushing a platform of white supremacy.

A favored tactic of white supremacists in the United States was to use photographs of Eleanor interacting with Black people to stoke hatred against her and to create a political backlash against President Roosevelt. One such image showed Eleanor being escorted by two Black honor guards at Howard University. The photo appeared in a pamphlet that was widely circulated throughout the South. Intended to stir "the black pot of race," it included photos of the president and the First Lady "consorting with Negroes" and proclaimed them "ardent Negrophiles" who allowed Black guests to dine and sleep at the White House. During a congressional investigation into lobbying activities, the Texan who produced the pamphlets defended his actions by unabashedly proclaiming, "I am a southerner and I am for white supremacy."

In response to segregationists, Eleanor retorted, "Why curse Hitler and support Jim Crow?" It was hypocritical, she pointed out, for the United States to denounce the appalling racial policies of the Nazis when its own segregation of Blacks contradicted democratic values. But American racism did more than merely call into question the country's moral authority. It also undermined the war effort.

It wasn't until six months into World War II that the marine corps reluctantly opened to Black men in June 1942, the last of the services to do so. The navy limited the duties of Black sailors, with the majority serving as mess attendants, stewards, and cooks. The U.S. Army Air Forces was mandated to open its training program to Black pilots but did not deploy them for combat missions. In March 1943, Eleanor was alerted that the 99th Pursuit Squadron, the first of the fighting units, was still idling at the Tuskegee Army Flying School in Alabama. "This seems to me a really crucial situation," she admonished Secretary of War Stimson. The next month, the 99th Pursuit Squadron headed for North Africa and Europe, where they primarily escorted bombers in flight to protect them from enemy aircraft and earned an impressive record. Furthermore, the entire U.S. armed forces was segregated.

Hitler's propaganda machine noticed the internal racial divisions and set out to exploit them. While American bigots spread divisive messages of hate at home, the Nazis dropped millions of leaflets aimed at Black servicemen abroad, asking why they would want to risk their lives for a country that did not treat them as equals. "Uncle Sam's colored soldiers are just CANNON FODDER," proclaimed a leaflet. Avoiding mention of their own racial prejudices, the intent was to persuade Black troops to desert and surrender.

It was this kind of demoralization that Eleanor's trip to the South Pacific intended to ameliorate. She undertook a grueling, dangerous journey to make sure that America's servicemen felt valued and respected by the nation they swore to defend. That mission inevitably collided with an Axis propaganda machine working diligently toward opposite ends on both the battlefield and the American home front.

Stateside, the U.S. government warned Americans about

enemy agents spreading false rumors. Still, many people believed the rumors and perpetuated them, "some innocently and some maliciously," noted a North Carolina newspaper.

Eleanor grew exasperated with the American public for believing wartime falsehoods. A rumor about the immorality of members of the Women's Army Auxiliary Corps (WAAC) suggested that some were sent home from North Africa due to pregnancy. Combined with the prevailing social mindset that women belonged in the home and that wearing a uniform was masculine, the rumors resulted in negative publicity for the WAAC. Asked to comment on the "whispering campaign," Eleanor replied that the rumors were Nazi propaganda intended to suppress recruiting. The country's first armed services unit established for women, the WAAC was a voluntary enrollment program whose members served in noncombatant roles.

"When you realize that the Axis would do anything to prevent our building up a force of women which will release that many men for actual combat, it is easy to understand that the Axis would be pleased if these rumors were to affect our enlistments," noted Eleanor. Similar rumors about women in the armed services had already made the rounds in Great Britain and Canada. She chastised gullible Americans for "playing Hitler's game" and "falling for such propaganda, just like children."

The Nazis rattled sabers at Eleanor for speaking out, demonstrating the threat her platform and reputation presented to them. In early 1939, with Hitler already menacing neighboring countries, a German newspaper warned Mrs. Franklin D. Roosevelt to "leave politics alone" after she wrote in "My Day" of being in favor of the United States selling military planes to France. "One should ask her to keep her pen away from things of which she is ignorant. There are many other better fields of work for a militant writer; for instance, social questions concerning the 12,000,000 unemployed, lynching, child labor and public morals. It is not good for a nation if not only the husband but also the wife enters the political china shop."

Unfazed, Eleanor continued speaking out against Hitler as his forces rampaged across Europe. She warned against the dangerous belief that peace with the German dictator was possible and maintained that, if necessary, the United States must be ready to meet force with force to protect itself. At an anti-Hitler rally in November 1941 in New York City, she told the crowd, "This nation is going to defend itself and that defense means preparation to see to it that the Nazis do not win."

Hitler's propaganda minister, Joseph Goebbels, raged over the First Lady's powerful influence on public opinion and professed his desire to silence her. "Mrs. Roosevelt is shooting her mouth off around the country," he wrote in his diary. "If she were my wife, it would be a different story." During her visit to Great Britain, he warned German journalists, "The hullabaloo about Eleanor Roosevelt should be left to die down gradually and should not result in Mrs. Roosevelt's journey being popularized or invested with a certain importance."

A prominent BBC broadcaster hypothesized on why the Germans "and their toadies" were exerting "all their guttersnipe talents to abuse her." The answer was simple, he told listeners. Eleanor's mere existence infuriated the enemy, since she was the antithesis to everything they stood for. She was kindly and warmhearted; they were cruel with hearts of ice. She was honest and decent; they were cunning and depraved. Above all, Eleanor infuriated the Nazis for leading a full, complete, and independent life and, as First Lady, for playing an important part in the leadership of the United States and among the Allied nations. The Nazis did not consider women to be free, self-respecting citizens, and they were excluded from political life by party doctrine. The example that Eleanor set and the values she represented "were contributing more than all the guns, planes, and tanks to our victory."

Eleanor's wartime arsenal included the ability to encourage, offer comfort, and build morale. Axis propagandists attempted to strip away her power to do that—dangerous tactics that pursued her to the Pacific.

CHAPTER 9

LIKE MUSHROOMS IN THE JUNGLE

"So many rumors have come in my mail lately of curious tales which supposedly have been circulated among your companions that I confess to wondering how many will be believing them."

—ELEANOR ROOSEVELT IN A LETTER TO JOSEPH P. LASH, AUGUST 4, 1943

Auckland, New Zealand, September 1–3

At a Red Cross club in New Zealand, Eleanor was told that an angry marine refused to be in the same room with her. She had set out for the Pacific with some apprehension because of malicious rumors circulating among servicemen. The allegation was that she had maligned the marines, saying that after the war was over, they would be too savage to return to civilian life right away. Another claim was that she wanted them quarantined for malaria before they could return home. In alternate versions of the rumor, the marines were swapped out for army men in the Pacific and the Caribbean and for paratroopers in Italy.

Eleanor battled back against the Axis propagandists sowing the discord. In her talk that day at the Red Cross club and all throughout the trip, she took care to dispel the falsehood. "I [have] a son in the Marines," she told them, "and he certainly would never allow me to have any such ideas."

The reach of enemy propaganda was extensive. While in New Zealand, Eleanor received a letter from a hostess at a Red Cross club warning her that the same rumor was circulating in Australia, where she was headed next. None of the marines with whom the hostess spoke had heard the falsehood directly but believed it anyway. Eleanor addressed the issue in "My Day," which appeared in newspapers in Australia and New Zealand. She included the entire letter and set the record straight. "I have never made such statements, either in public or in private, because such thoughts have never been in my mind," she wrote. "I am too anxious to get the many boys I know and love as individuals home, and they are serving in all branches of the services. My only regret is that any boys should be made bitter by such untruths."

That the enemy was utilizing propaganda within the armed forces was a given, asserted *Yank: The Army Weekly*. What was surprising was that servicemen fell not for clever rumors but the "out-and-out cock-and-bull stories" that were obviously false, like the tale about the First Lady and the marines. "How anybody could believe that one is beyond us," the magazine admonished. "If P. T. Barnum heard about the way some soldiers, sailors and marines swallow rumors, he would probably change his estimation of the birth rate of suckers. In the armed forces, there is one born every 30 seconds."

Marine correspondent Samuel E. Stavisky tried to find out where the rumors started but never pinpointed a source.

He initially heard of the First Lady's reputed remarks on Guadalcanal but thought nothing of it "since the individual who made it was a loudmouth who hated all the Roosevelts" for advocating racial equality "and the First Lady especially so." Stavisky chased the rumor, repeated in slightly different forms, while he was in the Pacific. Like the Red Cross hostess, he too failed to find a single marine who had heard it firsthand. "Again and again the allegation kept popping up, like mushrooms in the jungle, but not once could I find confirmation." When he asked why they thought she would say such an awful thing, the answer was always the same: that she was responsible for Blacks being allowed in the marine corps.

The rumor is believed to have been started by Japanese radio personality Tokyo Rose. (One sailor noted that the two women everyone on board his ship knew by their voices were Tokyo Rose and Eleanor Roosevelt.) Both Japan and Germany produced radio programs in English intended to weaken servicemen's morale. The sultry-sounding female broadcasters, collectively referred to among Allied troops as Tokyo Rose and Axis Sally respectively, interspersed popular American music with propaganda. "Hi GIs—if your government really cared about you, you'd be seeing [musician and navy man] Artie Shaw in San Francisco instead of being in that dirty foxhole," taunted one. Radio Tokyo was often the easiest, and sometimes the only, station that troops in the Pacific could tune in to.

Eleanor dealt with the rumor throughout the war. Those spreading the story "are evidently too stupid to realize that my only concern would be that such a story would hurt the men themselves," she lamented in "My Day" a year after the Pacific trip. "If our boys think that...the wife of the President, or any other woman, says or writes such arrant nonsense, they must be made extremely unhappy by it."

Although the thought of having even one man believe the rumors bothered Eleanor, the overwhelming majority of service personnel she encountered in the Pacific were pleased she was there. "Last Sunday Mrs. Roosevelt visited our camp and gave us a short but inspiring message. It was the first time I had seen her in person, so I as well as the rest of the fellows enjoyed it very much," a soldier serving in Australia reported in a letter printed in his Iowa hometown newspaper. A serviceman on New Caledonia wrote a stateside friend that if critics complained about the cost of her being there, "as far as our bunch is concerned we would all be willing to turn over our pay for the rest of the war to help compensate you fellows on the home front for any inconvenience you suffered by Mrs. Roosevelt's trip."

Eleanor was routinely met with resounding cheers and enthusiastic receptions. She signed thousands of short snorters (including one a Texan claimed was the longest in existence with twenty-two feet of dollar bills and fifteen hundred signatures) and autographed pay stubs, cigarette packages, bandages, casts, a mess cook's chef hat, an airman's pencil sketch of President Roosevelt, and whatever else was on hand. At an army camp, she was greeted by fifty soldiers carrying small cameras and eager for a photo op. A soldier from Washington State presented her with a bouquet of white sweet peas, telling her, "I want to give you these on behalf of my little boy, who is named after the President. He is 6½." They told her about their families, like one whose wife was seven months pregnant. "You could see the longing in his eyes," said Eleanor. Others showed her pictures of their children, and she praised newspapers for the popular practice of publishing photos of servicemen's babies born while they were overseas.

At an Auckland area hospital, a bed-bound U.S. Army private in a surgical ward propped himself up on his elbow and delivered a spontaneous speech thanking her for visiting. "I'm speaking on behalf of all the men, the staff and our padre," he said. "We sure do appreciate that you have come all this way to shake hands with us and to talk to us."

While in Auckland, Eleanor also kept up with seeing women's war work. Her inspections took her from a navy yard, where servicewomen and civilians performed shore-based tasks, to the largest canning factory in the Southern Hemisphere. Much of the factory's output went to the armed forces. Eleanor watched the making of cans, meat preparation, packing, labeling, and other processes. (Workers confided that they were making corned beef hash with potatoes and onions just to please American tastes.)

In a crowded dining room at the cannery, Eleanor used a tabletop as a dais from which to address the women. After the uproar of clapping, shouting, and another rendition of "She's a Jolly Good Fellow" abated, she expressed the appreciation of the United States for their efforts. "It is one of the reasons we are going to win—because all the people of the [Allied nations] are putting their best into this war effort," she said. "Good luck to you, and may all your loved ones soon be back with you."

Later, at a civic assembly for women, she singled out the cannery workers. "It is not pleasant work; it is hard work. But women have learned to do work they have never done before," she said. "In the nursing fields, in hospitals, in all voluntary work, women are doing fine work. In all these things women are earning the gratitude of men."

By the time Eleanor departed New Zealand, newspapers had praised everything from her "pedestrian powers" and "personal charm" to her keen insight into world affairs. "As you may know the New Zealanders by nature are quite a reserved people but they went overboard for her," Major George Durno, who accompanied Eleanor on the trip, told Tommy. "She did a magnificent job, saying the right thing at the right time and doing a hundred and one little things that endeared her to the people." A press officer with the Air Transport Command and a former political reporter, Durno had traveled with President Roosevelt earlier in the year on a clandestine journey to Casablanca for a conference with Prime Minister Churchill.

Eleanor left New Zealand with a final message of hope. She revealed to the audience at a civic reception in Auckland that she had received a cable from the president saying the recently concluded Quebec conference with Churchill and other Allied leaders was a success. "I used to think when Mr. Churchill gave his Victory sign he was bolstering up courage, but now when he does it, it is because it is his conviction," she said.

Eleanor's visit "would still further strengthen the bonds of friendship forged between the two countries," professed the mayor of Auckland at the reception. The audience, cheering and applauding, gave a standing ovation to Eleanor, who despite the strenuous tour looked "bright and cheerful."

In truth, Eleanor was beginning to weary and was still anxious about the possibility of not getting to Guadalcanal. She continued to press her case to Franklin, telling him, "All the men ask if I've been to Guadalcanal & say now it's safe & I should go, so I hope Ad. Halsey permits it on my return." Her weariness combined with self-doubt about whether she was accomplishing what the president wanted. Writing to Tommy, she confessed, "I dread Australia for 13 days, but they will come to an end. Even the British trip couldn't touch these schedules."

CHAPTER 10

NO FRAIL FLOWER

"Her visit here [Australia] was an historical event and she is undoubtedly going to be a person who will go down in history as one of the great women of her time."
—LIEUTENANT GENERAL ROBERT EICHELBERGER IN A LETTER TO HIS WIFE, EMMELINE, SEPTEMBER 26, 1943

Canberra and Melbourne, Australia, September 3–5

Unlike Eleanor's arrival in New Zealand, which was largely kept quiet until she arrived, her appearance in Australia was highly anticipated. When the transport plane, after a six-hour flight across the Tasman Sea, touched down briefly in Sydney on the way to Canberra, the airfield was packed with well-wishers. Despite the stop being unofficial and access tightly controlled by police officers questioning anyone seeking entry, a crowd of several hundred aircraft workers and others amassed at the field, cheering and throwing flowers when the First Lady debarked.

"They had come just to get a glimpse of her; they knew she was to leave in half an hour for Canberra," said Lieutenant General Eichelberger. "There was an electric welcome that any veteran of crowds could recognize at once as real and spontaneous."

Eleanor waved to the crowd, which was kept at bay by a cordon of military and civil police. Suddenly a young woman broke through the barrier, ducking under the arm of a burly officer, calling out to the First Lady, "Please, Mrs. Roosevelt, may I have your autograph?" Eleanor waved aside the policeman in pursuit of the twenty-two-year-old airport canteen worker. She penciled her name on the birthday party invitation she was presented and then spoke with the woman, whose husband had been taken as a prisoner of war in Singapore and perished in an internment camp.

Eleanor's official welcome to Australia took place at an aerodrome near the national capital, Canberra, where scout planes were sent up to seek warning of her approach from Sydney. She stepped from the plane, carrying a navy-blue handbag, down a four-rung metal ladder and onto the tarmac "with all the simplicity of a neighbour paying a call"—if the neighbor was accompanied by two generals and an admiral and had the prime minister, a Royal Australian Air Force honor guard, and a crowd of four hundred people awaiting her. Overhead, the air force escort that flew with her from the coast roared overhead and dipped in salute. Eleanor ignored the officials who wanted to whisk her away immediately, posing for press photos and shaking hands with bystanders. Despite it being a working day, a crowd lined the airport boundary fence to witness the official welcome ceremony.

As much as Eleanor wanted to avoid formalities, her visit, as it had been in New Zealand, was a momentous occasion, generating the most excitement in Australia since King George VI and Queen Elizabeth (then the Duke and Duchess of York) visited sixteen years earlier. Some of the capital's old-timers believed it even eclipsed the excitement of a royal visit. In Canberra, public buildings were spring-cleaned and adorned with bunting, and gardens were spruced up as the city took on an air of prewar festivity.

At Parliament House, where a state luncheon was planned, a red carpet was taken out of storage, ten thousand pieces of silver were polished to a sheen, paintings stored in the basement for safety in case of an air raid were rehung, and the ministers of state granted themselves special dispensation allowing liquor to be served on a Saturday afternoon. (Eleanor was the first woman ever invited to eat in the Parliament House dining room and the second American to appear before the Australian Parliament, after General MacArthur.) During the largest reception in Canberra since the start of the war, hosted by the governor-general, some women wore evening dresses for the first time in months (others like Eleanor wore their service-related uniforms) while men donned dinner jackets rescued from mothballs.

Eleanor's schedule in Canberra was heavy with fancy government receptions and other official functions, like the ceremonial planting of an American oak tree at the almost-completed U.S. embassy. Newspapers griped about the lack of "common contact" and castigated "official pooh-bahs" for stacking her itinerary with formal engagements and not public events.

"Any fussy stooges who are planning to wrap her up in cotton wool and keep her from the vulgar gaze should remember that Mrs. Roosevelt can do more to create goodwill between this country and the United States than a dozen high Government officials—if she is given the chance," chastised one. "She hasn't risked a trans-ocean crossing solely to have afternoon tea with the right people." She should be able "to meet and talk to the little people who matter, not exclusively to the big people who irritatingly think they matter."

The First Lady's presence was on par with royalty but with a notable difference. In contrast to the formality that characterized the visits of members of the British royal family, her friendly manner and unpretentiousness were a hit with the Australians. "The success of your visit to Canberra," Nelson Johnson, the U.S. minister to Australia, informed Eleanor, "was due very much to yourself and to the warm informality which you gave to the proceedings everywhere."

Newspapers cheered whenever Eleanor broke with protocol. Arriving at Government House in Canberra for her first event, a press conference, she spotted several uniformed women digging in a garden on the grounds. She broke away from the official party, striding over to them and striking up a conversation. Members of the Australian Women's Land Army, which was formed the year before to address wartime labor shortages in agricultural sectors, they presented her with a bunch of golden wattle blossoms, the national flower.

Inside Government House, Eleanor sidestepped protocol yet again. She was seated on a sofa in a lounge while nearly fifty members of the media were expected to stand at a respectful distance from her. Instead, she invited them to come closer and to sit on the carpet in a semicircle around her. Reporters were delighted, and even more so when she threw in some Australian slang, describing her plane landing in Canberra as "Good-o." They deemed it the liveliest and most informal press conference ever held in Australia.

Reporters did not hold back, firing off more than forty questions in thirty-five minutes. Eleanor answered their inquiries unreservedly, commenting on topics ranging from how the president dealt with coffee rationing (he drank milk with breakfast instead) to the sense that, unlike after the last world war, there seemed to be a greater willingness in the United States to acknowledge the need for a global outlook rather than a purely national one.

The press conference took a dramatic turn when a messenger entered the room with an announcement: Allied forces had invaded the "toe" of Italy, the first large-scale landing on mainland Europe, a victory that coincided with the fourth anniversary of the war's start. During a days-long "softening-up" process, coastal defenses and enemy positions were bombarded with artillery, preparing the way for ground troops to come ashore. Germany, which had been jubilant on the anniversary of the war's outbreak in previous years, also faced additional setbacks with the bombing of Berlin and the loss of nine hundred miles on the Russian front.

Asked about furthering goodwill between Americans and Australians, Eleanor replied that she had no specific strategy. "You must have a spirit of goodwill to begin with, and then take every opportunity to create a better understanding between people," she said. During the press conference, she reiterated her desire to meet ordinary people and servicemen while in Australia.

"She won't be satisfied just seeing places, but wants to meet everybody in them," explained Coletta Ryan, the Red Cross supervisor in the South Pacific, who joined the First Lady's party in New Caledonia and traveled with her in New Zealand. (When the plane stopped briefly in Sydney, Coletta debarked, saying that she was "too worn out to continue the official tour. I guess I'm just no match for Mrs. Roosevelt's vitality.")

To Eleanor's frustration, security was extraordinarily high throughout her travels in Australia. Buildings where functions took place were heavily guarded and entry regulated by a rigid pass system. Plainclothes officers mingled with crowds, and police motorcycle escorts rode along wherever she was driven. In Sydney, authorities planned to use a new device—the walkie-talkie—to help with crowd and traffic control.

Further insulating Eleanor from the everyday people and "plain soldiers" she wanted to meet was the brace of high-ranking U.S. Army officers and MPs that continuously accompanied her. Used to traveling unimpeded in the United States, where she declined Secret Service protection, she was furious at being treated "like a frail flower." (Eleanor won a showdown with the Secret Service over driving her own car and going about unaccompanied. The head of the Secret Service insisted that she at least carry a revolver in her car, and she learned how to use the weapon.) "I've never been so hedged around with protection in my life," Eleanor told Tommy. The coddling made her want to do something daring when she got home, "like making munitions." As she indignantly reported to Franklin, "I have an M.P. escort everywhere that would do you credit. I have all the pomp & restriction & none of the power!"

Australians wanted to interact with Eleanor too, and Canberra was burgeoning with out-of-towners. Those who couldn't get rooms in the fully booked hotels camped in cars and tents on the outskirts of the city. Like the plucky canteen worker who eluded officers to snag the First Lady's autograph at the Sydney airport, Australians found ways to circumvent the security surrounding her.

Eleanor's itinerary for her one full day in Canberra appeared in newspapers, alerting people as to where and when they could find her. At the American embassy, she met a trio of young women who journeyed seven hundred miles from a small tin and gem mining town to see her. A policeman warned them not to enter the embassy grounds but promised to look the other way if they slipped through a fence. Summoning their courage, they rushed up to Eleanor and introduced themselves. Later, near the entrance to the Australian War Memorial, crowds of children surrounded the First Lady as officials tried to shoo them away. A ten-year-old boy plucked up his courage and handed her a bunch of peach bloom and rosemary despite being concerned the other boys would call him a sissy. Built to commemorate World War I, the memorial opened in 1941 when the next world war was already underway. It was expanded in scope as a space for the remembrance of all Australian involvement in war.

Listed on Eleanor's itinerary in Canberra was this item: "11.50: Private visit to the Prime Minister (Mr. Curtin)." An important reason she was in Australia was to foster under-standing between the two nations and to aid in easing tensions between their leaders, whose wartime relationship was some-times strained.

With the attack on Pearl Harbor and the Japanese aggres-sion that quickly followed, including the sinking of two British Royal Navy warships, Prime Minister John Curtin's tanta-mount concern was for Australia's security. It seemed as if war was coming to the country's doorstep, an invasion thought to be a likely possibility. Roughly the same size as the continental United States, Australia then had a population of seven million, most of whom lived near the coast.

But Curtin had limited sway over war matters, even those involving Australia, which at the time had limited defenses. As with New Zealand, much of its military was overseas fighting alongside the British. Traditionally, Australia looked to Great Britain for leadership in world affairs and relied on the military protection that came with being part of the Commonwealth. Plus Prime Minister Churchill and President Roosevelt were the two primary figures leading the war.

Curtin incurred Churchill's displeasure by demanding the

return of Australian troops from Europe and North Africa. Great Britain was reluctant to release the troops since it was already stretched thin—fighting Axis forces in Europe and focused on protecting territories in the Far East that it considered to be at imminent risk. Days after Hong Kong, a British Crown colony, fell to the Japanese in late December 1941, Curtin angered Churchill yet again by taking his grievances public. He asserted in a newspaper article that Australia looked to the United States to help defend the Pacific.

"Australia is now inside the fighting lines," Curtin stated. "We know the problems that the United Kingdom faces. We know the constant threat of invasion. We know the dangers of dispersal of strength. But we know too that Australia can go, and Britain can still hold on. We are therefore determined that Australia shall not go, and we shall exert all our energies toward the shaping of a plan, with the United States as its keystone, which will give to our country some confidence of being able to hold out until the tide of battle swings against the enemy."

In early January 1942, the Japanese began bombing Rabaul, the capital of the Australian Mandated Territory of New Guinea, on the island of New Britain. Ground troops seized Rabaul within weeks, a prelude to operations on mainland New Guinea, which is separated from Australia by a scant ninety-three-mile-wide strait at its nearest point. Other enemy forces continued southward on the Malay Peninsula toward Singapore, where the British naval base was crucial to Australia's defense.

"After all the assurances we have been given, the evacuation of Singapore would be regarded here and elsewhere as an inexcusable betrayal," Curtin cabled Churchill. "We understood it was to be made impregnable and in any event it was to be capable of holding out for a prolonged period until the arrival of the main fleet."

Then came the dreaded news that Singapore was indeed lost, the vital British navy base with it. Among the prisoners of war were fifteen thousand Australians. Days later, Darwin in northern Australia was bombed in two separate raids that destroyed much of the town and the ships in its harbor, heavily damaged an air force field and barracks, and killed more than 240 civilians and service personnel. The attack, the first of sixty-four bombing raids on Darwin between February 1942 and late 1943, heightened the country's sense of vulnerability and isolation, as it was believed to be a softening up of defenses before an invasion.

Pressing Australian interests, Curtin remained at odds with Churchill, who insisted that British Commonwealth concerns were paramount over those of any one dominion. The tussle over where to deploy Australian troops continued, with Curtin successfully insisting they return to Australia to protect the country and to help repel Japan's southward progression.

The United States sent troops to Australia, which like New Zealand was used as a staging base for operations in the Pacific, with some eighty thousand arriving during the first three months of 1942. Another boon came in March when the famed General MacArthur, who had a flair for self-promotion, arrived and was greeted with great fanfare. Everywhere Eleanor went in Australia, she heard praise for MacArthur. One woman told her she felt as though fifty thousand men had arrived to defend them when he unexpectedly surfaced there.

MacArthur was sent to Australia after a massive rout in the Philippines. Despite a valiant effort by American and Filipino forces to hold Luzon, the main island, and its capital, Manila, wave after wave of Japanese land and sea attacks forced a retreat to the Bataan Peninsula. Balking at leaving his men, General MacArthur eventually acceded to President Roosevelt's order that he flee the Philippines. With defeat all but certain, the government could not risk having the general captured by the Japanese. MacArthur escaped by night aboard a PT boat and then flew to Australia, where he was named supreme commander of Allied forces in the Southwest Pacific.

Even as the threat of a Japanese invasion of Australia abated with Allied successes at Midway and the Coral Sea, the Australian government continued to push for an offensive strategy. Curtin's requests for additional resources were repeatedly denied, as were those of MacArthur, who continually criticized President Roosevelt and the War Department over the "Germany First" decision.

The massive defense program that would make the United States the "arsenal of democracy" had not yet been fully mobilized, and President Roosevelt was forced to prioritize resources. Believing that Germany posed the greater threat to the United States, he and Churchill secretly decided on a Europe-first strategy. "If Germany were defeated, the defeat of Japan would most surely follow," Roosevelt reasoned, "whereas on the other hand the defeat of Japan would not necessarily [ensure] Germany's defeat." His position was to hold steady in the Pacific until Germany was vanquished. Additional resources would then be diverted to the Pacific for all-out war against Japan. When Curtin found out about the pact, he fumed that "two men thousands of miles from here are inclined to think that Australia is in no great danger." Convinced that a face-to-face meeting with Curtin, one of the few Allied leaders he had yet to meet in person, could make a profound difference, President Roosevelt invited the prime minister to Washington. Curtin declined every invitation.

While the struggles between the prime ministers and the president primarily took place out of the public eye, other diplomatic issues were more apparent. In January 1943, Eleanor received a summary of remarks made at a gathering of media professionals in New York City stressing the need for greater understanding on the part of the United States toward Australia. Frank J. Cuhel, an American journalist based in Sydney, lashed out at newspapers that did not give Australian troops their fair share of credit for victories. "I saw the Australian peoples' reactions to these reports," Cuhel said, "and it certainly did not help strengthen a mutual trust. After all, it doesn't matter so much which one of us happens to capture a hill from the Japs, just so we make darned sure it's our side that wins."

Cuhel urged awareness of the "other fellow's problems" and a recognition of what happens when American ways are suddenly thrust upon another nation. "We expected the Australian to change overnight. We were used to drawing on a vast store of supplies that Australia did not have. We forgot that Australia lost almost a complete generation of men in the last war, and has lost in killed and captured, almost another generation in this one, all of which has left her short handed in man-power."

Summing up, Cuhel said, "We must remember we did not come to Australia specifically to save that country but to eliminate the Japs. This 'American Saviours' theme should be dissipated for the benefit of both countries."

Eleanor forwarded the report to Franklin with a two-sentence cover memo: "I think I can help this situation. Will you consider my going now?"

Whether Eleanor traveled to the Pacific—and when—was at the president's discretion. She anticipated traveling to China and Russia, a trip she was eager to make, only to have Franklin change his mind because he wanted to meet with the leaders of those countries first. Not long after vetoing that idea, Franklin turned to Eleanor in the White House elevator and said, "I think it would be well if you were to go to Australia, New Zealand, and the Pacific Islands."

Although Eleanor visited Australia unofficially—and stressed it publicly so as not to ruffle any ambassadorial feathers—to a large extent, her being there was viewed in diplomatic terms. An editorial declared her a "Valuable Ambassadress," noting, "Mrs. Roosevelt will be able to do at least as much to establish understanding and goodwill between her country and ours as any formally accredited Ambassador."

At the state luncheon in Canberra, Prime Minister Curtin welcomed Eleanor "not only in her own right—a very great right that she has established for herself in her own country and, indeed, throughout the world—but also as the Ambassadress of her husband and the people of the United States of America." Another speaker, former prime minister William Morris Hughes, bluntly stated that although her visit was presented as unofficial, it had great political significance. He then put in a plug to the American people to reelect Franklin.

In a private meeting with Prime Minister Curtin prior to the luncheon, Eleanor delivered a verbal message from President Roosevelt extending his regard for Curtin and for the Australian government. She emphasized her husband's admiration for Australia's war effort and his assurance that Australia's importance was prominent in his mind. Both Eleanor and Curtin agreed on the need for postwar planning and unity, and the principal topic of conversation was the position of all countries after the war. She stated to the press that she believed Australia would become an important postwar Pacific unit of manufacture and distribution.

The next day, Eleanor reported to Franklin about her

meeting with the prime minister. "I like Mr. Curtin very much & I hope you will ask him to come to the U.S. again," she wrote. "I think he would come."

Eleanor achieved the result Franklin wanted. In January 1944, after returning from meetings in Tehran with Joseph Stalin and in Cairo with Chiang Kai-shek, he extended another invitation to Curtin. This time, it was accepted. Three months later, Curtin arrived at the White House, where Eleanor greeted him and his wife. She then traveled to South Carolina with them to meet with the president, who was there resting due to poor health.

While Eleanor was in the Pacific, she and Franklin cabled each other every few days. Their notes were affectionate and informative, checking in on each other's health, sharing family news, and exchanging details about their respective activities. As the date approached for Eleanor's return to the United States, they made plans to see each other right away. After she had been abroad for a month in England, Franklin was anxious for her to come home. Deciding how to send her resulted in numerous transatlantic telephone calls between government officials, leading Franklin—who did not want her to travel on a military plane—to capitulate. "I don't care how you send her home, just send her," he declared. As the plane Eleanor shared with ferry pilots landed in Washington, DC, she saw several cars and Secret Service agents on the tarmac and was surprised and pleased that Franklin had taken time off to come meet her.

In Australia, while publicly Eleanor was as engaging and lively as always, privately she despaired that her visit wasn't having enough of an impact. "Truth to tell...I very much doubt that these trips have any real value & they certainly put our high ranking officials to much trouble & travail of spirit," she confided in Franklin.

Adding to Eleanor's discontent was the ever-present feeling

that, despite the dizzying pace she kept—living up to her reputation as "America's Public Energy No. 1"—she wasn't doing enough for the men in uniform. She asked to visit New Guinea, just hundreds of miles away, where General MacArthur was headquartered in the city of Port Moresby. Before leaving New Zealand, Eleanor spoke with Robert Patterson, the U.S. undersecretary of war, who recommended that she see Port Moresby, which was safe enough and would offer "a wonderful impression of activity."

Then word came from MacArthur denying Eleanor's request. The denial was especially stinging since the five roving senators, representing both political parties, were welcomed at Port Moresby around the same time. As Eleanor put it to a friend, "[He] was too busy to bother with a lady." Speculation arose that MacArthur's brush-off was politically motivated. He was being talked about as a contender for the 1944 Republican presidential nomination and would likely not have wanted press photos showing him with the First Lady.

Regardless of the reason, there was no way around MacArthur's decision. Eleanor vented her frustration to Franklin, particularly over the excuse that he couldn't spare the high-ranking officers required to escort her in Port Moresby. "This is the kind of thing that seems to me silly. I'd rather a sergeant & I'd see & hear more but I must have a general & I'm so scared I can't speak & he wouldn't tell me anything anyway." (She was correct that the brass weren't entirely forthcoming. Even the amiable Lieutenant General Eichelberger, who appreciated what she was doing for his troops, admitted, "I kept everything from her that I could.")

MacArthur's refusal to allow her to go to Port Moresby was especially distressing as she traveled through Australia and met servicemen who were soon going to New Guinea or had recently returned. She told Franklin, "It would have pleased the men & they can't understand it. They all say, 'but it is quite safe Mrs. Roosevelt & you ought to see the field we've made!'" Losing the chance to visit New Guinea raised the stakes on her getting to Guadalcanal.

Despite the personal discontent Eleanor was experiencing, she never let on while in public and left Canberra to praise. "America's First Lady has unwittingly given the Federal Capital's pseudo-aristocrats the biggest jolt their tough hides have had," declared a newspaper. "Mrs. Roosevelt showed them convincingly that a great woman could still be a human being without losing control of a situation. That it was still possible to move with kings, nor lose the common touch."

———

The next morning, after Eleanor landed in Melbourne, the city was quickly abuzz. A convoy of official army cars, motorcycle police, marshals toting tommy guns, and two large buses carrying correspondents, photographers, and army press relations officers was impossible to miss as it traveled from the airport to an army camp forty miles away.

"Jeepers, she's just like your mother, isn't she?" a young soldier exclaimed after glimpsing Eleanor. She insisted on lunching with the enlisted men, compelling the generals in attendance to take a seat at the same table as rank-and-file soldiers and eat their meal from the metal mess dishes the soldiers used. During the meal, she asked whether many marriages were taking place between American servicemen and Australian women, and the commanding officer informed her that 15 percent of the men of his battalion had applied for permission to tie the knot. After lunch, Eleanor visited the camp canteen, where she mingled with the soldiers and stood on a chair to deliver her greetings-from-the-president speech.

Eleanor circumvented the brass surrounding her whenever she could. In a hospital ward, a patient handed her a long letter he had received. She put on her glasses and read every word, visibly moved by the contents. Seeing the young man's distress, Eleanor asked everyone—generals included—to wait in the corridor while she spoke with him alone. Once stateside, she cautioned people not to unnecessarily burden their servicemen. Mail was a morale booster, but it had to be the right kind of mail, since they never knew when a letter would be read. It could be on a battlefield or in a hospital bed. It was important to share things with them, "to keep them close and make them feel they are part of your life every day." But "complaining letters" were better left unwritten, she cautioned. "Doctors told me they'd seen men buoyed up by letters from home, but also completely cast down."

At a Red Cross club, Eleanor arrived unannounced one morning. Following behind her was "a brace of generals and admirals manfully teetering on the edge of collapse," a sailor gleefully relayed in a letter home. When the group encountered two young marines standing in their underwear by an electric heater, waiting for their trousers to be mended, club management "gasped for shame and the entourage gasped for breath." Eleanor, who reminded her hosts that she had brought four sons up to manhood, chatted with the boys, who were "both paralyzed with amazement and chagrin but thrilled thru and thru." When the First Lady left, they clutched their scorched legs and burst into excited shouts. Wide-eyed, one exclaimed, "She—the wife of the President—talked to me!"

But some of the officers, relayed the correspondent, "could write copy for Colonel McCormick," a reference to Robert R. McCormick, a newspaper magnate and Roosevelt administration critic. "They caricature her speech, estimate the cost of the trip and—if they're gentle—ask what the hell she's doing tearing around; why doesn't she stay home." The cause, he believed, went back to the erroneous statements alleged to have been said by Eleanor concerning the marine corps.

Still, Eleanor's visit went over big with the local population, he continued. The enlisted men he knew liked her too and were excited and pleased she was there. "I keep thinking of those two boys without any pants and how they'll remember that morning perhaps when they're in a nasty fox hole trying not to do anything foolish or panicky. I think Eleanor created two damn good Marines in a few minutes that morning and I don't know an officer in the battalion who could do the same."

As with the mess hall meal, the men were delighted with the temporary shake-up in the military hierarchy. "It's somepin when a half a dozen general officers wait gasping for someone to complete a casual talk with two privates! It's somepin and it's Eleanor."

CHAPTER 11

WOMANPOWER

"Women in the United States are winning greater economic equality with men through their war work, but you must remember the United States is a big country, and in some parts equality is coming rather slowly."
—ELEANOR ROOSEVELT, *AUSTRALIAN WOMEN'S WEEKLY*, SEPTEMBER 11, 1943

Melbourne and Sydney, Australia, September 5–9

"The whole world is waking to the fact that women can do almost anything to which they turn their hands," Eleanor told a luncheon gathering with servicewomen in Melbourne. From what she had seen so far, Australian women, like those in New Zealand, were performing a greater variety of jobs than women in the United States, where the manpower shortage was less acute.

The last of "a hurricane rush" in Melbourne was "a woman's day" for Eleanor as she met with women employed in various branches of the military and in the defense industry and with Australian Red Cross volunteers. She saw women turning out ammunition for tommy guns at a factory and comforted a worker being treated for an on-the-job hand injury. She witnessed women at a laboratory performing high-precision work on optical munitions—such as telescopic sights for anti-tank guns and predictors that enabled the calculation of an enemy aircraft's future position—which were a vital component of modern scientific warfare. She inspected a base postal unit run by the Australian Women's Army Service, where the sorting of mail and parcels for the troops was taking place. At an ambulance car company, women ran the show, driving the vehicles, doing maintenance work, and transporting the wounded from hospital ships.

When Australia went to war, women sought to contribute to the cause and instead were met with resistance. At the time, it was largely unheard of for married women to work outside the home, and those who were employed did so mostly out of economic necessity. There was also debate about whether they were up to the task of taking on occupations formerly filled by men, with some questioning if women could handle "the intense physical and nervous strain" of wartime work.

When the formation of a Women's Land Army was being considered to address work shortages on farms, one detractor found it "ridiculous" to suggest that women could do the physical labor required. "Our women are wonderful; but is it fair to ask them to shear or crutch sheep, [to] plough the land?" he asked.

Those in support of having women do more sometimes wrapped their reasoning in misogyny. "In England and France women do splendid work in the camps, and thus relieve the soldiers and make them available for military activities. If in England and France why not in Australia?" asked a newspaper editorial. The piece quoted a high-ranking military officer who thought it seemed absurd that servicemen sat around peeling potatoes. "That is women's work," he said. "The men enlisted to do the fighting. Let them do that, and that only."

Ultimately, necessity ended the debate. The demands of war steadily increased, particularly after the Pacific became an additional battleground. Eventually even men in what were considered essential home-front jobs, initially exempt from military service, were called upon to enlist. Women stepped in to pick up the slack, supporting the war effort and keeping the country running.

In Australia and New Zealand, they sheared sheep, tended livestock, and harvested crops. In addition to supplying their own home-front populations, Great Britain needed food support and Allied servicemen in the Pacific had to be fed. Despite initial opposition in New Zealand to the creation of a Women's Land Service, even with limited resources and less farmhands, the output of meat, dairy, and wool increased during the war.

Both countries' armed forces recruited women for noncombatant roles in auxiliary branches of the army, navy, and air force. Women also worked in civilian occupations, such as tram conductors and postal carriers. Others took over the jobs their enlisted husbands had previously done, like ice vendors, a necessary service at a time when iceboxes were used in homes to keep food from spoiling.

A similar scenario played out in the United States as women entered the workforce in unprecedented numbers. Eleanor was an early predictor that circumstances would necessitate utilizing women in the war effort—and that women would meet the challenge. On a radio broadcast in February 1942, she suggested that women be registered for selective service, as England had done. Analyzing their capabilities and training and deciding in advance where they could be used would be efficient and save time. Initially receptive to the idea, the president changed his mind after being told by the War Manpower Commission that large numbers of unemployed men were still available. But the situation changed as more men entered the armed forces and decreased the number of workers in defense-production facilities.

"The U.S. manpower problem is rapidly coming round to the inevitable solution: womanpower," noted *Time* magazine. "Slacks and hairnets dot the nation's war plants now—and thousands on thousands of women stand ready" to make munitions as well as rear their children.

Eleanor used the lines of communication she had established with the nation's women to advise and encourage them to seek employment in war industries. Winning the war depended in large part on the United States' ability to rapidly produce ships, bombers and fighter planes (many aircraft could be lost in a single battle), ammunition, machine guns, and other weaponry, something that could only be accomplished if women filled factories and shipyards.

The shifting landscape also opened up roles for women in the military as a way to solve manpower shortages. When the United States entered the war in December 1941, the only American women in uniform were army and navy nurses. Each branch of the service subsequently opened to women during the war, with more than 350,000 serving in support roles such as clerks, cooks, messengers, telephone operators, and airplane spotters. Not surprisingly, racism was a factor, with some branches limiting the number of Black women they would hire. The marine corps refused to include Black women altogether and was the last holdout to allow any women at all. Higher-ups finally conceded after the heavy loss of life during the Solomons campaign and the realization that they would need to keep funneling untold numbers of men into combat duty.

A marine private in training wrote to the First Lady to complain about the policy change:

Naval Training School, Norman, Oklahoma
February 1, 1943

Dear Madam,

I'm writing to you with the hope that you can help us Marines. We object to the idea of having women Marines. There is no place in the Marine Corps for skirts. And naturally we don't need women.

The Marine Corps has a reputation of being the best fighting force in the world. We're trying to keep that reputation. How can we do it with women in here. We will appreciate anything you can do for our cause.

Thanking you for your trouble and attention, I remain
Pvt. Donald E. Blount
USMC

P.S. This is the opinion of all the Marines. They back me in all that I've said. We don't need women in the Marine Corps.

He found no sympathy with Eleanor, who sent this reply:

February 6, 1943

Dear Mr. Blount:

Women are proving useful in all branches of the Services.
Don't worry, they won't bother you!

Very sincerely yours,
Eleanor Roosevelt

The first branch of the armed services to accept women out-side nursing roles—and the only one to send them overseas—was the U.S. Army. Eleanor backed a bill proposed by Congresswoman Edith Nourse Rogers establishing the Women's Army Auxiliary Corps (WAAC), a voluntary enrollment program, which was presented to Congress in May 1941. (The name later changed to the Women's Army Corps when members were given full military status.) The bill languished with lawmakers, prompt-ing army chief of staff General George Marshall to demand, "I want a women's corps right away, and I don't want any excuses!" Congress continued to stall, even after the United States went to war. The bill was delayed due to obstruction by shortsighted congressmen more fearful of how the nation's laundry would get done than they were about addressing urgent wartime concerns. "Who will then do the cooking, the washing, the mending, the humble homey tasks to which every woman has devoted her-self?" asked one representative.

Congress finally signed into law the bill establishing the WAAC a year after it was introduced. Recruitment posters appealed to a sense of patriotism, asking, "Are you a girl with a Star-Spangled heart?" while others emphasized a "Woman's Place in War" and promised 239 different kinds of jobs.

"This is the army behind the fighting forces," said Eleanor after touring a WAAC training center in Des Moines, Iowa.

Even in defense of the nation, there was opposition to breaking down traditional social barriers by having women work outside the home in large numbers. Predictably, Westbrook Pegler ranted against the idea. "Mrs. Roosevelt proposed that all of us, men and women, be drafted for war work, which would mean that mothers should be taken out of the homes and the kids taken over by some kind of public mothering authority," he claimed. "Considering that broken homes are the main causes of juvenile delinquency and crime I am altogether against this proposal."

The Catholic Church also took exception. *Catholic World* deemed "women's work" evil primarily for alienating "the life of the wife from the life of the husband." The magazine editorial further claimed that women who worked outside the home "weaken family life, endanger their own marital happiness, rob themselves of a man's protective capabilities, and by consequence decrease the number of children."

Nearly everyone expected that women working in the war-production industries would still have to keep up with domestic duties. Eleanor pushed to ensure that women had the necessary resources and support, such as child care, that would allow them to both tend their households and join the assembly lines and that they receive equal pay.

Eleanor's encouragement of and support for women's participation in war work helped broaden the quest for gender equality, for which she had been advocating for more than two decades. After the war ended, some women would want to return to their homes, she acknowledged, while others would rather continue in the workforce. Regardless of where they found their place, she had a forthright message for all women: stay involved in civic life, and don't sit idly by while men alone determined the fates of their countries. As she told an Australian newspaper, "The political candidate of the future must answer to women."

Like many affluent women of the time, Eleanor candidly admitted that she was slow to come around to women's suffrage. When Franklin, a New York State senator at the time, expressed support for the movement, she was shocked. She had never given the matter serious thought since she "took it for granted that men were superior creatures and knew more about politics than women did." But if Franklin was a suffragist, that meant she must be one too.

In the ensuing years, Eleanor made up for her initial apathy by urging women to use the power of their vote. "I had learned that if you wanted to institute any kind of reform you could get far more attention if you had a vote than if you lacked one," she counseled. (New Zealand was the first country to grant women the right to vote, in 1893, twenty-six years before the United States did the same.)

In 1921, Eleanor was appointed a delegate to the League of Women Voters' national convention in Cleveland. She was in the audience listening as Carrie Chapman Catt, the league's leader, appealed to women to end the practice of war. Catt threw out her prepared speech and took the U.S. government to task for bowing to isolationists and refusing to join the League of Nations, an international diplomatic group formed after World War I to mediate disputes between countries to prevent open warfare. Catt urged women to work together and demand action from Congress. "Let us be silent no more!" she implored. "Men were born by instinct to slay. It seems to me God is giving a call to the women of the world to come forward, to stay the hand of men, to say, 'No, you shall no longer kill your fellow men.'"

Two decades later, Eleanor echoed a similar message. In the postwar era, she said while addressing the women's services luncheon in Melbourne, it would depend more than ever on women to build and maintain a peaceful world.

———

"No men allowed!" shouted a constable outside the town hall in Melbourne.

More than fifty thousand people lined the city's streets, traffic brought to a standstill, and thronged the vicinity of the town hall, anticipating Eleanor's arrival there. People sat on ledges and roofs and leaned from windows in tall buildings to catch a glimpse of the First Lady. When a reporter arrived, the scene at the main entrance was pandemonium as policemen on the steps tried to stem the rush and weed out the men trying to conceal themselves among the women.

A thunderous cheer rose from the crowd as Eleanor stepped from her car and waved several times before entering the building, where three thousand women waited. The event was open to any who wished to attend, and the hall filled in about fifteen minutes. Her speech was amplified through loudspeakers so that people who couldn't gain entry could still hear her address.

"Being a housewife in these difficult days is no mean war job," Eleanor told the audience, most of whom had hurried through housework to attend. They laughed when she told how, as a housewife herself, she had supervised a breakfast tray for Prime Minister Churchill at the White House. She heard him cheer when he found two eggs, which was two months' ration in England.

At the town hall address, a film taken during Eleanor's visit to Great Britain was shown. The film depicted war work being done by women, whose courage and steadfastness of spirit she greatly admired as they lived with war at close quarters. In all the time Eleanor mingled with women in England, Scotland, and

Northern Ireland, whether in factories or on farms, in the service or in their homes, she never heard a single murmur of hardship. "Their only thought was we must get on with the war."

One woman returned home after an air raid to find her house destroyed by a bomb. "Was your husband there?" Eleanor asked. "No, the coward," the woman replied. "He is in the Army."

———

"Mrs. Roosevelt Meets Heroines," announced a newspaper during Eleanor's stop in Sydney. The real-life heroines were members of the Australian Army Nursing Service: Sister Margaret Anderson, who was awarded a George Medal for bravery after shielding the wounded from dive-bombing enemy planes aboard a freighter on the way out of Singapore in February 1942, and Sister Ellen Savage, the only woman out of thirteen to survive the sinking of the Australian military hospital ship *Centaur*.

Four months earlier, in May 1943, the *Centaur* was sailing from Sydney to Port Moresby, New Guinea, to collect wounded and ill servicemen and transport them to hospitals in Australia. Under the Geneva Convention, hospital ships were to be respected by all sides during war and left unharmed. The *Centaur* traveled unescorted with 363 crew members, doctors, nurses, and other medical personnel on board. The ship was fully illuminated and prominently marked with red crosses in several places. The weather was clear and visibility excellent. At 4:10 a.m., forty miles off the coast of Australia, a Japanese submarine torpedoed the *Centaur*. Fire raced through the ship, which capsized and sank within three minutes of being hit.

Awakened in her cabin when the torpedo struck, Sister Savage grabbed her rosary beads and, with a friend, Sister King, made it to the top deck, where she saw the bridge aflame and knew the ship was sinking. She grabbed a life belt, and she and Sister King, who could not swim, jumped overboard. The suction dragged Sister Savage down into the dark water, and she was hit in the head by a piece of wreckage. She became entangled in ropes and debris before suddenly shooting to the surface. There was no sign of Sister King.

After spending two hours in the shark-infested water, Sister Savage was pulled aboard a raft. "We had no first aid equipment so we couldn't do much for the injured except bathe their burns with salt water," she said. She had lacerations on her head and was clad in torn silk pajamas. Fellow survivors gave her a pair of khaki trousers and a topcoat, which she shared with a fifteen-year-old crew member.

Sister Savage was put in charge of rationing the meager food and water supplies and credited with helping to keep up morale, particularly by leading prayers, as sharks circled and several search planes failed to spot the rafts. "She never told me at any stage that she was injured or in pain," said the sole surviving medical officer. It wasn't until she and the sixty-three other survivors were rescued after thirty-four hours at sea that the extent of her injuries became known—a fractured nose, burst eardrums, a broken palate, and cracked ribs. Sister Savage recovered and resumed nursing at a Sydney hospital three months later. In 1944, she was awarded a George Medal for "conspicuous service and high courage."

If Eleanor were young enough, she told "My Day" readers, she would have liked to be a nurse in the army or the navy "for they are allowed to share more nearly the men's existence."

In the Pacific theater, U.S. Army nurses followed closely behind the fighting forces, arriving in an area once it was under Allied control—outside a direct Japanese ground threat yet close enough to receive air evacuees. In these outposts, nurses

assumed responsibilities that would typically have been handled by doctors, administering anesthesia, performing surgical procedures, giving transfusions, dressing new, raw stumps,
and removing shrapnel. "They are not living very comfortably,"
said Eleanor. "They are seeing daily sights that must try their
fortitude."

At a Red Cross club for nurses in Sydney, Eleanor spent "a
very happy half hour" talking with women who had served in
New Guinea. Crowding a lounge, sitting in chairs and on the
floor, they ate chocolate cake while telling her about their experiences. In addition to the physical and mental rigors of caring
for the wounded, there were other challenges—rats absconding
with socks, snakes curled up beside a bed's mosquito netting,
insects eating uniforms hanging in closets, and always-damp
clothing due to the humidity. "Oh, the blessed relief of a hot
shower when you have had nothing but cold water for nine
months," said a nurse. Another told Eleanor that, for a time,
the only water available in hospitals had to be brought in carts,
every cupful treasured so as not to waste a drop. Many nurses
served overseas in stretches as long, or nearly as long, as some
of the men. They cared for the wounded as they were brought
in, regardless of the hour, and sometimes worked twenty-four
hours straight.

"Add to all this the hazards of air raids and you have a stern
test of hardihood," Eleanor said. "Yet I never heard a single nurse
complain."

Every woman at home owed a debt of gratitude to the nurses
in the Pacific and to the women working with the Red Cross,
Eleanor asserted. In her report to Norman Davis, she praised
Coletta Ryan, the Red Cross supervisor in the South Pacific.
Coletta hoped to convince army and navy officials to allow her
to set up facilities on Guadalcanal and elsewhere, part of which

meant persuading them that women could withstand the hardships of the conflict zones. (She established a Red Cross club on Guadalcanal several months later and after that went on to work in India and China.)

A former apartment-house manager in Washington, DC, and a Ziegfeld Follies performer, Coletta arrived on New Caledonia in the early days of the war. Overcoming a lack of materials and supply delays due to shipping difficulties, she set up an officers' rest home in a clifftop villa. Working with the Naval Construction Battalion, commonly called the Seabees, she built badminton, volleyball, and tennis courts, screened in the house and a wraparound porch, revamped the kitchen with a new stove, and installed a refrigerator. She oversaw a farm with chickens and cows, ensuring a supply of fresh milk and eggs, and planted a vegetable garden. In between, she tended to a local boy who ingested poison and helped to deliver a local woman's baby in the middle of the night.

Red Cross worker Mary Ferebee Howard lived a rugged life on New Caledonia, sleeping on a cot in a tent she shared with six other women. They showered at a pipe with holes punched in it, constantly battled mosquitoes, and worked seven days a week at a service club. One of the "most tragic" duties she performed was meeting the hospital ships that came to the island, carrying with her a large canvas bag filled with cigarettes, chewing gum, and candy. Debarking the wounded took several hours. First there were the men carried in litters, to whom she whispered a few words and patted for comfort. Next came those who could walk. "If you could call it walking," recalled Mary. "Most of these were minus an arm or leg and many had head wounds." Last to come off the ship were men in a dazed state, seemingly not seeing or hearing, whom she and the other greeters talked to at great length and hugged if possible. "By the time it was over and our canvas bags were empty, so were we. All night long I thought of the tragic and sad eyes of those young boys," said Mary.

"My hat is off to every woman working in this area," Eleanor declared. She thought it "ridiculous" that more women in military service were not permitted overseas. She attributed the restriction to "a false chivalry, which insists that women be protected from war hazards and hardships, even against their own wishes." Sheltering women from military service or even from defense industry employment as some wanted was shortsighted. Particularly after witnessing the effects of jungle warfare on the men in the Pacific, Eleanor believed a great postwar difficulty would be the readjustment of couples who had been separated not only for long periods of time but also by the experiences they underwent. The readjustment would be easier, she believed, if both had "experienced a similar discipline and acquired a similar attitude toward life."

Journalist Ruth Millett concurred with the First Lady, telling readers that of the letters she received from servicemen, at least half emphasized the fact that they didn't want their women involved in the war—they wanted to find them unchanged when they returned. "It seems to me that natural as their desire is, their attitude is far from wise. For it doesn't take into account the fact that they themselves are going to change—and change greatly," said Millett. "Wouldn't any returning soldier who had undergone battle find it easier to understand and be understood by a woman who had given up an easy life to help win the war than by a woman who had sat at home staying 'unchanged' for her man?"

Eleanor emphasized this point in a post-trip address by sharing the story of a soldier who was anxious rather than elated to be given leave. "I don't think I'm fit to go home," he lamented.

"For five months I haven't done anything but kill. People back home don't want me, I've changed too much."

Eleanor warned that everyone on the home front had a responsibility to help returning fighters adjust to civilian life. "We at home," she said, "have got to know how to be wise enough to deal with lots that has changed those men out there—men who had to do things they didn't want to do but they knew had to be done."

CHAPTER 12

THE HEROISM AND THE HORROR

"Let us hear no more disgusting criticism of Mrs. Roosevelt for visiting the war fronts. This is no pleasure jaunt for the wife of the President. She is subjecting herself to considerable inconvenience, discomfort and personal expense in an effort to cheer up the men in foreign service."

—*GAZETTE*, CHARLESTON, WEST VIRGINIA, SEPTEMBER 18, 1943

Rockhampton, Townsville, Mackay, Cairns, and Brisbane, Australia, September 9–14

Streetlamps gleamed, buildings and houses aglow, as the town of Rockhampton, for the first time since the Pacific war began and dimout bans were put in place, turned on all its lights on the evening of Eleanor's arrival. Situated in central Queensland, a subtropical state in northern Australia, Rockhampton was the site of a large

U.S. Army camp. The region's varied terrain—hills, jungle, open space, and beaches—was ideal ground to train American troops and close enough to New Guinea to use as a frontline staging area.

After a last-minute change of orders sent Lieutenant General Eichelberger to the South Pacific rather than North Africa, he set up headquarters in Rockhampton and set about instructing GIs in the ways of jungle warfare. Wary of the censors, he never described the town in the prolific letters he wrote to his wife. Eleanor performed the task for him. In "My Day," she relayed details about visiting Rockhampton, where houses were built on stilts (Eichelberger shared his rambling, one-story structure with five officers and three sergeants). The cooler, ground-level space was often used for storage and screened by flowers and vines. Residences stretched along the banks of the river flowing through town, and blooms flourished in abundance—hibiscus, bougainvillea, and the flame-colored poinciana tree. "My first impression is of the most beautiful and elaborate gardens I have ever seen," wrote Eleanor. Town officials turned over most of their city hall's first floor to the army to use as offices, and headquarters were established in a botanical garden.

Returning to the beauty and order of Rockhampton was like a balm for Eichelberger following the "savagery and anarchy" of living and fighting on New Guinea. After long stretches in the jungle, he said, "most of us had forgotten what civilized living was like."

New Guinea is the second largest island in the world, outsized only by Greenland. At the time war broke out, the western half of the island was Dutch New Guinea, a colony of the Netherlands, and the eastern half was divided into two sections: New Guinea in the north and Papua New Guinea in the south, both administered by the Australian government. Fighting on New Guinea took place on various parts of the island and lasted nearly the entirety of the Pacific war. Allied forces were aided by native New Guineans, who fought alongside them, trekked supplies to the front on foot and by canoe, and transported back wounded and deceased soldiers.

New Guinea "is immense," a member of General MacArthur's staff told Senator James Mead when the lawmaker visited there. The island stretches thirteen hundred miles, about the same distance as from Boston to Miami. "And four hundred miles across—except that a ridge of sixteen-thousand-foot mountains runs down its entire length, with glaciers of perpetual snow on their tops, even though we're about on the Equator," the staff member explained. "It's wild as anywhere on earth—whole tracts still never explored."

After taking territory on the island's northeastern coast, Japan set its sights on Port Moresby, a seaside town in southern Papua. Seizing Port Moresby would deprive the Allies of a critical forward base and disrupt shipping lanes. The Japanese intended to isolate Australia and, from this vantage point, could launch an attack farther into the Australian mainland and target key bases from Brisbane to Melbourne.

When an attempt to capture Port Moresby from the water ended in defeat at the Battle of the Coral Sea, the Japanese tried again by trekking overland from the beachhead at Buna on the Papuan coast. Looming between Buna and Port Moresby is the formidable Owen Stanley Range. Japanese forces made a torturous advance across the mountains along the Kokoda Track, an old native trail, coming within twenty miles of Port Moresby, which was being defended by Australian forces. But fervency and discipline can only take troops so far, noted Lieutenant General Eichelberger. Much of the narrow dirt track across the mountains could only be traveled on foot. Replenishing supplies and weapons from

Japanese bases on the coast became increasingly difficult as the soldiers trekked inland, and the mission was hindered further still by Allied strafing. Japanese high command, which was pouring resources into Guadalcanal, eventually ordered its forces in the Owen Stanleys to retreat.

General MacArthur went on the offensive and ordered an attack. The going was slow and arduous as American and Australian troops, including a division of forces Prime Minister Curtin insisted return from North Africa, pursued the retreating Japanese on two separate tracks across the harsh mountainous terrain. They joined forces on the other side, along with troops that had come up the coast, and readied for an assault on the enemy's stronghold at Buna.

The swift victory Allied command anticipated was hampered by inaccurate intelligence. Estimated at three hundred, the number of Japanese troops in the area was actually ten times that amount. "It is perhaps not surprising that aerial photography failed to disclose the location and strength of the Jap defenses," said Eichelberger. "In a dense jungle where a bunker or entrenchment cannot be seen from thirty yards away, aerial photography must be swallowed with a full shaker of salt."

The Japanese occupied a three-mile coastal strip surrounded by water on three sides—the sea at their back and on their left flank and two unfordable streams on the right. Almost their entire position was in a coconut plantation, fortified with a series of bunkers and connecting trenches that were nearly invisible among the abundant camouflage of trees and tall grass. "Such enemy concealment may seem implausible to people who have never seen wet, luxuriant, close-branched jungle," explained Eichelberger. A sniper shot one of his aides from a "spider hole" under the roots of a tree with giant palm fronds concealing the opening.

Shielding the Japanese in front were mangrove bogs,

impenetrable except for a few trails along which Allied forces could advance from the jungle. "It was easy for the Japs, secure in buried log bunkers, able to move reinforcements swiftly along a motor road, to command our approaches with heavy automatic weapons fire," recalled Eichelberger.

When the battle at Buna began, Eichelberger was in Rockhampton, where he had been ordered to continue training troops. Then, ten days into the faltering fight, he was summoned to General MacArthur's headquarters in Port Moresby and ordered to take over command at Buna. MacArthur bluntly made sure the assignment was understood. "Bob," he said, "I want you to take Buna, or not come back alive."

Arriving in New Guinea, Eichelberger found troops demoralized and disorganized, insufficiently trained and undersupplied, unkempt and clothing tattered, and with little discipline or military courtesy. Cases of malaria, dengue fever, tropical dysentery, and jungle ulcers were rampant. Eichelberger ordered medics "to take the temperatures of an entire company of hollow-eyed men near the front." Every member of the company, some 150 men, was running a fever. There was no choice but to have them forge ahead. "To evacuate all those with fever at Buna would have meant immediate victory for the enemy. I had to encourage most of those troops back into combat," Eichelberger said. (A field commander fought the entire campaign with a malarial fever "well above the human boiling point.")

Eichelberger briefly stopped all fighting to reorganize troops and replace some ranking officers. He increased supplies and procured better rations for the half-starved men, and he stepped up the ground reconnaissance patrols that were crucial for gathering knowledge of enemy positions and the terrain ahead.

Daunted by the perils and the strangeness of swamp and jungle, troops were reluctant to undertake the patrolling, but it was the patrolling and the information it yielded that would help keep them alive. Years later, reflecting on Buna, Eichelberger was "inclined to believe" that the men were frightened less of the Japanese fighters than they were of the jungle. "It was the terror of the new and the unknown," he explained. "There is nothing pleasant about sinking into a foul-smelling bog up to your knees. There is nothing pleasant about lying in a slit trench, half submerged, while a tropical rain turns it into a river. Jungle night noises were strange to Americans—and in the moist hot darkness the rustling of small animals in the bush was easily misinterpreted as the stealthy approach of the enemy."

When Eichelberger's troops attacked the enemy several days later, he fought alongside "the lads" in his command. Reported a correspondent on the scene, "The commanding general himself took a tommy gun and mixed it with the Japanese." (A few weeks later, on Christmas morning, newspapers reported that three American generals had been wounded at Buna and so had Eichelberger's aide. Eichelberger's wife, Emmeline, correctly figured he was in the fray and worriedly telephoned the War Department, which dispensed the falsehood that he was still in Australia. A couple of days later, an article was published detailing a correspondent's trip to the front at Buna. He accompanied a "tall, gray-haired general" who stopped to speak to the sick and the wounded being transported along the trail, telling them, "Good morning, lads. I only hope you will all be home next Christmas." Emmeline knew her husband was alive as of Christmas morning since he was the only general known to address soldiers using the term *lads*.)

According to an ancient military maxim, a commander must be seen by his troops in combat. When Eichelberger arrived at Buna, officers were prohibited from wearing insignia of rank at the front because it could draw enemy fire. "I was glad on that particular day that there were three stars on my collar which glittered in the sun," said Eichelberger. "How else would those sick and cast-down soldiers have known their commander was in there with them? They knew, being sensible men, that a bullet is no respecter of rank."

The day's fighting yielded a hard-won and important success: a small group of infantrymen led by Sergeant Herman Bottcher found a fissure in the Japanese defenses and drove through to the sea. "The breakthrough was, possibly, lucky: the holding of the position was accomplished by intelligence and sheer guts," said Eichelberger. Censorship rules prevented newspapers from printing Eichelberger's name but not that of Sergeant Bottcher. Under heavy machine gun fire, Bottcher and his "bearded, grimy crew" fought their way from the jungle to the coast. They dug in and repelled enemy attacks to hold a strategic stretch of beach, cutting off communications between two Japanese garrisons. (Eleanor later asked to meet Sergeant Bottcher and found him at the ice cream counter in a Red Cross club in Sydney. A little over a year later, he was killed by a burst of mortar fire while fighting in the Philippines.)

The breakthrough on the beach at Buna "was only the beginning," recalled Eichelberger. Retreat back over the mountains was impossible. The only option was to keep battling and to drive the enemy from its entrenched coastal positions—or suffer defeat and death in the swamps. Troops proceeded to slowly move forward, day after day, painstakingly pushing toward the sea. Significantly, morale improved even as the weather worsened, torrential nightly rains turning "all the jungle into a tanglefoot morass" and causing a spike in cases of tropical illness.

The fight for Buna lasted another agonizing month. "In battle the margin between victory and defeat is often narrow," noted Eichelberger. "Under the terrific pressures of combat, officers and men alike tend to forget that the enemy is hard pressed too. Sometimes just plain stubbornness wins the battle that awareness and wisdom might have lost. That's what happened at Buna. The Japanese morale cracked before ours did." Another factor in the Allied favor was that the Japanese forces, while highly trained and courageous, strictly adhered to battle plans and rarely improvised to meet unexpected situations.

Six days after the conflict at Buna ended, Eichelberger received a note from General MacArthur that read in part, "I am so glad that you were not injured in the fighting. I always feared your incessant exposure might result fatally. With a hearty slap on the back. Most cordially, MacArthur."

For Eichelberger, victory at Buna went beyond personal satisfaction for having completed a successful command or gratitude for having survived. His joy came from the fact that the brave men with whom he fought "could see the sea again. They had proved themselves."

Fighting in the Pacific was a vastly different kind of combat than in other parts of the world, Eleanor told the audience at a Democratic Women's Day gathering after her return. On battlefields in Europe, tank battalions were pitted against one another and massive armies moved and maneuvered in unison. In contrast, jungle warfare was fought individually or in small clusters.

Soldiers went into the jungle on foot, laden with loads of supplies and weapons. They endured week after week of mud-filled foxholes, insect bites and skin sores, and scared, sleepless nights. Clothing and shoes disintegrated from frequent downpours and from wading through swamps, and they had to guard against infected food and water. So abundant was the rain in Papua that wounded men sometimes drowned before being found by the litter bearers. "No war is a good war, and death ignores geography," said Eichelberger. "But out there I was convinced, as were my soldiers, that death was pleasanter in the Temperate Zone."

Jungle warfare was "a sly and sneaky kind of combat," as Eichelberger described it. Soldiers lived and fought in the jungle, playing a "grim hide-and-seek" with the enemy. To survive, they had to melt into their surroundings, using ground and vegetation to best advantage—giant trees and palms, tangled undergrowth, tall and thick grass, bottomless marshes, and trenches. They crept and crawled through the jungle, stealthily moving from point to point, listening and stalking, fighting at close range from behind trees, bushes, logs, and natural embankments, and sometimes hand to hand. Maintaining direction was difficult due to an absence of landmarks, with even mountain peaks invisible in the dense foliage and visibility restricted to ten or fifteen feet.

"The invisibility of the Japanese gave a haunting and fearsome quality to any advance," said Eichelberger. "Every GI knew there were snipers high in the trees, but he could not see them. And there seemed to him no rhyme or reason in their tactics. For three days a patrol might proceed forward and backward over a trail without molestation. On the fourth day enemy bullets would turn the swamp mud red, and our survivors would shoot angrily but unseeingly into the impenetrable green above." The technique was calculated to mystify and to heighten the sense of insecurity. "I can say this: the technique worked."

For the troops at Buna and at Guadalcanal, early jungle battles of the Pacific war, it was essentially baptism by fire. Other than a few World War I veterans, the men faced an enemy force for the first time at Buna. Time was pressing, and although trained in general infantry, they received limited instruction in jungle tactics before being sent into battle. Officers and men learned as they went along, adapting equipment, weapons, and fighting methods to the demands of the tropics. Because of these experiences, future troops went into the jungle better trained for combat and better equipped with weapons and clothing more suited to the climate.

"The first boys who went into New Guinea probably had no idea of what they were going into," Eleanor told the Democratic Women's Day audience. "Now they are getting the kind of training that really prepares them for that kind of fighting. And the boys who have been in it persuade the new boys that it's worthwhile to be well trained."

Eleanor saw troops in training throughout Queensland and was particularly interested in observing jungle warfare tactics. Along a narrow trail cutting through jungle, she followed a few paces behind a camouflage-clad sniper as he fired at concealed and moving targets. She watched as the men were taught how to hide themselves and to remain motionless. When they were learning how to detect the enemy while staying unseen, traps were set, and anyone who failed to implicitly follow instructions was marked as dead. Her son James had described to her the experience of pushing through the jungle, like the boys at Buna had done, and how it took all night to travel half a mile. "Someone making a new path must cut through, step by step," she relayed in a post-trip article. "I didn't understand it then. I understand it now."

In one training area, Eleanor was warned there would be shooting nearby. "But even so I nearly stepped on one boy before I saw him, and the gun seemed to go off right under my feet," she later recalled. She wished she had witnessed the intensive instruction before answering an irate letter she received from a soldier's mother. The outraged woman blasted the training her son was receiving in the Louisiana swamps as cruel, inhuman, and unnecessary. Said Eleanor, "I might have been able to explain to her that [it] was for her son's own safety in the future."

In Rockhampton, Eleanor embarked on a nonstop, seven-hour tour of U.S. Army installations, venturing by jeep along dusty track roads to reach military camps in the bush. In a dentist's tent, she surprised the patient in the chair, a soldier who had a blackened molar removed without uttering a sound. "It hurt like hell," he said afterward, "but with Mrs. Roosevelt watching I had to act tough."

At an army camp near Brisbane, Eleanor climbed up on a tank destroyer, a highly mobile, lightly armored vehicle, for an up-close look at the long-barreled, high-velocity gun mounted in an open turret. Elsewhere she saw a demonstration of the use of heavy Japanese machine guns and automatic rifles captured by U.S. troops on New Guinea. One of the most interesting types of training she witnessed was on a beach north of Cairns. An army engineer unit performed an amphibious landing operation— waves of troops coming ashore, the laying of roads on the beach, bringing equipment onto land, setting up aid stations, and digging in defenses—while under simulated enemy resistance. "It seemed to me to require not only skill and courage, but a great deal of training and physical hardening, for the tasks performed were the toughest kind of work," Eleanor told "My Day" readers.

Just as Eleanor endeavored to make people on the home front fully understand and appreciate the conditions under which the troops lived and fought and suffered, *Life* magazine used the Battle of Buna to do the same.

Victory at Buna "ended a campaign small in Pacific

strategy but unsurpassed in merciless intensity of fighting,"
Life reported in February 1943. Articles on the battle in two
back-to-back issues were illustrated with photographs taken
by George Strock, who lived with the troops and accompanied
them into battle. "His pictures of the campaign, made under
fire, reveal better than any previous sets of pictures the heroism
and the horror of this strange jungle war," declared the magazine. "Studying them, it is as if Papua had been transported
5,000 miles back to the home front—the horror, the patience,
the ingenuity, the simple American courage that got those boys
through to the sea."

In the second of its issues featuring the Battle of Buna, *Life*
wrote about Bill, a young man from Wisconsin farm country,
who made it out of the jungle and to the water's edge. Running
onto the smooth white sand, he was taken down in a burst of
fire from a machine-gun nest. One of Strock's photos depicted
the lifeless bodies of Bill and two other soldiers lying on the
beach at Buna, killed as the job was nearly finished. But the
magazine was forbidden from printing the heartbreaking photo.
In that same issue, an editorial told readers why there was no
visual of Bill's final moment: it was against army policy to show
American dead. The U.S. government sheltered the public from
the harshest realities of war, permitting the media to publish
only images of blanket-covered bodies and flag-draped coffins.
Reporters were also restricted in what they could write, and coverage was generally upbeat and bloodless. The extreme measures
were taken in order to keep Americans from becoming demoralized by the graphic realities of combat and to keep public
approval for the war high.

"The job of men like Strock is to bring the war back to us, so
that we who are thousands of miles removed from the dangers
and the smell of death may know what is at stake," *Life* told its

readers. "Why should the home front be coddled, wrapped up in cotton wool, protected from the shock of the fight? If Bill had the guts to take it, we ought to have the guts to look at it."

Seven months later, just prior to Eleanor's return from the Pacific, readers finally saw Bill and his fallen comrades. Nearly two years after the United States entered the war, the Office of Censorship ended its edict and permitted *Life* to print the photo. "The reason we print it now is that, last week, President Roosevelt and Elmer Davis and the War Department decided that the American people ought to be able to see their own boys as they fall in battle; to come directly and without words into the presence of their own dead," explained the magazine. "And so here it is. This is the reality that lies behind the names that come to rest at last on monuments in the leafy squares of busy American towns."

Those who made it through the fighting were hardly spared. Eleanor saw the haunting effects of the savagery and the strain of jungle warfare etched into the faces of men recently returned from New Guinea. "I wonder if you have ever noticed what shadowed eyes some of those boys have," she remarked to a stateside audience.

Troops given a break from battle were sent to Mackay, a lush, coastal resort town in northern Queensland, for ten-day getaways before returning to the New Guinea front. The Red Cross occupied fourteen buildings within two city blocks, accommodating some eight hundred guests per day. The local population aided the Red Cross in entertaining the servicemen, including five hundred young women who formed the Air Force Victorettes (Eleanor was deemed an honorary member). They hosted dances and beach parties and participated in horseback riding, tennis, cycling, deep-sea fishing trips, and other events and outings with the servicemen.

The idyllic surroundings were a temporary reprieve, but they couldn't erase the horrors of battle endured in the New Guinea jungles. "Without exception," said a Red Cross worker, "they had that jungle look—faces pallid, drawn, and thin, and eyes somewhat apathetic."

———

Eager-faced troops headed for the front in New Guinea filled trucks in a convoy at a U.S. Army base near Townsville, another large military outpost in Queensland. Eleanor insisted on stopping to greet the men, who were wearing steel helmets and battle dress and weighed down with the full packs they would carry into the jungle. She walked down a rough road, her shoes covered in dust and scuffed by rocks, pausing next to each truck to say goodbye and wish the soldiers luck.

A corporal from New York City attracted her attention with his headwear, a wide-brimmed, felt slouch hat worn by the Australian army. "I traded a carton of cigarettes for this hat. I like it. It's much cooler than a steel helmet," he told her.

A private from New Jersey declared, "Well, this is the swellest send-off any outfit could ask for. I have never seen so much 'brass' all together in my life."

At one point, Eleanor's voice quavered, but she quickly recovered and continued down the line of trucks. She insisted on returning along the other side of the convoy and taking the time to wave to those she had missed.

Lieutenant General Eichelberger assured her, "This is what these boys have been waiting and training for for months. They wouldn't stay behind now even if you asked them to."

Prior to farewelling the troops, Eleanor went through a hospital where men wounded in various parts of New Guinea were being treated. When she asked a sergeant from California how he was making out, he grinned and said, "Don't worry about me, ma'am. If it hadn't been for an Aussie I wouldn't be here now." After his left knee was smashed by enemy machine gun bullets, his Australian comrade had gone in under fire and pulled him to safety.

During Eleanor's time in Townsville, she conveyed a message of admiration to the citizenry, who had endured several enemy raids the prior year. Around midnight, beneath a nearly full moon and an almost cloudless sky, air-raid sirens sounded. The town was quickly blacked out before searchlights illuminated the first of four bombers, which made an initial pass over the town and then returned to drop their bombs. The Townsville population "took their first Japanese air raid calmly" as they sought cover in backyard dugouts, slit trenches, and concrete shelters. For the first time on the Australian mainland, service women other than nurses were on duty during an air raid. One hundred and twenty women were among the eleven hundred air-raid wardens who manned their posts within minutes of the sirens sounding. Subsequent air raids followed in the next two out of three nights. Bombs fell into the sea and on uninhabited land, and there was no damage or casualties (other than a lone coconut tree).

Australia's first "air raid baby" was born shortly after six bombs exploded less than a mile away on the night of the initial attack. While driving to the hospital, the newborn girl's parents were frequently stopped by vigilant wardens, who waved the couple on with good wishes when they learned why they were on the road during a blackout. The hospital's maternity ward was otherwise empty. As soon as the alert sounded, seventeen infants, ranging from twenty-four hours to fourteen days old, were taken to a specially constructed shelter beneath the building.

Elsewhere that evening, several big dances were interrupted by the sirens. Some women in evening dress and their soldier escorts decamped to a concrete shelter. Another young woman was bidding good night to her American soldier boyfriend when the sirens sounded. "Gosh," she said. "He was just going to kiss me."

An air battle ensued on the night of the third raid when two fighter pilots "poured lead" into an enemy plane, which was forced to drop its bombs into the sea and was last seen losing altitude over the water.

Located on the northeast coast of Queensland, Townsville was transformed into a major military center. As part of the country's defensive preparations, an airstrip created for civil use was developed into a base for the Royal Australian Air Force. In 1942, the U.S. Army came to town, setting up additional airfields, hangars, hospitals, camps, docks, warehouses, and a depot where Eleanor saw bombers being fitted for action.

Eleanor commended Townsville's residents for their courage withstanding the bombing raids, and she thanked them for the hospitality they showed American servicemen "under the most unusual and trying circumstances." Although the war commonly caused shortages, the disparity was particularly acute in Townsville, where the military buildup surged the population. Soldiers significantly outnumbered civilians, leading to strained resources and shortages in goods and services. In addition, the government commandeered a city block in a residential suburb, converting thirty private homes into a U.S. Army hospital. The hospital's commanding officer "took pride not only in his well-appointed wards but also in his new morgue, with a refrigerator box, and the graduate embalmer he had located."

At a U.S. Army camp near Townsville, the ever-present shadow of racism led to a violent incident in 1942 which was kept concealed. After months of enduring racial taunts and abuse, Black GIs who were part of a labor battalion commanded by white officers mutinied. The long-simmering tensions boiled over when an officer assaulted one of the men in his unit. The soldiers fired machine guns into the tents of their superiors, setting off an eight-hour siege that killed one person and injured dozens of others. No word of the "Townsville mutiny" appeared in the press. Robert Sherrod, a *Time-Life* reporter, handed his write-up of what occurred to visiting U.S. congressman Lyndon B. Johnson, a lieutenant commander in the Naval Reserve and part of a presidentially appointed survey mission in the Southwest Pacific. Johnson agreed to get Sherrod's dispatch to his editors in New York but instead suppressed the report.

———

When a fleet of U.S. Army troop-carrier ships docked in Melbourne in February 1942, Black soldiers were forced to remain on board while the two governments wrangled over their fate. Although the Australian government welcomed the presence of the American military, they asked that Black soldiers be deployed elsewhere in accordance with the country's White Australia policy. In 1901, passage of the Immigration Restriction Act limited non-British migration to Australia, a law primarily targeting Asians and Pacific Islanders but applicable to all nonwhites. The racist attitude extended to the country's indigenous people, Aboriginal Australians, who were subject to discrimination and segregated from certain public places in much the same way as Black Americans.

General MacArthur refused the request to send away Black troops but compromised by agreeing that they would generally be dispatched to more remote areas of the country. Despite the whites-only policy, Black soldiers generally received favorable and friendly treatment from the Australian people.

While en route to Australia, the members of a U.S. Army regiment were cautioned that it was "a white man's country." Landing in Sydney, Private Travis Dixon found an entirely different situation. "We were allowed to go into any place that we thought we could afford," he wrote to his father in Nebraska. When Black troops first arrived, "they were treated like human beings," reported the *New York Amsterdam News*. "They were freely invited to the Australians' homes to dinner, hospitably accepted in hotels, bars, dance halls and other public places."

U.S. military commanders were swift to impose their own segregation policy in Australia, confining Black troops to specific sections in cities and barring them from recreation venues. (A white MP tapped a Black serviceman on the shoulder at a Red Cross club in Brisbane, telling him there was one for him "in the Jim Crow section.") Racism was rampant down the ranks, and some servicemen took offense to the Australians' sociability toward Black Americans. Stories circulated that Blacks were cannibals, that they had tails, and that they carried razors and were quick to kill. U.S. Army officers visited local schools and lectured children to stay away from Black troops. White soldiers had a particular grievance about Australian women associating with Black men and cursed them out in public.

Private Dixon's letter sent from Australia failed to reach his father. The hard-at-work censors confiscated correspondence referring to the "race problem" or criticizing military segregation. They also blocked any missives that mentioned Australians' congeniality toward Black troops for fear it would lead to a postwar upset of racial order in the United States.

Overall, it was somewhat of a losing battle. The Black press reported on the favorable treatment of Black troops in Australia, and the men offered accounts of their experiences in interviews and in letters that slipped by the censors. "We were greeted enthusiastically, lived in the best hotels and associated freely with the Australian citizens, with the American soldiers there as the only ones objecting," a merchant seaman told the *Baltimore Afro-American*.

The same was true in Great Britain, where Black Americans were generally embraced by local populations but faced discrimination from fellow servicemen. Some GIs were "very indignant" to learn that Black soldiers "were not looked upon with terror by the girls in England and Ireland and Scotland," Eleanor informed Secretary of War Stimson. "I think we will have to do a little educating among our Southern white men and officers."

When Stimson learned of Eleanor's impending trip to Great Britain in 1942, he strongly suggested to the president that she refrain from addressing the issue of race in the military while she was abroad or making known "the differential treatment" Black servicemen received in Great Britain compared to in the United States. The president was sympathetic to "our attitude," Stimson recorded in his diary. Eleanor met with Black troops on numerous occasions while in Great Britain but honored the president's wishes to refrain from publicly discussing race, a position that changed during the Pacific trip.

While in Australia, Eleanor made a point of speaking with Black newspaper correspondents at press conferences and was photographed with Black servicemen. Even off-duty recreation venues in the military were segregated, and stops at Red Cross clubs for Black troops in Townsville and Brisbane were included on her itinerary. She specifically asked to visit the Dr. Carver Club in Brisbane, a facility run by the Red Cross and named for George Washington Carver, the agricultural scientist and inventor, who had passed away earlier that year. Along with the usual amenities, a second-floor ballroom, painted sky blue with moonlight effects on the ceiling, had a specially constructed dance floor that accommodated five hundred people, a stage equipped with amplifiers, and balcony seating. The club was off-limits to white American servicemen, except by formal invitation, but was open to all Australians. Jazz and swing bands regularly played at the club, and it became a popular night spot during the war.

Eleanor's final act in Australia was delivering a rousing and powerful speech, addressing an audience of thousands in Brisbane. She touched on topics familiarized throughout the trip, from postwar economics to the need for global cooperation, and delivered "an eloquent plea for racial tolerance." Minority groups in the United States were not always treated as they should be, she told the audience. "Among other things, the war has taught us that we must approach all persons as human beings" and that "it is our responsibility" to see that they have the opportunities for development to which they are entitled and protection from exploitation. In order to make the sacrifices of war truly matter, she said, "We need a changed attitude to the people of all races."

———

Mystery shrouded Eleanor's departure from Australia. "I must be off the record again when I leave here," she told Tommy. The transport plane, now designated Flight 246 for increased security, left from an airfield "somewhere in Australia," heading for an unannounced destination.

A large gathering amassed at the airfield to see the First Lady off. Among them was Captain Robert White, who was grudgingly assigned to the group that accompanied her in Australia. "It's a hell of a way to kill Japs, I thought, when they ordered me south to handle the press for Mrs. Roosevelt's tour of Australia." Nearly two weeks, three thousand miles, and countless stops later, Captain White shared a changed attitude in a letter to his wife.

"Mrs. Roosevelt is certainly one of the most brilliant and competent individuals I ever met," he wrote. "I no longer think of her as the wife of the President, but rather as a highly efficient and perfectly competent public official."

When Captain White and his fellow servicemen arrived in Australia, they expected to make quick work of the war and return home in timely fashion. "We should have known better, but our wishful thinking had the best of us," he admitted. Instead there was training in jungle warfare, the brutality at Buna, then more training and more fighting.

After more than a year overseas, the United States had "evolved into a distant dreamland," and the men lived for letters from loved ones. "In short, we are lonesome. We don't admit it. We like to cover it up with fast chatter, quips, bravado, and the saga of adventure that pulp writers find in war, but underneath we all know the truth."

This was the scene into which Eleanor arrived. Troops knew of her as the First Lady, as a columnist, and as a Washington socialite. "She may be all of these things," said Captain White, "but over here she was something more—something none of us had seen in over a year, an American mother."

At the Australian airfield, Captain White stood with a group of army men as Flight 246 taxied down the runway with Eleanor aboard. As the plane took off, a sergeant mused aloud, "Damn, she's fine, ain't she."

MONGOLIA

(KURIL IS.)
(Jap.)

MANCHUKUO

OBI OR SHAMO
(DESERT)

Harbin

Hsinking

HOKKAIDO

Vladivostok

GREAT KHINGAN MTS.

Mukden

INNER MONGOLIA

Hakodate
Ominato

Peiping

Tientsin

Dairen
(Jap.)

CHOSEN

Keijo

HONSHŪ

Hwang Ho

Taingtao

Keishu

Kyoto

Tokyō

Sian

Yellow

Kobe

Yokohama

Sasebo

Osaka

CHINA

Nanking Nagasaki KYŪSHŪ

Chungking

Hankow

Shanghai

Yangtze Kiang

Changsha

RYŪKYŪ IS.

OGASAWARA JIMA
(Jap.)

Kunming

Foochow

Canton

TAIWAN
(FORMOSA)
(Jap.)

HONG KONG (Br.)

MARIANAS IS.
(Jap. Mand.)

Hanoi

Kwangchowan (Fr.)

FRENCH

Aparri

LUZON

GUAM
(U.S.A.)

THAILAND
(SIAM)

Manila

PHILIPPINE

Bangkok

Legaspi

IS.
(U.S.A.)

PALAU IS.

YAP

INDOCHINA

Saigon

Davao

MINDANAO

CAROLINE ISLANDS

TRUK IS.

PONAPE

Gulf of Siam

MALAY
STATES
(Br.)

BR. N. BORNEO

(Jap. Mand.)

Brunei
(Br.)

Sandakan

SARAWAK
(Br.)

Singapore

Kuching

HALMAHERA

BORNEO
(Neth.)

CELEBES
(Neth.)

AMBOINA

BISMARCK ARCH.

NEW IRELAND

SUMATRA
(Neth.)

NETHERLANDS INDIES

NETH.

PAPUA

TER. OF NEW GUINEA
(Austl. Mand.)

Rabaul

NEW
BRITAIN

BOUGAINVILLE

SOLOMON

Palembang

Java Sea
(Neth.)

Batavia

Soerabaja

NEW GUINEA

TER.
OF PAPUA
(Austl.)

Lae

Buna

YSABEL I.

MALAITA

JAVA

SUNDA IS.

TIMOR
(Neth.)

Arafura Sea

Port
Moresby

GUADALCANAL

CHRISTMAS
I.

NEW

COCOS IS.
(Br.)

Darwin

Gulf of
Carpentaria

Coral Sea

INDIAN

Broome

Daly Waters

Townsville

NORTH WEST CAPE

GREAT

Alice Springs

EASTERN

Noumea

OCEAN

AUSTRALIA

DESERT

Lake Eyre

Brisbane

HIGHLANDS

Fremantle

Perth

Darling R.

LORD HOWE I.
(Austl.)

CAPE LEEUWIN

Great

Adelaide

Murray R.

Sydney

Australian Bight

Canberra

Melbourne

Bass Strait

Tasman Sea

TASMANIA

Hobart

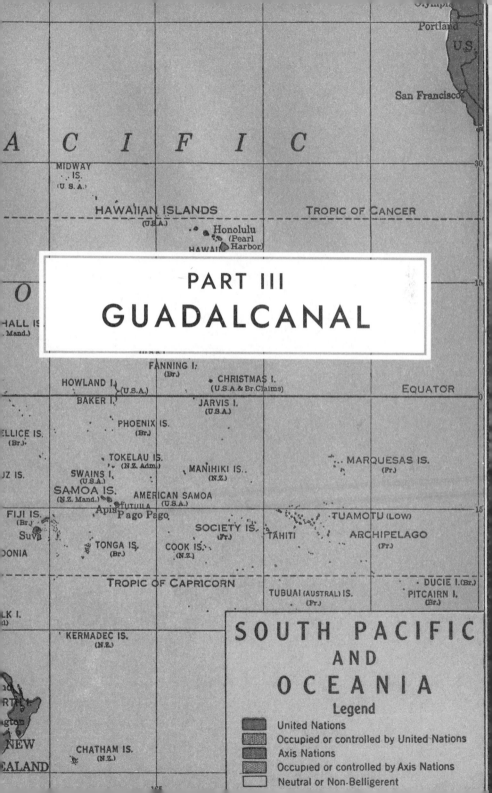

PART III
GUADALCANAL

CHAPTER 13

MORALE WINS WARS

"Well, we saw her tracks in the sand at one of the islands, but we couldn't tell which way they were headed."
—GARY COOPER WHEN ASKED "HOW'S ELEANOR?" WHILE PERFORMING FOR THE TROOPS IN THE SOUTH PACIFIC IN LATE 1943

New Caledonia, Efate, and Espiritu Santo, September 14–17

Back on New Caledonia, Eleanor received the much-hoped-for news from Admiral Halsey: she was going to Guadalcanal. By the time she returned to the island from Australia, the New Georgia campaign was complete. The admiral consented to the visit, although he still had misgivings. Now, though, the misgivings were solely out of concern for the First Lady's safety. She was to be ready by 8:00 a.m. and would make stops on the islands of Efate and Espiritu Santo along the way.

Why the change of heart? Admiral Halsey had seen for

himself, corroborated by media coverage from New Zealand and Australia and accounts from other military personnel, that Eleanor's Pacific tour was not the superficial political trip he initially believed it to be. He especially commended the meticulous way she toured a hospital.

"When I say that she inspected those hospitals, I don't mean that she shook hands with the chief medical officer, glanced into a sun-parlor, and left. I mean that she went into every ward, stopped at every bed, and spoke to every patient: What was his name? How did he feel? Was there anything he needed? Could she take a message home for him?"

Admiral Halsey praised Eleanor's determination and devotion to his men as she walked miles of hospital wards and "saw patients who were grievously and gruesomely wounded."

Plus, provided there were no mishaps while Eleanor was on Guadalcanal, her visit there would generate a tremendous amount of press coverage. Good public relations was an important factor in maintaining the public's approval for the war and keeping funding flowing. When Admiral Halsey first visited Guadalcanal after taking command, he told reporters, "I wish to God that every man, woman and child in our great country could know and see" what the troops were doing there. They couldn't, but Eleanor had the reach to bring a renewed focus to the island and to the events that occurred there.

And the most important reason for Halsey's about-face: morale wins wars, and he could see the uplifting effect the First Lady's presence had on troops. He "marveled most" at the expressions on the men's faces as she leaned over them in their hospital beds. "It was a sight I will never forget," he said. On Halsey's return to his headquarters after his first visit to Guadalcanal, he stopped on Efate to do the same. In a naval hospital, he went from bed to bed expressing his gratitude, giving a boost not only to the wounded he met but to the servicemen on Guadalcanal who later heard about it.

Partly to make amends for his earlier brusque behavior when he and Eleanor initially met on New Caledonia, Admiral Halsey invited her to participate in a high-profile medal ceremony for U.S. Navy Lieutenant Hugh Barr Miller.

Around the time Eleanor left Hyde Park for the Pacific, Lieutenant Miller was rescued from a Japanese-occupied island. Forty-three days earlier, the USS *Strong*, the destroyer on which he served, was torpedoed and sank into the Pacific. What transpired afterward earned Miller the Navy Cross, the second-highest decoration awarded by the navy for extraordinary heroism in combat. He was presented with the medal during a ceremony in a hospital ward in Nouméa, standing at the bedside of a sailor who survived the *Strong*'s sinking.

After the *Strong* was hit by a Japanese torpedo during a nighttime engagement near New Georgia Island, Miller aided in abandon-ship operations and remained with the vessel until it went down (241 men, about three-quarters of the crew, were rescued by another destroyer). After four days adrift in the ocean clustered on life nets and pieces of raft, Miller and several others washed up on enemy-occupied Arundel Island. Suffering from internal injuries caused by underwater explosions as the *Strong* sank, feverish and vomiting oil, Miller experienced a severe hemorrhage and believed he was near death. As the ranking officer, he ordered the three men with him to take their remaining equipment—including his shoes and socks, which he gave to a barefoot sailor—and proceed without him. They were never seen again, their fate unknown.

Miller then stretched out on the ground in the jungle, waiting for death. To his surprise, he was still there the next day and began to rally. "My situation looked pretty hopeless, but I [was] determined to do something about it," he recalled. Miller lived on coconuts and tins of meat taken from Japanese soldiers killed in skirmishes with American PT boats and sheltered in a hidden "palm-frond lean-to" he built at the base of a giant mangrove tree. Nearly caught after his tracks were seen on the beach, Miller, a former college quarterback on a Rose Bowl championship team, lobbed a grenade he had scavenged into the center of the five-man patrol searching for him. Several times, he made nighttime raids, creeping close to machine-gun nests on the beach, tossing grenades into them and then running "like hell."

After thirty-nine days on the island, Miller was spotted by the pilot of a low-flying U.S. torpedo bomber. At first, the pilot thought the figure on the beach was an enemy combatant and intended to cut him down until he saw Miller's "red beard and shining forehead." A seaplane returned an hour later to fetch Miller. When a marine motored in an inflatable boat from the plane to the shore to pick up the castaway, Miller insisted that the gear and intelligence material he gathered from Japanese troops be taken to the plane first before coming back to retrieve him.

Miller's "gallant and courageous conduct was in keeping with the highest traditions of the United States Naval Service," concluded the citation. When Admiral Halsey finished reading, Eleanor pinned the Navy Cross and a Purple Heart with a gold star on Miller's khaki uniform shirt as the men in nearby beds applauded.

Typically, Admiral Halsey pinned medals on his men but ceded the job to Eleanor that day as a sign of his respect for her. "I was ashamed of my original surliness," he admitted. The admiral shrewdly and correctly surmised too that—combined with Miller's compelling story—having the First Lady present the prestigious valor award would garner wider press coverage.

That day, Eleanor outpaced her escorts around Nouméa as

she went from hospital to hospital, from a convalescent camp to a receiving center for new arrivals, from a mail sorting facility (where an office worker discovered he was listed as "missing") to a salvage depot making tires and repurposing discarded clothes and shoes. A member of a medical base detachment on the island set a Republican friend straight, writing, "Do you think it's a cinch to come over here, and especially a woman? It's dangerous and tiresome and it's a wonder a person her age could stand it."

Before Eleanor and the admiral—who was not inclined to change his mind easily—parted ways, he told her it was impossible for him to express his appreciation for what she was doing for his men. "She alone had accomplished more good than any other person, or any group of civilians, who had passed through my area," said Halsey. During his remaining tenure as commander of the South Pacific forces, he added, "nothing caused me to modify this opinion."

From New Caledonia, Eleanor started on the two most strenuous days of the trip. First she flew to Efate, a small volcanic island and a top secret one. Admiral Halsey personally asked Eleanor to visit Efate, the site of some of the largest military hospitals in the region, which the Japanese did not know was occupied by American forces. The first hospital was built in record time along with airfields and other vital necessities for fighting a war. "We couldn't start a land offensive against the Japs until we had the hospital ready," explained a Naval Reserve engineer.

"Colorful as this place is, I'm damned if I know what to do here," groused Mack Morriss, a *Yank* magazine correspondent, while on Efate. The censors "won't stand for too much detail, so I'm sort of up a tree." Eleanor as well was specifically cautioned not to mention the island's name in print.

Like other troops stationed on support bases, the men on Efate were there primarily to ensure the security of the island.

"I was told, and can see that they don't think they're doing much in the war," Morriss wrote in his diary. "At least they feel that down inside, altho they know very well that it is vital that they should be here." As close as Efate was to battlegrounds in the Solomons, hardly a man stationed on the island had seen combat—except for those in the hospitals.

Admiral Halsey admired Eleanor's hardiness, but in truth, hospital visits took an immense toll on her. "One saw the results of the war in the hospitals," she said. She had been visiting wounded servicemen throughout the war, as she did during World War I. In San Francisco earlier that year, she toured two navy hospitals before heading to her son John's house to see him and his family. "I did my best to be an appreciative Grandmother," she told a friend, "but there is something not only physically exhausting but emotionally draining in these hospital visits!"

In particular, Eleanor steeled herself before making her way through burn wards, and she never forgot the smell of burned flesh. At a West Coast hospital, she was shown a video tutorial on how burns were treated and then explained it to "My Day" readers. A wax-like coating was sprayed on the affected skin, which relieved pain and made it so patients could stretch the muscles and the skin and reduce the buildup of scar tissue. Due to sulfa drugs, which were introduced in the mid-1930s, infection was better controlled than it had been in the past.

Worse than the physical fatigue from walking through miles of wards was "the horrible consciousness of waste" and the "feeling of resentment that burned within" Eleanor as she "wondered why men could not sit down around a table and settle their differences before an infinite number of the youth of many nations had to suffer." Seeing so many young men wounded in body and mind, especially those "who had broken mentally and emotionally," caused her to lie awake nights.

Eleanor relayed to Franklin graphic accounts of troops' battle fatigue and shell shock, which eventually came to be known as post-traumatic stress disorder (PTSD). The president immediately asked the secretary of war and the secretary of the navy to act on the issue. Regarding "the subject of fatigue and stress," he requested, "I wish that further special consideration be given in all combat services." Additional attention was to be focused on rotating more often troops in tropical combat areas with heavy fighting and where malaria and other diseases were serious factors. He also asked for a further study of commands on small islands and in other remote places, regardless of climate, and relieving personnel if they had been there more than a year.

Other times, as Eleanor walked the hospital wards, it was difficult for her to keep from showing how deeply saddened she was for the wounded. "I knew that that was the last thing they wanted and that their brave front of casual cheerfulness was put on to prevent people from showing that they were sorry."

When Eleanor left a hospital, she carried with her a tangible reminder of the men she met. While in England, she began collecting the names of the wounded, and she continued the practice in the Pacific. Noted were the nature of each man's injuries, where and how he received them, and the name and address of a family member for her to contact when she returned home. Since communications from the Pacific were often delayed and difficult—mail took about three weeks to wend its way from Guadalcanal to the United States—it was a perk to have the First Lady contact a family with an update about a loved one. By the end of the trip, she had amassed "quite a collection" of detailed logbooks with entries such as this one:

2nd Lt. LeRoy D. Mitchell:
Gunshot wound, face. Ruptured eye, right. Wounded in action over Rabaul, attacked by seven Zeros. Bombardier in B-17. Nearest relative: (Father) Mr. Angelo Mitchell, Box 204, Larrimore, Pa.

Eleanor described injuries and combat conditions during a radio broadcast benefiting a war bonds campaign two days after returning to Washington. During the address, she gave the home front a dose of reality. "No bombs are falling on your head," she said. Nor were they the ones lying on their backs in a jungle swamp while an enemy camouflaged in the trees took shots at them. Anyone who complained about rationing should think about the boys fighting in the New Guinea jungles, who had only bread and tea on Christmas Day because every bit of food had to be dropped from an airplane. She told of a young man she met in a first-line hospital, wearing ragged clothes and so recently injured that he was still in the set of bandages from when he fell in battle. He was in pain and had nothing except a Red Cross comfort kit, yet he managed to muster a smile and thank whoever did anything for him. She recalled her surprise when she asked another wounded man his age and was told nineteen. With those shadowed eyes and a face drawn in pain, he looked much older.

Amid the horrors of war, one of the greatest morale factors is "the American sense of humor," Eleanor said in the same broadcast, "and it expresses itself in a thousand ways every day." Like at a marine hospital camp, where buildings were labeled with posters illustrated by a former Disney cartoonist. The doctors' quarters were announced as "Lil Mayo Clinic," and the hospital office as the "Snafu Department—requests always interpreted in an interesting way." A fiendish-looking face covered with a gauze mask adorned a poster outside the surgery, also known as the "Butcher Shop." In Buna, after Sergeant Bottcher and his men broke through the enemy defenses, a superior promised them steaks or whatever else they wanted to hold their position. A soldier did a handstand and held the pose, the seat of his trousers rotted away by swamp water. "Pants," he said. "For God's sake, General, pants!"

The first time Eleanor landed on New Caledonia, a crew with whom she took a flight to a smaller airport on the island made her an honorary member of their unit. They were the U.S. Army Air Forces 13th Troop Carrier Squadron, nicknamed the "Thirsty 13th," the first army transport squadron in the South Pacific. In unarmed planes, regardless of the weather and over large stretches of water and treacherous terrain, they flew critically needed supplies to the troops fighting on Guadalcanal and afterward supported six additional battles in the Pacific.

For Eleanor's return trip to New Caledonia, the imaginative airmen decorated the nose art on the plane in which they flew her on the same short trip. A figure representing the First Lady faces toward a globe, a knitting bag on her arm, and beneath the image was written "Our Eleanor." She and the crew posed for a photo with the plane. "It gave them a laugh," she recalled during the war bonds address. And in the future, when they were heading home after a hard mission, "perhaps there will be some jokes about the fact that 'Our Eleanor' has done a good many miles and perhaps she will pull through the next ones."

Eleanor could go on endlessly telling stories "that will make you laugh and stories that will make you cry," she told listeners. "What is true of our boys in the Southwest Pacific is true of our boys wherever they fight. Their spirit is the same wherever they are."

———

Unlike Efate, Eleanor's next destination, Espiritu Santo, was hardly hush-hush. A reconnaissance team searching for a suitable site to establish a base farther north from Efate zeroed in on Espiritu Santo—an undertaking immortalized by James Michener in *Tales of the South Pacific*, which he began writing while stationed on the island. "I also knew Admiral (John) McCain in a very minor way. He was an ugly old aviator," wrote Michener. "One day he flew over Santo and pointed down at that island wilderness and said, 'That's where we'll build our base.' And the base was built there, and millions of dollars were spent there, and everyone agrees that Santo was the best base the Navy ever built in the region."

Espiritu Santo was within easier striking distance of Guadalcanal, which was essential for providing support for ground operations. Before any bullets were fired, the battle for Guadalcanal began as a construction race. While the Japanese were hurrying to complete an airfield there in mid-1942, construction crews on Espiritu Santo feverishly tackled the jungle to do the same. Whichever side finished first and launched its bombers in the air would have the advantage in striking enemy bases.

Working around the clock by floodlight and with limited equipment, in just twenty days, Seabees erected the first of four airfields on the island. Docks, roads, and unloading facilities had yet to be built, but time was of the essence, and the bombers needed fueling. Fuel drums were dumped over the sides of ships, hauled ashore in nets, and lugged inland. The drums were loaded

onto a truck, rolled up on a stand, and their contents emptied
into tank wagons that then serviced the aircraft. For twenty
hours straight on August 6, all available hands, including a general and a colonel, worked a bucket line through a rainstorm to
put twenty-five thousand gallons of fuel aboard the bombers.
The next morning, the marines landed on Guadalcanal to begin
the fight for the island.

By the time of Eleanor's visit, quiet, peaceful Espiritu Santo
was transformed into the largest U.S. naval operating base outside Hawaii. It had the services and infrastructure of a small
American city—excellent roads, telephone and teletype systems,
a retail store, steam laundry, hospitals, an optical laboratory,
movie houses, and dining and beer halls. But there was no mis-
taking the purpose of this boomtown. War supplies spilled over
to an island across the channel where mass amounts of ammunition and fuel were stored. Nearby was a recreation center where
troops could rest and relax, swim, and play a variety of sports,
including baseball on one of eight diamonds.

Once the fight on Guadalcanal was underway, the Navy
Department publicly disclosed the existence of the base on
Espiritu Santo, part of the New Hebrides chain, and that it was
the jumping-off point for some of the air forces assisting the
marines on the island. A map accompanying the announcement
in the *New York Times* prominently marked the location of
Espiritu Santo with a cross.

Espiritu Santo was within range of enemy fighters, who
dropped numerous bombs near a hospital the day before
Eleanor's visit but didn't cause any damage or casualties. Docked
warships and cargo vessels were darkened at night, "lit only by
the big, yellow moon of the South Seas," noted Senator Mead.
"Against the big black shadows of the fleet there you could see
a thousand tiny pin-pricks of light going up and down and in

and out where sailors with masked flashlights were going about their work."

After dining on an aircraft carrier, Mead was taken back to shore, "bounding in a jeep, in the blackout, up the trail to our little shack," a thatched hut next door to the one Eleanor occupied. Mead's roommate, a fellow senator, was "a terrific snorer" who courteously gave him ten minutes to fall asleep before he turned in. "Owen," said Mead, "I hope for Mrs. Roosevelt's sake that she has already drifted off."

Eleanor didn't have long to rest. After just two hours of sleep, she was summoned for a 1:30 a.m. takeoff for a six-hundred-mile ride. Destination: Guadalcanal.

CHAPTER 14
REST IN PEACE

"On Guadalcanal, as in many other places, I said a prayer in my heart for the growth of the human spirit so that we might do away with force in settling disputes in the future."

—ELEANOR ROOSEVELT, IN A DIARY SHE KEPT WHILE TRAVELING IN THE PACIFIC

Guadalcanal, September 17–18

In the predawn hours, a U.S. Navy bomber sliced through the darkened skies, flying with lights out to evade detection. Two hundred miles south of Guadalcanal, six fighter planes appeared and flanked the aircraft, three on each side. Admiral Halsey's insistence that a plane carrying the First Lady could only enter the island's airspace with a fighter escort was warranted. Several nights before and after Eleanor's visit, Guadalcanal was bombed by the Japanese, the first enemy action against the island in two months. The timing led the admiral to wonder "if our team was the only one with code-breakers."

Inside the covert aircraft, Eleanor perched on a tiny make-shift seat, fastened to a plywood cargo liner, over the bomb bay opposite Coletta Ryan. The two women sat stiff and straight in the confined, spartan space, the compartment tightly sealed with no light and no way of looking out. Below them was a set of doors that rolled and rumbled open when bombs were sent to seek their targets.

The plane's exterior was decorated with images of a Japanese flag, representing an enemy sea plane recently shot down, three bombs for three high-altitude bombing raids, and a naked woman bending forward, hands on her knees. The bomber's name, "Open Bottom," was deemed indelicate and covered over, but the painted-on figure remained for the flight. The day before piloting Eleanor to Guadalcanal, Harry Sears, the commanding officer of Patrol Bombing Squadron 104 ("The Buccaneers"), took the borrowed plane on two check flights. A week earlier, Sears was on a routine mission when one of the four engines on his plane quit during takeoff. While attempting to land, with full bomb and fuel loads, he crashed into a row of sandbags at the end of the runway, collapsing the landing gear.

On the way to Guadalcanal, Eleanor and Coletta were each given a flight jacket. To further help ward off the bone-chilling cold in the unheated plane, thick blankets were draped around them. In her hands, Eleanor held a cup of hot coffee brought to her by the crew's nineteen-year-old radio operator. She thanked the young man, speaking loudly to be heard over the roar of the engines. Despite the difficulties of the three-hour ride, ears ringing and shivering in the dark, Eleanor was elated at achieving her goal of getting to Guadalcanal.

On arriving, Eleanor breakfasted with an air force general

before touring the island. As her car left the airfield, a truck loaded with construction workers arrived from the opposite direction. She and Coletta leaned out of the vehicle and waved, catching the passersby off guard. "Hi, babe!" shouted some of the men in greeting. "Gosh, there's Eleanor," exclaimed others when they realized the identity of the uniform-clad figure. The commanding officer was appalled that she was treated with such levity, but Eleanor took it in stride, saying, "They were so evidently pleased to see women there one had to laugh and go on waving."

The First Lady's arrival was kept secret, although the men at the evening movie were informed that shirts and shorts were required the next day. "However, it didn't have the desired effect on all of them," Eleanor said in a post-trip speech to audience laughter.

Some cleanup of the island's male-only environment occurred on her behalf. Improvised urinals, made of pipes with funnels that emptied into a pit of rocks, were obscured behind target cloth, and a sign strung between two coconut trees above the busiest roadway—rallying troops to KILL THE BASTARDS!—was taken down.

During the fiercest fighting on Guadalcanal, Eleanor's name rang out in the jungle. Japanese infantrymen would launch their attacks with taunts in English: "Marine, you die!" and "Blood for the Emperor!" The marines yelled back, "To hell with the Emperor! Blood for Franklin and Eleanor!"

Accompanying the marines who staged the initial assault on Guadalcanal was Richard Tregaskis, a six-foot-seven, bespectacled correspondent. Formerly a reporter in Boston, the twenty-six-year-old volunteered for the risky assignment, an insulin kit stashed deep in a pocket. As the ship on which Tregaskis was traveling drew closer to its destination, the marines sharpened their bayonets, oiled their knives, and cleaned and sighted their rifles. They were given a tutorial on how best to traverse the daunting terrain and warned against booby traps. The officer in charge of paperwork tallied likely casualties, estimating that one out of four men would not survive the assault. The Sunday before the invasion, onboard church services were crowded. Priests, ministers, and rabbis were commissioned by the armed forces as chaplains to enhance morale. They served alongside the troops, including in combat zones under enemy fire, offering comfort to men dying on battlefields, transporting the wounded to medical aid stations, burying bodies, and writing to bereaved families.

"This is going to be a difficult matter," a lieutenant colonel counseled his platoon leaders during a final pep talk before reaching Guadalcanal. "But it can be done and it must be done and we've got to lead the way.

"There's only one thing to do. Get out of the boat, say 'Follow me,' run like hell and take these people with you," he concluded. "It's the first time in history we've ever had a huge expedition of this kind accompanied by transports. It's of world-wide importance. You'd be surprised if you knew how many people all over the world are following this. You cannot fail them."

The fleet of ships closed in on Guadalcanal beneath an overcast sky and no trace of a moon, ideal conditions for a stealth attack that were predicted by a weather forecaster. "Unless the Japs had come very close, they could not have spotted us," reported Tregaskis in his book *Guadalcanal Diary*. The next morning, as dawn broke, cruisers accompanying the troop ships aimed a barrage of gun and mortar fire toward the shore. Dive-bombers swooped low over the beach, strafing the ground to dispel enemy troops and pave the way for the landing forces.

"I walked among the troops gathered on the forward deck, and found them silent and nervous—a contrast to the gaiety and song which had filled the few preceding days. There did not seem to be much to say, although a few lads came up with the inevitable, 'Well, this is it,'" recalled Tregaskis. "The first of our marines clambered over the rail and swung down the rope nets into the boats. The boats pulled away and more came up, and the seeping waterfall of marines continued to slide over the side."

Once onshore, troops made their way across the beach, waded through boggy streams and rivers, navigated coconut groves and fields of tall grass, and marched for miles through the jungle. No encounters were had with enemy soldiers, although signs indicated they had recently been there, like freshly chopped trees holding a gun emplacement. Soon word came from a unit farther ahead that the airfield near the coast, the "prize of the Guadalcanal invasion," was reached and taken without force. The breakfasting Japanese were caught off guard by the surprise air attack, leaving half-eaten dishes of food in the mess hall as they abandoned the airfield.

Guadalcanal's code name was "Cactus," and as Admiral Halsey noted, "God knows it was a thorny spot." Following the swift initial success was a torturous, six-month-long fight by sea, air, and land forces. Later the admiral grimly jested that the fight for Guadalcanal should have been called "Operation Shoestring." The commanders in charge repeatedly requested additional men and materials but were denied. "Europe was Washington's darling; the South Pacific was only a stepchild," concluded Halsey. The marines might have won much sooner if they were protected, supplied, and reinforced. "We didn't have the ships, either cargo or combat," he said, "and the enemy did."

While the Japanese quickly lost control of the airfield, they retained their hold on other parts of the island, steadily bringing men and supplies during nighttime runs. As air and sea battles took place in the surrounding area, the marines dug in and fought alone on the ground for two months until army reinforcements reached the island. Like the men at Buna, the first troops on Guadalcanal had limited training in jungle warfare and learned on the spot. They were hindered by similar challenges with terrain, climate, and vegetation and faced a foe that used ruses—playing dead, pretending to surrender, and drawing them into ambushes.

One month into the campaign, correspondent F. Tillman Durdin described "a typical night" on Guadalcanal: marines tumbled from bed rolls to foxholes on two separate occasions as large flights of Japanese aircraft materialized overhead; bombs struck their encampment, killing a few men and injuring several others; three enemy warships landed soldiers and supplies fifteen miles east; and U.S. planes took flight to counterattack the air and sea raiders. "Life is reduced to essentials," reported Durdin, "and Guadalcanal's greatest pleasure is just in still being alive."

Gradually roles reversed, with the Japanese unable to deliver supplies and reinforcements. Some of the remaining enemy troops—tired, hungry, defeated by incessant shelling and aerial bombing, and with loudspeakers and leaflets calling on them to give up—began to surrender despite the fact that doing so was a violation of their country's warrior code. "We were told that the Americans on Guadalcanal would be easy to defeat. We were not told about American artillery, which was a complete surprise and which killed and wounded so many of us," said a Japanese soldier. A U.S. Navy captain posited that there were at least three occasions when the chances of holding Guadalcanal "were not worth five cents." But the men on Guadalcanal "didn't figure that way," refusing to capitulate and ultimately coming out victorious.

Months after the fighting ceased, swamps and jungles were still being searched for men who had fallen in battle. They were buried on the spot and the sites marked. "But then the fight had to go forward," Eleanor bluntly told "My Day" readers. "Though they still search constantly, they are not sure all the temporary graves can be found."

At a cemetery on the island, Eleanor walked slowly among the graves, dabbing her eyes with a handkerchief. The burial ground was within view of the ocean with coconut palms shading the area and purple-shrouded mountains rising in the background. The tranquility seemed in stark contrast to the violence suffered by its occupants.

Crosses marking the graves were made by friends of the deceased from materials at hand: packing box slats painted green and nailed together and shell casings intricately fashioned into shape. Draped over one cross was a rusted and weathered rosary, while other markers carried the lone word "unidentified." Some resting places were commemorated with Stars of David whittled from bamboo. Eleanor paused in front of a grave adorned with a bent propeller in honor of an aviator who died in a flaming crash while defending the island's airfield, which was named Henderson Field for the first marine pilot killed during the Battle of Midway.

"As you look at the crosses row on row," Eleanor relayed in "My Day," "you think of the women's hearts buried here as well and are grateful for signs everywhere that show the boys are surrounded by affection." Personal belongings and mementos were left at the graves of the fallen servicemen. Nailed on many of the crosses were aluminum plaques made from mess kits they no longer needed, on which "their buddies engrave inscriptions, such as 'A swell pal, a good guy, rest in peace.'"

For a long time afterward, Eleanor would often recall the

cemetery on Guadalcanal, particularly when she heard someone spewing bigotry. As soon as they started to speak, she would envision the cemetery, where men of varying religions, nationalities, races, and backgrounds once fought side by side and now laid together in death.

By the time Eleanor arrived, Guadalcanal was transformed from "a stinking, muddy, mosquito-ridden, war-infested island" into a sizable military base with ample services and infrastructure. Previously, accommodations were tiny pup tents on the muddy ground or in rigged-up caves in the hillsides. Now, there were screened, framed tents with wooden floors and electricity and stores for replenishing toothpaste, tobacco, and "other luxuries formerly denied." At first, the men wore fatigues "until they rotted off with perspiration and mud and insect attack." Now, starched and well-laundered khaki was "the vogue." Then, the standard meal, both morning and night, was stale saltines and jam washed down with chlorinated tepid water. Now, a typical meal consisted of meat, vegetables, fruit, bread, and butter—and much-appreciated ice water. Then, a jeep could barely be found, and transportation was dragging "one weary leg after the other through at least two feet of jungle mud." Now, vehicles were plentiful and traversed miles of drained and crowned roads. Then, cargo ships were exposed targets, quickly unloading without weighing anchor to "dash away" from frequent air raids. Now, the vessels remained to fully unload, never pausing to scan the sky.

Despite a substantial amount of cleanup, the destruction of war and the ongoing hardships were still evident on the island. With a gun-toting army private, Eleanor inspected the burned-out hulk of a Japanese Zero, a single-seat fighter plane, that had been shot down. Three months earlier, she had worried and waited for a letter from Joe Lash after reading about an intense air battle over Guadalcanal that claimed ninety-four Japanese planes. She sought to reassure Trude Pratt, Joe's fiancée and her close confidante, by relaying information from her son James: during an air raid, most of the men, except for pilots and those servicing machines on the ground, would be in underground shelters and safe from all but a direct hit. "The chance of that is 1,000 to one," she told Trude, "so we can go on saying our prayers but you can feel more assurance for his safety I think."

When Eleanor left New Caledonia for Guadalcanal, she was unsure if Joe was still stationed on the island or if he had been transferred. Due to her rapid travels and the slow pace of mail, she had not heard from him in weeks and hoped for the best.

"For me it was a grand day," Joe wrote to Trude. He learned early in the morning that Eleanor was there and dashed madly out to shave. As he sat in a colonel's tent, fidgeting impatiently, waiting for the First Lady's luncheon with senior officers to conclude, he heard her hearty laugh. "You know how it rings out and dominates the whole table—the robust Roosevelt laugh."

A note was slipped to Eleanor that Joe was there, and they broke army protocol by embracing. The press was in attendance but did not get any photographs of the pair hugging, Joe told Trude. But it made news anyway. The same congressman who took exception to Eleanor's being given a Māori greeting indignantly bellowed, "She kissed Joe Lash." (He also didn't like that she wore a grass skirt over her uniform on a South Seas island.) Westbrook Pegler was nowhere near a war zone and yet grasped the opportunity to malign the First Lady, quoting a correspondent at the scene who reported that she "kissed her radical political protégé."

Eleanor's friendship with Joe began several years earlier when he, along with members of other youth organizations, was called before the House Un-American Activities Committee to answer questions about possible Communist influence in student groups. Conservative critics took her association with liberal student activists like Joe as evidence that she had Communist leanings. ("Mrs. Roosevelt and the Reds" shrieked an article headline about a summer student leadership gathering held at Campobello.)

FBI head J. Edgar Hoover, who was suspicious of Eleanor's political activities, seized on the opportunity to try to prove it. On his orders, FBI officials compiled an eleven-page memorandum on Joe, and agents broke into the headquarters of the American Youth Congress and photographed Eleanor's correspondence with the group's leaders. (The FBI's file on her totaled more than thirty-two hundred pages over four decades and was one of the largest ever compiled by the agency on an individual.) Even Joe and Trude's romance was subject to media scrutiny, with a newspaper noting that Joe was stationed on Guadalcanal and speculating if and when "Eleanor's tax-the-rich pals" would wed.

On Guadalcanal, Joe accompanied Eleanor to the rendezvous point where she was meeting Admiral Halsey, riding in a station wagon (one of the snazziest Joe had ever seen) with General Archie Howard, the island base commander. "The poor General must have been baffled by the conversation between us which was of color schemes for the 11th Street house, furniture and a person named 'Trude.'" It was Trude, seeking a divorce, who Eleanor had joined in Nevada prior to leaving for the Pacific; she was also helping to decorate the New York City residence where Trude and Joe planned to live after his return.

At the rendezvous, Joe remained in the car. Then to his horror, Admiral Halsey, "a legendary figure in these parts," walked over to the station wagon with Eleanor. "Now a Sergeant doesn't smugly remain seated when a four-star Admiral comes over," he said. So he "decided to hell with the press" and "jumped out and stood at attention." Photographers snapped their cameras as Eleanor made introductions and the two men shook hands.

After dropping Eleanor and General Howard at a hospital, Joe was alone with the admiral. "I gulped and said nothing, knowing the man has great cares, anyway a Sergeant doesn't speak until spoken to. He asked me about my work as an 'aerologist' (Navy term for weather man) and then said some amusing things about the Senators, who seem to have left him severely alone. Admiral Halsey is a jovial man but with a reputation for remarkable bluntness and directness so I guess the Senators decided it was best not to tangle with the old seadog."

Later, with Joe at the wheel of a car borrowed from the weather station where he worked—and the MPs accompanying Eleanor glad to be relieved of duty for a while—she took a detour from her official schedule to see a young soldier she knew, Private Cecil Peterson. Eleanor had several wartime pen pals, servicemen with whom she regularly corresponded to hear firsthand about their experiences. Orphaned at an early age, Cecil spent much of his childhood in foster homes and New York state-run institutions before becoming a student leader for a national youth organization and attending a vocational school to study radio. After his attempt to enlist as an air force pilot was denied and he decided against the navy for restricting the roles of Black sailors, he was inducted into the army. Cecil was a recruit at the Tuskegee Army Flying School in 1942, training as part of base personnel, when Eleanor first reached out as part of the Youth Morale Corps. The corps was founded when Viola Ilma, director of the Young Men's Vocational Foundation, an organization that found jobs for boys out of reform school, was told by a young serviceman, "I don't get any mail, but sometimes the other boys let me read theirs, and that feels good."

Eleanor was one of the first to join the Morale Corps, which consisted of some 115 women, mostly from New York City. They wrote and sent packages to three hundred correspondents and sometimes entertained them when they were on furlough. (One man became engaged to his letter-writing friend's daughter.) The year before, while Cecil was visiting New York City, he took Eleanor up on her invitation to pay a call at her Greenwich Village residence. So did Bill Coyne, a merchant marine who served in Russia and another of the First Lady's correspondents. He attended a speech she gave in New York, after which they took a taxi to her apartment, where they raided the icebox and then had a lengthy talk. Bill confided in Viola Ilma that he "simply couldn't get over the way Mrs. Roosevelt talked to me just as if I were somebody."

After visiting with Private Peterson, next on Eleanor's itinerary was a stop at the weather station where Joe's forecasting supported B-24 bomber missions. (She also wanted to "take a peek" at the tent quarters he shared with his unit so she could describe it to Trude.) Joe performed a cutting-edge job in the military. For the first time, meteorology, the science of predicting the weather, was widely and actively used in war and played a vital role.

The army air forces trained thousands of forecasters and set up weather bureaus from Alaska to Australia, Greenland to Guadalcanal. "Between them they tell us what the weather is everywhere—even pretty accurately in enemy territory," explained an army air forces colonel. "It's possible, now, for the first time in history, to have a complete picture of the weather all over the world at the same time."

The information was used to make predictions for both ground and flying operations. Frozen swamps were easier for tanks to traverse. Rain might delay trucks delivering ammunition. Fog could provide cover for an enemy attack. Blitzkriegs were best started when skies were fair and land was dry. No bomber left the ground until a weather officer ensured that flying conditions were favorable. Airmen needed to know what to expect at their aerial battleground—not at takeoff but what the conditions would be like when they arrived on the scene. It was a meteorologist's job to forewarn where lethal weather elements like turbulence and icing lurked.

At the weather station on Guadalcanal, marines, GIs, and sailors clustered around the First Lady, wanting to know how the "weather men" rated. "Lucky that no one thought to ask her for an autograph," said Joe, "for I never would have been able to get her back to the General by 5:15."

Joe drove Eleanor back from the weather station to resume her schedule, "disregarding the speed limit of 25 miles as I could afford to with Mrs. R. in the car." As they were passing a river, some fifty bathing marines hurriedly dove into the water when they spotted Eleanor. Down the road, three sailors signaled for a ride before they noticed who was in the passenger seat. "They clambered in raucously, saw Mrs. R., gulped and were the silentest swabbies I have met in the service as Mrs. R. told them about things back home," Joe relayed to Trude.

Later, as Eleanor entered the grounds of a hospital, a military policeman sped by on a motorcycle, shouting, "Air raid!" She was quickly ushered into an underground shelter with hospital personnel and patients who could walk or use crutches to get there. As they sat in the dark, the atmosphere was "rather tense" until "somebody started to sing, and we all joined in," Eleanor recalled. Once the all clear was given, she wasted no time getting to work in the wards. She especially wanted to know what the effects of the air raids were on the two men who could not leave their beds. One was unconscious, moaning and turning his head from side to side and being comforted by a nurse, and another was pacing the floor in a tiny room. The latter man she tried to engage in conversation, hoping "to change the current of his thought." But she was unable to get through to him and finally had to give up trying.

"Hospitals and cemeteries are closely tied together in my head on this trip," Eleanor recorded in her diary. She thought of the wounded and the broken even when talking with "boys who were well and strong and in training, ready to go wherever they had to go to win the war."

That night, Eleanor talked with Joe until around midnight on the screened porch of a guest cottage on the hospital grounds. Seeing her so tired and weary prompted him to write Trude with some alarm. "She must have been going a terrific pace, because while she was going through hospitals here this afternoon, the officers who have been with her gratefully took time out to sleep," Joe said. "You and Tommy must make her rest, really rest, when she returns, impatient though she may be to tell the American people about the boys here."

CHAPTER 15

THE REAL TRAGEDY

"This visit to the Pacific, like her previous visit in England, has proved of value not only to the American boys she meets and cheers and invigorates, but to her country as a whole—a wartime report to the nation from the First Lady of that nation."

—HONOLULU STAR-BULLETIN,
SEPTEMBER 21, 1943

The final Pacific leg: Espiritu Santo, Wallis Island, Christmas Island, and Honolulu, September 18–22

Ever the adventurer, Eleanor upgraded on the flight leaving Guadalcanal, trading the makeshift perch in the bomb bay for the copilot's seat. For the last two hours of the ride and on landing, she had an expansive view from the solarium-like cockpit made of bullet-resistant glass on three sides and on the roof for clear visibility.

Back on Espiritu Santo, an "exciting" moment occurred when Eleanor stood in the spot where her son James, on a dark, rainy evening and illuminated by a jeep's headlights, received a Navy Cross along with fifteen other servicemen. The executive officer of the 2nd Marine Raider Battalion, a special forces unit that conducted raids behind enemy lines, James received the medal for his part in an attack on Makin Island during the Solomons campaign. After the Raiders arrived by submarine and then transferred to rubber boats and slipped ashore, James had continually exposed himself to intense sniper and machine-gun fire while commanding operations and later rescued three men from drowning in the heavy surf during evacuation. Regarding the medal ceremony, Eleanor told "My Day" readers, "How I wish I could have been there." Capping off the evening on Espiritu Santo was a farewell dinner for a departing officer, during which an admiral sang the Lord's Prayer. Recalled Eleanor, "Out here with boys engaged in dangerous missions sitting about, it was a very moving experience."

Back in the larger, familiar transport plane, Eleanor started on the long journey home, stopping first at Wallis Island, where a heavy storm beset the travelers. From there, the planned route to Honolulu via Canton Island was changed last minute due to concerns about Japanese fighter aircraft in the vicinity for possible retaliatory raids. Instead the plane was refueled on Christmas Island, where weeks earlier, Eleanor had begun her tour of the region.

Word of Eleanor's success connecting with the troops preceded her. The new commanding officer took advantage of the chance arrival and asked her to meet with a certain soldier. During maneuvers, the young man had been pinned beneath an overturned tank for an hour and a half, fully conscious the entire time, before the vehicle was lifted from his body. He later awoke in the hospital to learn that one of his legs had been amputated. Even with blood transfusions and other treatment, infection set in and his temperature shot up. Doctors believed he was slipping, losing his desire to live, which was jeopardizing his recovery.

Eleanor assured him that he would get well.

"Yes, Ma'am," he murmured politely.

"Where is your home?" asked Eleanor.

"Brooklyn," he answered in the same listless tone.

"Is there a wife or a mother waiting for you there?" she inquired.

"My mother," he whispered.

"Would you like me to see your mother when I get back, and tell her that I have seen you?"

The boy's face lit up, and he turned toward Eleanor. "Would you do that?"

Eleanor assured him that she would on one condition. He had to try to get well so that she could bring good news to his mother.

"I will get well, Mrs. Roosevelt," he promised.

Eleanor held his hand for a moment before leaving. "I felt so sure that he would keep his word that I was almost happy as I climbed into our plane," she recalled. He kept his word and so did she, meeting with his mother and siblings at her New York City apartment.

Eleanor shared the soldier's story to highlight a matter she spoke about frequently and fervently: the treatment of servicemen with disabilities after they returned home. "Science has taught us how to kill very effectively, but it has also taught us how to save human lives," she said in a post-trip speech. Advances in surgical and medical science, along with medics tending troops on the frontline and the quick evacuation of the wounded from battlefields, meant that "after the war we will have more handicapped men among us than we have ever had before," she noted during a press conference. She urged Americans to treat soldiers with disabilities with understanding and helpfulness, not pity.

Another lifesaving measure was a vast blood donation program administered by the Red Cross. Blood was processed into dried plasma, which was storable for extended periods without refrigeration; it was then transported to the war fronts, where it was reconstituted for administering transfusions. During the bitter fighting on Guadalcanal, dried plasma was kept hidden in foxholes and dugouts to safeguard it from enemy gunfire and bombings. "Next to our ammunition it was perhaps our most precious possession," said a navy medical corpsman who served with the marines. The effects on the wounded were dramatic, allowing them to survive being carried on the long, difficult jungle trails to a medical station, and so were the effects on the uninjured. Because they knew blood plasma was at the ready and could be given at a moment's notice, "they felt that their chances of coming home alive were immeasurably increased."

At a Red Cross blood bank in Washington, DC, Eleanor took her place in line, rolled up her sleeve, and had a pint of blood drawn. She regularly donated blood, deeming it "the easiest service that one could render," until she turned sixty and an embarrassed attendant told her she was over the age limit. After returning from the Pacific, Eleanor thanked "My Day" readers for doing the same, assuring them, "I would like to tell you from personal observation that you are saving many a life."

———

Digging deep into her reserves of energy, Eleanor finished her Pacific foray with a fast-paced flourish in Honolulu. After she landed, there was just enough time "to have the dust from several islands removed" from her clothing before a press conference began at the Royal Hawaiian. A grand, pink-hued hotel on Waikiki Beach, the Royal Hawaiian once catered to the luxury tourist trade. In wartime, the resort was used by the military and reserved "for those who have performed hazardous duties at sea." Sailors, marines, and, in particular, submarine crewmembers came to the Royal Hawaiian to rest and recuperate.

"We think of it as a huge drydock," said a navy officer, "and it works that way. Nerves are re-wired, engines tuned up and a nice coat of sun-tan paint slapped on."

Senator James Mead was at Pearl Harbor when a submarine returned from a successful mission and docked amid cheers from bystanders. "The boys were all on deck, white as ghosts after spending weeks shut off from the light of day." The submarines, high tech at the time, were essentially surface ships that could travel underwater for limited amounts of time and were highly effective. During World War II, submarines sank more Japanese ships, including eight aircraft carriers, than did surface vessels and planes, and they destroyed millions of tons of goods and supplies. Crews endured seventy-five-day stretches of grueling, dangerous duty and had a 20 percent chance of not returning. The crewmembers Mead saw welcomed at Pearl Harbor were loaded into navy cars and sped to the Royal Hawaiian.

"I have watched them all these past few days, watched taut nerves relax, light come back into shadowed eyes and smiles to tight lips," reported a marine correspondent at the Royal Hawaiian. The transition to a life of sunshine and spaciousness was not always easy after extended periods in confined underwater quarters. Some submariners discovered they couldn't sleep at first on soft mattresses with so much space around them.

Instead they piled their belongings on the bed and stretched out on the floor until they got rid of their "bunk muscles."

No one else, "not even we senators," could stay at the Royal Hawaiian, said Mead. He wasn't allowed, but another nonmilitary guest was invited to stay there. As a reporter noted, though, to say that Eleanor was "staying" at the Royal Hawaiian was "probably wholly inaccurate because Mrs. Roosevelt never 'stays' anywhere."

By now, five fast-paced weeks of traveling left the First Lady weary, she admitted to a friend. Once during the press conference, "she seemed to drop her guard after answering a question in which it was evident she had no particular interest, and an expression of fatigue draped her face," observed a correspondent. "But she quickly recovered and an instant later was her usual alert self."

The press conference was open to accredited war correspondents—which "meant men only." Undeterred, reporters Virginia Bennett Hill and Gwenfread E. Allen were given permission the next morning to trail the First Lady around town if they could manage to do so without the benefit of war credentials. The intrepid duo scrambled for transportation, finally finding a taxi, which were in short supply due to gasoline rationing. Eleanor was expected at various venues around town, but no exact arrival times had been announced and she was already on the move. When their taxi pulled up in front of the Honolulu Academy of Arts, an art museum and wartime headquarters of the local Red Cross, the bustling activity and air of excitement suggested "something was brewing." A few minutes later, a car drove up to the entrance, and a naval aide jumped from the front seat and opened the back door. Out stepped Eleanor, accompanied by the governor of Hawaii and his wife. Red Cross officials were ready to greet her, and as she entered the building, one placed several leis—garlands of white jasmine, orchids, and yellow and white ginger blossoms—around her neck.

The reporter duo discreetly followed the First Lady's group from room to room, although they were warned not to speak with her. Eleanor met with workers and heads of the various sections, one of the busiest of which was the communications department. There they handled trans-Pacific nuptials (proxy marriages were common since it was difficult for servicemen to obtain leave to return home), prisoner of war messages, welfare inquiries, and notices of birth, death, and serious illness, with a month's worth of messages and inquiries totaling eleven thousand. On one occasion, nearly one hundred men waited in line outside an executive secretary's office in hopes she could connect them with friends and relatives who might be in the region.

Eleanor was allotted a few minutes to peruse the Academy of Art's treasures, guided by director Edgar C. Schenck through the galleries, where an ancient Roman mosaic and an antique Chinese relief caught her eye. On December 7, 1941, as the city was under attack, Schenck had raced to the museum to enact a predetermined plan for safeguarding the collection in case of an air raid. Precious objects were stowed away, vulnerable areas were reinforced with sandbags, and masterpieces in the galleries were swapped out with secondary works. The museum reopened two days later, featuring eleven new displays, and was kept open to build morale.

Virginia and Gwenfread turned out a lengthy, colorful article about their day with the First Lady that was more entertaining and informative than a credentialed colleague's perfunctory piece. Racing from the Academy of Arts back to the office to meet an early print deadline, he did let them use his car for further reporting. With a slight screeching of the clutch, they were off, driving at a respectful distance behind the official three-car convoy. The destination was the Queen Emma Summer Palace, once a retreat for Hawaiian royalty in the lush, mountainous Nuuanu Valley outside Honolulu. Seeing the Red Cross work taking place came with a tour of the historic house museum, beginning with the Edinburgh Room. The elegant chamber was added for an 1869 visit by the Duke of Edinburgh, Queen Victoria's son, and it was currently being used as the surgical dressing unit. Additional rooms housed a collection of royal regalia, antique furnishings, and the queen's wedding gown and other personal belongings.

After leaving Queen Emma's abode, Virginia and Gwenfread retrieved their car from an out-of-the-way parking space. By the time they made it onto the roadway, the convoy was well ahead of them. Stepping on the gas, they caught up as the official party returned to the city for a visit at another Red Cross facility. News soon spread that Eleanor was in the building. When she emerged, a roar of applause rose from the crowd gathered on the street as she smiled and bowed from side to side.

Earlier in the day, while Virginia and Gwenfread were arranging transportation to trail Eleanor, she visited the Office of Civilian Defense, where she was fingerprinted and issued a territorial identification certificate—a requirement for all civilians in Hawaii and part of the martial law that took effect within hours of the attack on Pearl Harbor.

Hawaii had anticipated war for years, readying its defenses and preparing its citizens for conflict in the region. Night maneuvers took place at Pearl Harbor, while army planes power-dived over Honolulu in practice bombing raids. The number of servicemen on duty topped one hundred thousand, augmented by thousands more people who came to work in the defense industry. Despite the military might, civic leaders warned residents,

"The Army and Navy are not here to protect the population of Honolulu; their duty is to defend Hawaii as one of the most vital parts of the American Defense system. In case of emergency the civilian population must be prepared to care for itself."

In 1940, an emergency disaster plan was adopted in Honolulu. The local Red Cross enlisted women to make surgical bandages and dressings, provided first aid classes, formed a women's motor corps, and established a blood bank. The seven sugar plantations on Oahu organized and trained a provisional police force to help protect against an invasion. An intensive, islands-wide blackout exercise, initiated by the army and civilian controlled, took place in May 1941. During this third—and final—annual drill, Red Cross workers set up emergency stations, and highways and streets were patrolled for compliance. After pretend attackers dropped flares to emulate explosives, trucks with emergency supplies hastened to the "bombed" areas.

Honolulans received mixed messages. The November 30, 1941, edition of the Honolulu Advertiser announced, "JAPANESE MAY STRIKE OVER WEEKEND." On December 2, the paper proclaimed, "Japan Gives Two Weeks More to Negotiations" and reported that the country still hoped for peace with the United States.

Joseph Grew, the American ambassador to Japan, had warned as far back as January 1941 that there was talk in Tokyo of a surprise attack on Pearl Harbor. On November 3, he informed the U.S. secretary of state that recent troop movements indicated Japan was in a position to launch an attack "in either Siberia or the Southwest Pacific or in both," and that war might come with "dramatic and dangerous suddenness."

The Sunday morning stillness in Honolulu was shattered on December 7, when the first of two waves of Japanese planes appeared in the skies overhead. Bombs and torpedoes rained down on the naval base at Pearl Harbor, the primary target of the attack, and on several airfields. The attack came at a time when fewer personnel were on duty, emulating Adolf Hitler's tactic of striking over a weekend. The mission hinged on the element of surprise, and it worked.

For nearly two hours, hundreds of Japanese torpedo planes, bombers, and fighters unleashed havoc and destruction. Eight of the U.S. Pacific Fleet's nine battleships were in the harbor at the time. Three of them—USS *Arizona*, USS *Oklahoma*, and USS *Nevada*—had returned from training exercises only forty-eight hours earlier. All eight battleships were damaged or sunk, along with cruisers, destroyers, and other vessels. On Battleship Row, which bore the brunt of the attack, the USS *Arizona* was struck by a 1,760-pound bomb on its forward deck. The hit breached the ammunition storage, triggering a massive explosion that lifted the ship out of the water before it sank nine minutes later. A total of 1,177 sailors and marines perished on the *Arizona*, most of them cremated in the blast, accounting for about half of the day's casualties. The *Oklahoma*, with one side sheared open, rolled over, trapping hundreds of men as it sank to the harbor floor. Torpedoed and bombed, the USS *West Virginia* also sank as chunks of steel from the *Arizona* rained down on it. Due to quickly implemented counterflooding measures, she stayed upright as she descended, allowing more men to escape. Still, more than one hundred of her crewmembers perished, among them three sailors who survived in a storeroom for sixteen days until they ran out of air. The *Nevada*, damaged but functional, tried to make a run for open water. During the second wave of attack, dive-bombing enemy pilots zeroed in on the moving target and inflicted further damage. Leaking and ablaze, the battleship was deliberately run aground to avoid blocking the channel.

Tragically, warning signs were missed that morning. At the harbor's entrance, a Japanese midget sub was spotted and sunk an hour and a half before the first bombers arrived. Nor did a radar station report of incoming aircraft shortly before the attack set off any alarm bells, as the planes were presumed to be B-17s scheduled to arrive from California. Meanwhile, Japanese communications intercepted in Washington hinted that something big was going to take place that morning, but the message wasn't passed along to Pacific Fleet commanders until after the attack was underway.

The next morning, Edward C. Raymer, a navy salvage diver who was part of a unit flown in haste from San Diego, stared from an airplane window in horror as Pearl Harbor came into view. "I was numbed by shock and disbelief at the panorama of wholesale destruction below," he said. Clouds of black smoke billowed in the air. Orange flames surged on the water's surface, fed from ruptured fuel tanks on the *Arizona*, which burned for another day and a half. Blazes were still being battled aboard the *West Virginia*, the *Tennessee*, and the *California*. On the *Oklahoma*, whose masts touched bottom and left the hull above the water, rescuers raced against the clock to try to reach the men trapped inside. On nearby airfields, the tangled remains of wrecked and burned-out planes were scattered about.

Unlike the stateside population, whom Eleanor repeatedly reminded of their good fortune in not having war on their doorsteps, the people on Oahu experienced firsthand an enemy attack. As Japanese planes swept in from the sea past Diamond Head, a volcanic crater on the outskirts of Honolulu, they headed in the direction of Pearl Harbor. Pilots swooped over Waikiki Beach and the city's streets, flying so low the rising sun insignia on the wings was visible from the ground, and sprayed machine-gun bullets. Forty-nine civilians were killed and thirty-five wounded that day on Oahu: workers on military bases, employees at sugar mills mistakenly targeted for attack, hobbyist fliers in the air, and people in the path of friendly fire from antiaircraft rounds that malfunctioned and landed in residential areas.

Margaret Lutz, a Red Cross field director at an army hospital, was awakened by a neighbor's radio as the announcer urgently intoned, "This is no joke! This is the real McCoy! We are being attacked! Stay off the streets and the telephone. Keep calm, keep calm, keep calm!" Margaret dressed hurriedly and drove to the hospital, where ambulances were bringing in casualties. "Blood was everywhere," she recalled. "Bloody clothing that had been cut from wounded bodies lay in piles along the corridors." When Margaret asked what she could do, she was told, "If you have any cigarettes, give them out. The boys have been asking for them." She broke open two cases of cigarettes and freely passed them around.

Patients who could be moved were transferred to a school building about a mile and a half away and the wards cleared for more wounded. "Several beds held boys who were beyond human help. After each bed had been vacated, we got fresh linen and made it up for the next occupant," Margaret said. Meanwhile, Japanese planes strafed the hospital, shooting holes in the roof of the surgery and the dental offices and killing a patient who was helping unload an ambulance.

In the days and weeks that followed, Honolulu looked and acted "like any European city under attack." Throughout the Hawaiian Islands, easily accessible coastlines were strung with barbed wire, including Waikiki's beaches. Armed sentries were stationed throughout the city, and military trucks armed with machine guns patrolled the streets. The FBI took close to five hundred people into custody, the majority of them of Japanese descent. Eleanor tried to dissuade the president from issuing an executive order in February 1942 authorizing the removal of 120,000 Japanese Americans—most of them U.S.-born citizens—from their mainland West Coast homes and imprisoning them in military-operated camps. In Hawaii, the head of the territory's FBI branch and the military governor determined that mass detention of Japanese Americans was unnecessary. Security risks were low, and since they made up nearly 40 percent of the population, they were integral to the islands' wartime economy.

With martial law in effect, the entire population was required to adhere to certain practices and restrictions. Civil courts were closed and elections suspended. Newspapers and radio broadcasts were censored, mail and phone calls were monitored, and a permit was required to develop a roll of film. Gas masks were issued to every resident, including children, with instructions to carry them at all times. A strict blackout order was issued, the mandate so thorough that civilian life essentially ended at nightfall.

Blackout restrictions were still in effect when actress Judith Anderson arrived in Honolulu in July 1943. Despite regulations posted on her hotel room door, threatening imprisonment for offenders, she opened the blacked-out windows in the stuffy room after dark, lighting up the area, and received a stern reprimand from the military.

After watching army rangers training under live fire, Eleanor lunched at a hospital canteen with Anderson, whom she had seen perform in the Broadway comedy *Family Portrait* and as Mrs. Danvers in the feature film *Rebecca*. Now, she reported, Anderson was "making a great hit with the boys" starring as Lady Macbeth. "Many of them have never seen a real theatrical performance before, nor heard of Shakespeare she told me. They come and beg her to give another show, as they didn't get it all the first time."

An Australian-born stage and screen actress, Anderson had concluded a record-setting turn on Broadway in *The Three Sisters*, the longest-running Chekhov play to date, several months earlier. She was being sought for other roles when she read in the newspaper that Maurice Evans, a Shakespearean actor and a captain in the Army Specialist Corps, was in Hawaii organizing entertainment for the troops. Anderson immediately offered to join Evans and work with him and his GI cast and crew to stage *Macbeth*. The two thespians had starred together in a Broadway production of the Shakespeare drama in 1941. The next year, they brought the story "about the powers of darkness, murder, and violence," as Evans described it, to an army camp at Fort Meade, Maryland. The nine hundred soldiers in the audience frequently broke into applause—particularly after Lady Macbeth's sleepwalking scene—and gave the show a standing ovation, summoning the cast again and again for curtain calls.

Since the start of the war, Anderson had been eager to do something for the "boys who fought so gallantly for us." But she was unsure how to be useful, since all she knew was serious acting. She joined the patriotic fervor for knitting, making sweaters, socks, and other items for the troops, and sold war bonds. As the war progressed, thinking of the enormous demands placed on the men on battlefields, she didn't feel that was enough. "I wanted to be closer to the war," she said. "I wanted to be closer to the boys, the same boys who had supported me in the theater, who had applauded me. I wanted to go to them, let them know I appreciated what they were doing for me and my country—to applaud them."

Prior to a performance of *Macbeth* at an army camp on Oahu, Anderson was sitting in a jeep studying her lines when a young soldier walked up and shyly asked permission to speak with her. "Of course," she replied. He eagerly expressed his delight in seeing a great actress at such close range. "First we had three months to wait," he said, "then a month, then a week, then a day, and now I am talking to you—boy, will I have something to write home about!" The encounter, Anderson told a reporter, was the greatest moment of her career.

Like Eleanor, Anderson connected personally with the troops. She regularly visited hospitals, taking special care to see those with mental maladies, and recreation centers, where she ate and danced and talked and laughed with servicemen. "I found out I did not need an act," she said. "I had found my job. I knew that these boys and many more like them, appreciated entertainment, but what they needed, and craved most, was companionship. A friendly word, a pat of the hand, the sound of a soft voice."

Anderson later volunteered for the United Service Organizations, which provided live entertainment for the armed forces, and returned to the Pacific. In jungle amphitheaters in New Guinea, she staged variety shows with a troupe of entertainers, covering everything from classical and swing played by a pianist to bawdy tunes belted out by an Italian singer. Added to the lineup was a one-act play from *Macbeth* that Anderson produced with a naval officer she once worked with in the theater. "It turned out to be by far the best thing that has been given. In fact, there has been nothing that would even run second to it. The soldiers reacted ten times better than they did to the Bob Hope show," Lieutenant General Eichelberger wrote to his wife.

To Anderson, the real tragedy was "more overwhelming than any ever set down on paper: a whole generation of high-hearted young men threatened and decimated by death, mutilation, madness. I shall never forget those wonderful, gallant, smiling faces, or the hurt ones, or the dead ones." Like Eleanor, she saw the cost of war not in ships or guns but in the lives being sacrificed.

One of Eleanor's final undertakings in Honolulu was a stark reminder of the tragic toll: standing on the deck of the USS *Oklahoma* in Pearl Harbor, where "the blow had fallen" nearly two years earlier. On that fateful day, the *Oklahoma* was being prepared for an inspection scheduled to take place the following morning. Many of the doors and hatches were wide open, accelerating the rate at which the battleship sank after being slammed again and again with torpedoes. While 32 men trapped on the *Oklahoma* were freed in the hours after the attack, 429 went down with the ship.

Efforts to resurrect the capsized vessel, the largest and most difficult of the Pearl Harbor salvage operations, took about eighteen months until it could be moved and drydocked. At the time of Eleanor's visit, the *Oklahoma* was raised from the harbor floor, upright but not yet afloat. The massive battlewagon was secured in place by an extensive system of cables and winches rigged between the ship and the shore on nearby Ford Island.

Edward Raymer, the navy salvage diver, reluctantly acceded to a superior's order to provide the First Lady with a tour of the *Oklahoma*. He disagreed with her politically (as did his staunchly conservative grandmother, a Westbrook Pegler fan). But by tour's end, like many a serviceman before him, he was won over by her sincerity and by the intelligent questions she asked about the recovery operation. As part of the process, Raymer explained, medics sorted through the sludge and debris searching for human remains. They placed approximately two hundred bones, representing the number in the human body, in individual bags. The bags were then sent to an army hospital, where a chaplain performed funeral services for these men who were lost as the war began.

Today, a memorial overlooking the water at Pearl Harbor is inscribed with a prayer Eleanor carried in her wallet throughout the war:

> *Dear Lord*
> *Lest I continue*
> *My complacent way*
> *Help me to remember*
> *Somehow out there*
> *A man died for me today.*
> *As long as there be war*
> *I then must*
> *Ask and answer*
> *Am I worth dying for?*

EPILOGUE

"The Pacific trip," said Eleanor, "left a mark from which I think I shall never be free."

In the weeks and months following the journey, she felt its effects acutely. She had lost thirty pounds while abroad and was as exhausted as she had ever been in her life.

The physical fatigue was easier to overcome than the emotional exhaustion. Eleanor fell into a deep depression, haunted by the suffering she had witnessed. "As long as she had to keep going—her iron will carried her through in spite of her deep horror at what she saw and the great sadness at the continuing bloodshed and dying," explained a close friend.

The "soul-stirring" Pacific trip made Eleanor more determined than ever to see the war through and to strive for peace. She reminded the nation of the "tremendous obligation" they owed the men at the front and cautioned that they must not let up on their duties until the war ended. "Your work may be hard," she stated, "but believe me, it doesn't touch the work of your boys."

Eleanor thought of the men buried at the cemetery on

Guadalcanal and the thousands more she met in hospitals, who would forever carry with them the results of the war. "If we do not achieve the ends for which they sacrificed—a peaceful world in which there exists freedom from fear of both aggression and want—we have failed."

A necessary near-term goal was to see a support program established for returning servicemen. Eleanor used the power of her platform to help ensure that it was done, bringing pressure to bear on politicians and rallying citizens to make their wishes known to their representatives. Legislation needed to be passed immediately and not after the war ended, both to boost the confidence of those on the fighting fronts and to assist the great number of veterans who were already returning.

As a soldier explained to Eleanor, "There is one great fear in the heart of every serviceman and it is not that he will be killed or maimed, but that when he is finally allowed to go home and piece together what he can of life, he will be made to feel that he was a 'sucker' for the sacrifice that he has made." Having millions of veterans satisfied that their interests were safeguarded while they were bearing the brunt of the war on battlefronts would contribute to a stabilized and thriving postwar society and economy.

The Servicemen's Readjustment Act, or the GI Bill of Rights, was finally passed by Congress and signed into law in June 1944. The bill provided veterans with funds for education and training, loan guarantees for homes and businesses, job-finding assistance, unemployment pay, and other benefits, and it also mandated the improvement of Veterans Administration hospitals.

Recalling the conversations with men in mess halls and service clubs across the Pacific whose chief concern was postwar employment, Eleanor worked to see that done too. She raised the issue publicly, once again spurring Congress to act, while behind the scenes, she brought together key figures who could help ensure an effective conversion of industry from war footing to peacetime production.

Keeping the peace was Eleanor's primary long-term goal.

Her wartime trips reinforced her belief that women everywhere, just as they broke new ground while helping to win the war, needed to play a greater part in the postwar era. "Through the years men have made the wars; it is only fair to suggest that women can help to make a lasting peace," she reasoned. She hosted a two-hundred-person summit at the White House, "How Women May Share in Post-War Policy-Making," and actively worked to have women included as delegates and advisers to postwar international conferences and as members of national policy-making bodies.

In a significant step forward, representatives from numerous women's organizations were asked by the U.S. State Department to act as consultants to the American delegation at the opening of the United Nations in San Francisco on April 25, 1945.

Both Eleanor and Franklin believed an international organization was crucial to maintaining world peace. She was elated that they were to attend together the United Nations conference, where fifty countries would be represented. "A United Nations organization is for the very purpose of making it possible that all the world's opinion will have a clearing place. It will supply every nation with a free expression of the people," she remarked to the press on April 12.

Several hours later, Franklin unexpectedly passed away.

"The story is over," Eleanor told reporters before shutting the door of her New York City apartment building hours after leaving the White House for the final time.

But Eleanor's story was far from over.

While she was in Rockhampton, Australia, the town's mayor declared that he "would like to see Mrs. Roosevelt at the peace conference table" and that he was sure it was a widely held opinion. The mayor's words proved prescient.

In December 1945, Eleanor was appointed by President Harry S. Truman as a delegate to the United Nations. She was the only woman among five U.S. delegates at the inaugural session of the General Assembly in London the next month.

In addition to acting as a delegate to the General Assembly, Eleanor served as chairperson of the Human Rights Commission. She was the driving force in creating the 1948 Universal Declaration of Human Rights. The milestone text, which became the foundational document of human rights law, encompassed on a global scale the humanitarian ideals Eleanor had long championed.

"Recognition of the inherent dignity and of the equal and inalienable rights of all members of the human family is the foundation of freedom, justice and peace in the world," begins the Declaration. It sets forth standard requirements for all nations in how their citizens should be treated regardless of their race, color, sex, religion, political beliefs, or other factors.

In 1949, Eleanor accepted a nomination by President Truman for a second term at the United Nations. "You have rendered a service to your country in a difficult time which could not have been performed by any other citizen. Nor can I think of anyone who could carry on in your place," said President Truman. "Your country needs you—indeed, this troubled world needs you and the counsel which you can bring to the UN, out of your rich experience and deep sympathy with the needs of humanity."

Eleanor served six years at the United Nations, her tenure concluding with the election of a Republican president.

While at the United Nations and in the ensuing years, Eleanor lived up to her globe-trotting reputation. She traveled to Germany, Israel, Jordan, India, Pakistan, Japan, the Soviet Union, Thailand, Hong Kong, and other far-flung locales. She took her last international trip, to Europe and Israel, nine months before her death at age seventy-eight. Everywhere Eleanor went, she met people from all walks of life, assessing and learning and creating greater cross-cultural understanding, all in service of creating a more peaceful world. In doing so, she truly became, as a newspaper stated during the Pacific trip, "a woman who has made the world her personal study."

Eleanor on Guadalcanal

The First Lady speaks with Pvt. Clarence D. Robertson of Tulsa, Oklahoma, next to the wreckage of a Japanese fighter plane.

Photo © Bettmann / Contributor / Getty Images

"Our Eleanor"

Eleanor with Lt. General Millard F. Harmon (left) and Admiral William F. Halsey in front of a plane decorated in her honor by the U.S. Army Air Forces 13th Troop Carrier Squadron on New Caledonia.

Photo courtesy of Franklin D. Roosevelt Presidential Library & Museum / National Archives and Records Administration

Eleanor with the crew of the main transport plane

Eleanor poses with photographer S.Sgt. Evans Houghton (far left),
press relations officer Maj. George Durno (third from left), and the
crew that flew her throughout her tour of the Pacific, including Capt.
Roy Pickering (fifth from left).

Eleanor being greeted by cheering crowds

Eleanor faces well-wishers from the balcony of the Town Hall in Sydney, Australia. News reports estimated that as many as 20,000 people turned out to see her, many of whom waited for hours. Some got creative in staking out spots, like an Army nurse and others who

witnessed Eleanor's arrival from the roof of the town hall.

Photo © Fairfax Media / Getty Images

Eleanor Roosevelt and Rangitīaria Dennan

Eleanor receives a traditional Māori greeting in Rotorua, New Zealand, from the renowned Guide Rangi. The photograph ignited a media frenzy when it was published in *Look* magazine in December 1943.

Photo © Bettmann / Contributor / Getty Images

Eleanor lunching with servicemen

Dining in mess halls was one way Eleanor interacted directly with servicemen and learned about their current and post-war concerns. Seated with her here at a U.S. military camp in Australia are servicemen from Michigan, Illinois, and Texas.

Eleanor chatting with nurses

During afternoon tea at an American Red Cross club in Sydney, a group of army and navy nurses shared with Eleanor their experiences serving in New Guinea. "I have the greatest respect and admiration for them," she told the American public. Although they suffered from homesickness, endured the hardships of severe climates, and faced the perils of war, she "never heard a single nurse complain."

Photo © Bettmann / Contributor / Getty Images

LEFT:

Eleanor on Christmas Island

The First Lady with a soldier on Christmas Island. Many of "your boys out there...are living a Robinson Crusoe life," she told an audience in New York City after her return from the Pacific.

Photo courtesy of Franklin D. Roosevelt Presidential Library & Museum / National Archives and Records Administration

BELOW:

Touring Christmas Island

Eleanor in a lookout tower with Arthur Cunningham, the American Red Cross director on the island.

Photo courtesy of Fold3 / Department of Defense. Department of the Air Force. 9/26/1947 / National Archives and Records Administration

The Guadalcanal Campaign

U.S. Marines rest in a field on Guadalcanal. For six months, beginning in August 1942, troops fought in the swamps, jungles, and hills on a hellish battlefield the Japanese called "Death Island." In Eleanor's trip reporting, she recalled the "shadowed eyes" of men who had endured the savagery of jungle warfare.

Photo courtesy of National Archives and Records Administration

Medical buildings on Guadalcanal

Photo courtesy of Fold3 / Department of Defense. Department of the Air Force. 9/26/1947 / National Archives and Records Administration

FACING PAGE, TOP:

Eleanor talks with a wounded serviceman

At a South Pacific hospital, Eleanor speaks with a sailor from Fort Worth, Texas, who was injured while unloading a ship. Admiral Halsey recalled being awed by the expressions on the men's faces as the First Lady leaned over them in hospital beds.

Photo © Everett/Shutterstock

FACING PAGE, BOTTOM:

Eleanor with Hugh Barr Miller and Admiral Halsey

In a hospital on New Caledonia, Eleanor congratulates Lt. Miller after pinning a Navy Cross and a Purple Heart on his uniform. Admiral Halsey invited her to participate in the medal ceremony as a sign of his respect for her (and to make amends for his previous surliness).

Photo courtesy of Fold3 / Department of Defense. Department of the Air Force. 9/26/1947 / National Archives and Records Administration

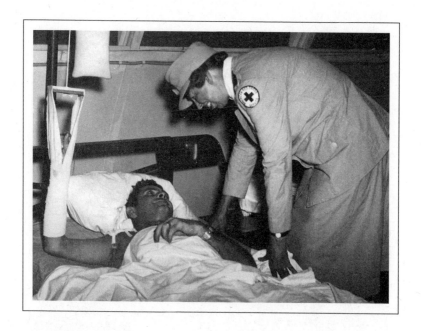

The Battle of Buna

Life magazine was not permitted to use this photo when it reported on the Battle of Buna in February 1943, due to U.S. government regulations against showing photos of dead servicemen. The image finally appeared in print later that year after the restriction was lifted.

Photo © Keystone-France / Contributor / Getty Images

Eleanor at the cemetery on Guadalcanal

An especially emotional experience for Eleanor was walking along the rows and rows of graves, adorned with handmade crosses and mementos left by servicemen for their fallen friends.

Eleanor on the USS *Oklahoma* at Pearl Harbor

Moored at Pearl Harbor on December 7, 1941, the USS *Oklahoma* was torpedoed and sank. At the time of Eleanor's visit the battleship was undergoing a salvage operation, raised from the harbor floor but not yet afloat.

Photo © Bettmann / Contributor / Getty Images

ACKNOWLEDGMENTS

Researching and writing *The First Lady of World War II* was a fabulous four-year journey.

The first stop along the way was the Franklin D. Roosevelt Presidential Library and Museum in Hyde Park, New York. Among its historical riches is an extensive file with original materials pertaining to Eleanor Roosevelt's Pacific trip—a time capsule that contains everything from her trip diary and notes she wrote to the president to itineraries, formal dinner seating charts, and a list of the bomber crewmembers who flew her to Guadalcanal. The wonderful staff at the FDR Library deserve an enormous thank you. During in-person research visits, they were extremely welcoming and helpful with queries large and small. Then, when the library closed during the pandemic, they didn't miss a beat and kept fulfilling research requests electronically.

Another pivotal place was the New York Public Library. Both before and after the height of the pandemic, the Rose Main Reading Room at the Forty-Second Street branch in New York City was my primary research hub. I utilized just about every service the library offers, including an important resource acquired via interlibrary loan. After the pandemic began, the library greatly expanded its remote services and access to databases.

I'm immensely grateful to the entire talented team at Sourcebooks, who partnered with me to make this book possible. I especially thank my editor, Meg Gibbons, who in her perfect offer letter revealed that she is an ardent Eleanor Roosevelt admirer. Her insights and guidance have made for a richer book.

I also owe a huge thank you to my agent, Dan Lazar, who enthusiastically embraced this project from the start and helped hone its vision.

And the biggest thanks of all go to my husband, Brian, whose encouragement and support are boundless.

SOURCE NOTES

This book came together through the wealth of information available at libraries, archives, and museums near and far—books, newspaper articles, correspondence, oral histories, congressional records, and much more. Librarians, archivists, and curators are the superheroes of the information world, many of whom kept resources flowing to researchers even when their institutions were required to close their doors during the pandemic.

Places of note include the Franklin D. Roosevelt Presidential Library and Museum in Hyde Park, New York, where Patrick Fahy in particular answered many of my queries; the Nimitz Library at the U.S. Naval Academy, where Dr. Jennifer A. Bryan generously provided an important chapter from a book I was having a hard time locating; the David M. Rubenstein Rare Book & Manuscript Library at Duke University, where Elizabeth B. Dunn assisted with information about Lieutenant General Robert Eichelberger's papers; the Rotorua Museum in New Zealand, where Natascha Hartzuiker graciously replied to my numerous emails; the Te

Papa Museum in Wellington, where Dougal Austin offered insights on the hei tiki; the National Library of New Zealand; the National Library of Australia; the State Library Victoria; the National Museum of the Pacific War in Fredericksburg, Texas; the National World War II Museum in New Orleans, where the exhibit "Guadalcanal: Green Hell" immerses visitors in the jungle environment; the U.S. National Archives; the New York Public Library; and the Hoboken Public Library.

Newspaper and magazine articles came from a variety of sources, including scrapbooks presented to Eleanor Roosevelt by the governments of New Zealand and Great Britain; the national libraries of New Zealand and Australia; the *New York Times*, which offers subscribers access to the TimesMachine, a digital replica of every issue from 1851 to 2002; databases and periodicals provided by the New York Public Library; and vintage magazines bought on eBay.

Primary Sources

The archives of the Franklin D. Roosevelt Presidential Library and Museum were the key to this book, particularly the Pacific Trip File, the Pacific Area Scrapbook (sent post-trip by the New Zealand government), and the Speech and Article File, among the Papers of Eleanor Roosevelt.

Another invaluable resource was a searchable online collection of Eleanor Roosevelt's "My Day" columns, which totaled more than 8,000 over a period of 27 years. Unless otherwise noted, "My Day" excerpts are from the database at Eleanor Roosevelt Papers Project, Columbian College of Arts and Sciences, George Washington University, Washington, DC, https://erpapers.columbian.gwu.edu/my-day.

The Autobiography of Eleanor Roosevelt (New York: Harper Perennial, 2014).

This I Remember by Eleanor Roosevelt (New York: Harper & Brothers, 1949).

Eleanor and Franklin by Joseph P. Lash (New York: W. W. Norton, 1971).

A World of Love: Eleanor Roosevelt and Her Friends 1943–1962 by Joseph P. Lash (Garden City, NY: Doubleday, 1984).

Eleanor Roosevelt, Vol. 3, *The War Years and After 1939–1962* by Blanche Wiesen Cook (New York: Penguin Books, 2017).

No Ordinary Time: Franklin and Eleanor Roosevelt: The Home Front in World War II by Doris Kearns Goodwin (New York: Simon & Schuster, 2013).

Trove: Newspapers & Gazettes: National Library of Australia, https://trove.nla.gov.au.

Papers Past: National Library of New Zealand (Te Puna Mātauranga o Aotearoa), https://paperspast.natlib.govt.nz.

Books

Banning, William, ed. *Heritage Years: Second Marine Division Commemorative Anthology 1940–1949*. Paducah, KY: Turner, 1988.

Beasley, Maurine H. *Eleanor Roosevelt and the Media: A Public Quest for Self-Fulfillment*. Urbana: University of Illinois Press, 1987.

Beasley, Maurine H., Holly C. Shulman, and Henry R. Beasley. *The Eleanor Roosevelt Encyclopedia*. Westport, CT: Greenwood, 2001.

Birdsall, Steve. *Log of the Liberators: An Illustrated History of the B-24*. Garden City, NY: Doubleday, 1973.

Borneman, Walter R. *MacArthur at War: World War II in the Pacific*. New York: Little, Brown, 2016.

Brawley, Sean, and Chris Dixon. *Hollywood's South Seas and the Pacific War: Searching for Dorothy Lamour*. New York: Palgrave Macmillan, 2012.

Buhite, Russell D., and David W. Levy, eds. *FDR's Fireside Chats*. Norman: University of Oklahoma Press, 1992.

Bureau of Yards and Docks, Department of the Navy. *Building the Navy's Bases in World War II: History of the Bureau of Yards and Docks and the Civil Engineer Corps 1940–1946*. Vol. II. Washington, DC: U.S. Government Printing Office, 1947.

Butler, Susan. *East to the Dawn: The Life of Amelia Earhart*. Cambridge: Da Capo, 1997.

Condon-Rall, Mary Ellen, and Albert E. Cowdrey. *The Medical Department: Medical Service in the War Against Japan*. Washington, DC: U.S. Army Center of Military History, 1998.

Cook, Blanche Wiesen. *Eleanor Roosevelt*. Vol. 1, *The Early Years 1884–1933*. New York: Penguin Books, 1993.

———. *Eleanor Roosevelt*. Vol. 2, *The Defining Years 1933–1938*. New York: Penguin Books, 2000.

Craven, Wesley Frank, and James Lea Cate, eds. *The Army Air Forces in World War II*. Vol. 4, *The Pacific, Guadalcanal to Saipan, August 1942 to July 1944*. Washington, DC: Office of Air Force History, 1983.

Crosby, Donald F. *Battlefield Chaplains: Catholic Priests in World War II*. Lawrence: University Press of Kansas, 1994.

Deacon, Desley. *Judith Anderson: Australian Star: First Lady of the American Stage*. Melbourne: Kerr, 2019.

Dennan, Rangitiaria. *Guide Rangi of Rotorua*. With Ross Annabell. Christchurch: Whitcombe and Tombs, 1968.

Dixon, Chris. *African Americans and the Pacific War, 1941–1945:*

Race, Nationality, and the Fight for Freedom. Cambridge, UK: Cambridge University Press, 2018.

Dod, Karl C. *United States Army in World War II: The Technical Services/The Corps of Engineers: The War Against Japan*. Washington, DC: U.S. Army Office of the Chief of Military History, 1966.

Driscoll, Joseph, *Pacific Victory: 1945*. Philadelphia: J. B. Lippincott, 1944.

Drury, Bob, and Tom Clavin. *Halsey's Typhoon: The True Story of a Fighting Admiral, an Epic Storm, and an Untold Rescue*. New York: Atlantic Monthly, 2007.

Dye, Bob, ed. *Hawaii Chronicles III: World War Two in Hawaii, from the pages of* Paradise of the Pacific. Honolulu: University of Hawaii Press, 2000.

Eichelberger, Robert L. *Our Jungle Road to Tokyo*. With Milton MacKaye. New York: Viking, 1950.

Emblidge, David, ed. *My Day: The Best of Eleanor Roosevelt's Acclaimed Newspaper Columns, 1936-1962*. Boston: Da Capo, 2001.

Evans, Maurice. *All This—And Evans Too: A Memoir*. Columbia: University of South Carolina Press, 1987.

Frank, Richard B. *MacArthur*. New York: Palgrave Macmillan, 2007.

Gann, Ernest K. *Fate Is the Hunter: A Pilot's Memoir*. New York: Simon & Schuster Paperbacks, 1961.

Ginter, Steve. *Consolidated PB4Y-1/1P (Naval Fighters Number 105)*. Simi Valley, CA: Ginter Books, 2017.

Glasser, Arthur F. *And Some Believed: A Chaplain's Experiences with the Marines in the South Pacific*. Chicago: Moody Press, 1946.

Gomery, Douglas, and Clara Pafort-Overduin. *Movie History: A Survey*. 2nd ed. New York: Routledge, 2011.

Halsey, William F., and J. Bryan III. *Admiral Halsey's Story*. New York: McGraw-Hill, 1947.

Harding, Stephen. *The Castaway's War: One Man's Battle Against Imperial Japan*. Boston: Da Capo, 2016.

Hixson, Walter L., ed. *The American Experience in World War II*. Vol. 4, *Pearl Harbor in History and Memory*. New York: Routledge, 2003.

Holmes, W. J. *Double-Edged Secrets: U.S. Naval Intelligence Operations in the Pacific During World War II*. Annapolis, MD: Bluejacket Books, 2012.

Howard, Mary Ferebee. *No Drums, No Trumpets: Red Cross Adventure*. Rocky Mount: North Carolina Wesleyan College Press, 1992.

Hughes, Thomas Alexander. *Admiral Bill Halsey: A Naval Life*. Cambridge, MA: Harvard University Press, 2016.

Huie, William Bradford. *Can Do! The Story of the Seabees*. Los Angeles: P-47 Press, 2018.

Huston, John W., ed. *American Airpower Comes of Age: General Henry H. "Hap" Arnold's World War II Diaries*. Vol. 1. Maxwell Air Force Base, AL: Air University Press, 2002.

Johnson, William Bruce. *The Pacific Campaign in World War II: From Pearl Harbor to Guadalcanal*. London: Routledge, 2006.

Korson, George. *At His Side: The American Red Cross Overseas in World War II*. New York: Coward-McCann, 1945.

Lash, Joseph P. *Love, Eleanor: Eleanor Roosevelt and Her Friends*. Garden City, NY: Doubleday, 1982.

Levi, Werner. *American-Australian Relations*. Minneapolis: University of Minnesota Press, 1947.

Lloyd, Clem, and Richard Hall. *Backroom Briefings: John Curtin's War*. Canberra: National Library of Australia, 1997.

Luvaas, Jay, ed. *Dear Miss Em: General Eichelberger's War in the Pacific, 1942–1945*. Westport, CT: Greenwood, 1972.

Mason, John T., Jr. *The Pacific War Remembered: An Oral History Collection*. Annapolis, MD: Naval Institute Press, 1986.

McManus, John C. *Fire and Fortitude: The US Army in the Pacific War, 1941–1943*. New York: Caliber, 2020.

Mead, James M. *Tell the Folks Back Home*. New York: D. Appleton-Century, 1944.

Michaelis, David. *Eleanor*. New York: Simon & Schuster, 2020.

Morriss, Mack. *South Pacific Diary 1942–1943*. Edited by Ronnie Day. Lexington: University Press of Kentucky, 1996.

Morton, Louis. *United States Army in World War II: The War in the Pacific: Strategy and Command: The First Two Years*. Washington, DC: U.S. Army Center of Military History, 1962.

Perry, Mark. *The Most Dangerous Man in America: The Making of Douglas MacArthur*. New York: Basic Books, 2014.

Persico, Joseph E. *Roosevelt's Centurions: FDR and the Commanders He Led to Victory in World War II*. New York: Random House, 2013.

Pryor, Elizabeth Brown. *Clara Barton: Professional Angel*. Philadelphia: University of Pennsylvania Press, 1987.

Raymer, Edward C. *Descent into Darkness: Pearl Harbor, 1941: A Navy Diver's Memoir*. Annapolis, MD: Naval Institute Press, 2012.

Rich, Doris L. *Amelia Earhart: A Biography*. Washington, DC: Smithsonian Institution Press, 1989.

Roosevelt, Eleanor. *This Is My Story*. New York: Harper & Brothers, 1937.

Roosevelt, Elliott, and James Brough. *An Untold Story: The Roosevelts of Hyde Park*. New York: G. P. Putnam & Sons, 1973.

Rottman, Gordon L. *World War II Pacific Island Guide: A Geo-Military Study*. Westport, CT: Greenwood, 2002.

Rowan, Terry. *World War II Goes to the Movies & Television Guide.* Vol. II: L–Z. Self-published, Lulu.com, 2012.

Rowley, Hazel. *Franklin & Eleanor: An Extraordinary Marriage.* New York: Farrar, Straus and Giroux, 2010.

Schneider, Carl J., and Dorothy Schneider. *World War II: An Eyewitness History.* New York: Facts on File, 2003.

Schrijvers, Peter. *The GI War Against Japan: American Soldiers in Asia and the Pacific During World War II.* New York: New York University Press, 2002.

Serling, Robert J. *When the Airlines Went to War: The Story of America's Civilian Air Warriors.* New York: Kensington Books, 1997.

Smith, Stephen Drury, ed. *The First Lady of Radio: Eleanor Roosevelt's Historic Broadcasts.* New York: New Press, 2014.

Special Service Division, Army Service Forces. *A Pocket Guide to New Guinea and the Solomons.* Washington, DC: U.S. Government Printing Office, 1944.

Stavisky, Samuel E. *Marine Combat Correspondent: World War II in the Pacific.* New York: Ivy Books, 1999.

St. John, Philip A. *The Liberator Legend: B-24 Liberator: The Plane—The People.* Paducah, KY: Turner, 1999.

Steinberg, Alfred. *Mrs. R: The Life of Eleanor Roosevelt.* New York: G. P. Putnam's Sons, 1958.

Stinnett, Ronald F. *Democrats, Dinners & Dollars: A History of the Democratic Party, Its Dinners, Its Ritual.* Ames: Iowa State University Press, 1967.

Summers, Anthony. *Official and Confidential: The Secret Life of J. Edgar Hoover.* New York: Open Road Media, 2012.

Third Marine Division Association. *Third Marine Division's Two Score and Ten History, U.S. Marine Corps.* Paducah, KY: Turner, 1992.

Thompson, Henry J. *The Buccaneers of Harry Sears.* Coronado, CA: Charlie Horse Books, 1997.

Tomblin, Barbara Brooks. *G.I. Nightingales: The Army Nurse Corps in World War II*. Lexington: University Press of Kentucky, 1996.

Tregaskis, Richard. *Guadalcanal Diary*. New York: Modern Library, 2000.

Van der Vat, Dan. *The Pacific Campaign: World War II: The U.S.-Japanese Naval War 1941–1945*. New York: Simon & Schuster, 1991.

Washburne, Seth. *The Thirsty 13th: The U.S. Army Air Forces 13th Troop Carrier Squadron 1940–1945*. Dallas, TX: Thirsty 13th, 2011.

Wu, Judy Tzu-Chun. *Doctor Mom Chung of the Fair-Haired Bastards: The Life of a Wartime Celebrity*. Oakland: University of California Press, 2005.

Wukovits, John. *Admiral "Bull" Halsey: The Life and Wars of the Navy's Most Controversial Commander*. New York: Palgrave Macmillan, 2010.

Web Resources

History.navy.mil and History.army.mil both have extensive resources pertaining to World War II, including the booklets *New Guinea* (history.army.mil/brochures/new-guinea /ng.htm) and *Guadalcanal* (history.army.mil/brochures /72–8/72–8.htm) in "The U.S. Army Campaigns of World War II" series and *The Army Nurse Corps: A Commemoration of World War II Service* (history.army.mil/books/wwii/72 –14/72–14.HTM).

Congressional Records: www.congress.gov/congressional-record /archive.

Life magazine archives: books.google.com/books/about/LIFE .html?id=N0EEAAAAMBAJ.

Yank: The Army Weekly archives: www.unz.com/print/Yank.

FDR's Fireside Chats, recordings and transcripts: millercenter
.org/the-presidency/presidential-speeches.

The Internet Archive (archive.org) has a wealth of historical books
and other materials, such as the FBI's file on Eleanor Roosevelt.

National First Ladies' Library: www.firstladies.org.

New Zealand Electronic Text Collection, part of Victoria
University of Wellington Library: nzetc.org.

Meet New Zealand guide: nzhistory.govt.nz/media/interactive
/meet-new-zealand-guide.

Australian Government Department of Foreign Affairs and
Trade, Historical Documents: www.dfat.gov.au/about-us
/publications/historical-documents/Pages/historical
-documents.

Australia at War: www.ozatwar.com.

Pacific Wrecks: www.pacificwrecks.com.

World War II Database: www.ww2db.com.

SouthPacificWWIIMuseum.com.

"The Prime Minister and the President: John Curtin and
Franklin D. Roosevelt in World War II," John Curtin Prime
Ministerial Library: john.curtin.edu.au/roosevelt.

New Zealand History: nzhistory.govt.nz (Manatū Taonga,
Ministry for Culture and Heritage).

Te Ara: The Encyclopedia of New Zealand: teara.govt.nz
/en (Manatū Taonga, Ministry for Culture and Heritage).

Queensland WWII Historic Places: www.ww2places.qld.gov.au.

Articles

Barclay, G. St. J. "Australia Looks to America: The Wartime
Relationship, 1939–1942." *Pacific Historical Review* 46, no. 2
(May 1977): 251–71. https://www.jstor.org/stable/3637934.

Bradley, La Verne. "San Francisco: Gibraltar of the West Coast." *National Geographic* 83, no. 3 (March 1943): 296.

Brawley, Sean, and Chris Dixon. "Jim Crow Downunder? African American Encounters with White Australia, 1942–1945." *Pacific Historical Review* 71, no. 4 (2002): 607–32. https://www.jstor.org/stable/10.1525/phr.2002.71.4.607.

Bugbee, Emma. "America's Most Traveled First Lady." *Literary Digest* 117, no. 17 (April 28, 1934): 9, 39.

Cavanaugh, Joanne P. "Women of War." *Johns Hopkins Magazine* (November 1998). https://pages.jh.edu/jhumag/1198web/nurses.html.

Colton, F. Barrows. "Weather Fights and Works for Man." *National Geographic Magazine* 84, no. 6 (December 1943): 641–70.

Davis, Luther. "Weather in Your Hat." *Air Force* 27, no. 7 (July 1944): 26–33.

Fagelson, William Friedman. "Fighting Films: The Everyday Tactics of World War II Soldiers." *Cinema Journal* 40, no. 3 (Spring 2001): 94–112. https://www.jstor.org/stable/1350196.

"Flares Instead of Explosives Drop as Hawaii Tests Blackout." *Christian Science Monitor*, May 22, 1941.

"Guadalcanal's Dead in Hallowed Graves; Cemetery Is Devoutly Tended by Buddies." *New York Times*, January 1, 1943.

Harsch, Joseph C. "Blackouts Find Honolulu Ready for Any Challenge." *Christian Science Monitor*, December 15, 1941.

Kimball, Warren F. "'Merely a Facade?' Roosevelt and the Southwest Pacific." *Journal of American-East Asian Relations* 3, no. 2 (Summer 1994): 103–26. https://www.jstor.org/stable/23613382.

"Life on the Newsfronts of the World: How the Heroic Boys of Buna Drove the Japs into the Sea," *Life* (February 22, 1943): 24.

Maga, Timothy. "Humanism and Peace: Eleanor Roosevelt's Mission to the Pacific, August–September, 1943." *Maryland Historian* 19, no. 2 (Fall/Winter 1988): 33–47.

Montgomerie, Deborah. "GI Joe Down Under: American Infantrymen in New Zealand During World War II." *New Zealand Journal of History* 34, no. 2 (2000): 262–76. https://www.nzjh.auckland.ac.nz/docs/2000/NZJH_34_2_04.pdf.

Pasley, Virginia. "First Lady to the Common Man." *American Mercury*, March 1944, 275–83. https://www.unz.com/print/AmMercury-1944mar-00275.

"Red Cross Helps in Tent or Big City." *New York Times*, March 10, 1943.

Roosevelt, Eleanor. "Flying Is Fun." *Collier's*, April 22, 1939.

Saunders, Kay and Helen Taylor. "The Reception of Black American Servicemen in Australia During World War II: The Resilience of 'White Australia.'" *Journal of Black Studies* 25, no. 3 (January 1995): 331–348.

Tremaine, Frank. "The Battle of Arundel Island." *Life*, November 8, 1943.

NOTES

ABBREVIATIONS

ER   Eleanor Roosevelt

FDR   Franklin D. Roosevelt

FDRL Franklin D. Roosevelt Presidential Library and Museum

ER Papers Eleanor Roosevelt Papers, Franklin D. Roosevelt Presidential Library and Museum, Hyde Park, NY

FDR Papers Franklin D. Roosevelt Papers, Franklin D. Roosevelt Presidential Library and Museum, Hyde Park, NY

Prologue

"a prisoner in the White House": Frances Perkins, *The Roosevelt I Knew* (New York: Viking, 1946), 69.

she considered divorcing: Allida Black, "Eleanor Roosevelt and Franklin Roosevelt: Partnership in Politics and Crises," in *The White House: Actors and Observers*, ed. William Seale (Boston: Northeastern University Press, 2002), 140.

"I had watched": *The Autobiography of Eleanor Roosevelt* (New York: Harper Perennial, 2014), 163.

"unaccustomed to": Emma Bugbee, "America's Most Traveled First Lady," *Literary Digest*, April 28, 1934.

"Mr. President": Telegram from Mr. and Mrs. Geo. B. Rogers, December 24 [no year noted], President's Personal File 2, Folder: Roosevelt, Eleanor/Foreign Travel, 1942–1944, FDR Papers (hereafter cited as PPF 2).

"listening post": Joseph P. Lash, *Eleanor and Franklin* (New York: W. W. Norton, 1971), 357.

"the moving force": "Mrs. Roosevelt Plans to Keep in Touch with the Public from the White House," *New York Times*, January 22, 1933.

"I want to know": "Mrs. Roosevelt Bids Radio Hearers Adieu," *New York Times*, March 4, 1933.

explored a coal mine: "Mrs. Roosevelt Goes into Mine to See Workers Underground," *Richmond Times-Dispatch*, May 22, 1935.

"to understand people": "First Lady of Land Rides into Heart of Coal Mine to Study Conditions," *Pittsburgh Post-Gazette*, May 22, 1935.

"reporter at large": Jay Franklin, "First, Second and Third Lady— Mrs. Roosevelt," *Vanity Fair*, January 1936.

She was already: Emma Bugbee, "Mrs. Roosevelt Flies to Capital in 'Bumpy' Air," *New York Herald Tribune*, March 17, 1933.

"America's Most Traveled First Lady": Bugbee, "America's Most Traveled First Lady."

forty thousand miles: Bugbee, "America's Most Traveled First Lady."

averaged annually: "A Well Kept Secret," *New York Times*, August 28, 1943.

"More than any woman": Bugbee, "America's Most Traveled First Lady." Note: spelling of "tabus" changed to "taboos" for readability.

"You know my Missus": Perkins, *The Roosevelt I Knew*, 70.

"Mrs. Franklin D. Roosevelt": "Mrs. Roosevelt Is Both Praised and Blamed for Her Activities," *New York Times*, December 9, 1942.

"Mrs. Smith": "Eleanor Sees Son in London," *Republic* (Columbus, IN), October 24, 1942.

"You certainly have": Lash, *Eleanor and Franklin*, 668.

"an event of great": "Reporter for the President," *Daily Mail*, October 24, 1942.

"the most unconventional": "Reporter for the President."

"I think it would be well": Kay Pain, "Mrs. Roosevelt Finds Our Slang 'Good-o,'" *Sunday Sun* (Sydney), September 5, 1943.

"a symbol of the war": Joseph P. Lash, *A World of Love: Eleanor Roosevelt and Her Friends 1943–1962* (Garden City, NY: Doubleday, 1984), 71.

"the growing impudence": "Blood on Her Hands," *Jackson Daily News*, June 22, 1943.

some government officials: John Morton Blum, ed., *The Price of Vision: The Diary of Henry A. Wallace 1942–1946* (Boston: Houghton Mifflin, 1973), 243.

"stay at home": "ODT Criticized for the Travels Undertaken by Mrs. Roosevelt," *New York Times*, July 27, 1943.

nearly two thousand strikes: Bureau of Labor Statistics, "Strikes in 1943," U.S. Department of Labor, May 1944, https://www.bls.gov/wsp/publications/annual-summaries/pdf/strikes-1943.pdf.

"They say I shall": ER, "My Day," August 28, 1943.

Chapter 1: The Nearest Thing to Heaven

"Eleanor Roosevelt [is]": "America's Most Unusual Woman," *Daily Telegraph* (Sydney), August 28, 1943.

When she moved: "First Lady Moves to New Home Amid a Buzz of Excitement," *New York Times*, April 15, 1942.

"With all the world news": ER, "My Day," April 16, 1942.

"I can now say": ER, "My Day," August 17, 1943.

first took to the skies: "Wife of Governor Christens Airplane, Then Has First Ride," *Ithaca Journal-News*, June 5, 1929.

no flight, no christening: "Flashes of Life," *Elmira Star-Gazette*, June 1, 1929.

a second invitation: "Mrs. Roosevelt Names Plane 'Governor,' Starts Here by Air, Forced Down at Poughkeepsie," *New York Times*, June 6, 1929.

the bravest and most athletic: Emilie Watson, "Amelia Earhart: The Flying Feminist," Flight Paths: Purdue University's Aerospace Pioneers, September 13, 2016, https://flightpaths.lib.purdue.edu/blog/2016/09/13/amelia-earhart-the-flying-feminist/.

made front-page news: "Governor Will Fly to Convention Today," *New York Times*, July 2, 1932.

gave denial to whispers: "Roosevelt Is Ready for Chicago Flight," *New York Times*, June 30, 1932.

"First Lady of the Land": The advertisement appeared in numerous publications, including *Life*, October 2, 1939, 26.

"If you have never flown": ER, "Flying Is Fun," *Collier's*, April 22, 1939, 15.

"She has done": Susan Butler, *East to the Dawn: The Life of Amelia Earhart* (Cambridge: Da Capo, 1997), 281.

"a real sense": ER, *This I Remember* (New York: Harper & Brothers, 1949), 215.

"the First Lady of the Land": "First Lady Flies with Miss Earhart," *New York Times*, April 21, 1933.

"It does mark an epoch": Emma Bugbee, "Mrs. Roosevelt in Night Flight with Amelia Earhart as Pilot," *New York Herald Tribune*, April 21, 1933.

"Her rapid air tour": Amon G. Carter, "All-American Woman," *Fort Worth Star-Telegram*, June 16, 1933.

"Here is what": "Mr. Rogers Lists First Lady as New Heroine in Aviation," *New York Times*, June 8, 1933.

designated for the president: Barney Driscoll, "389th Green Dragon Flares," *Second Air Division Association Journal* 38, no. 4 (Winter 1999–2000): 28, https://b24.net/2ndADA-Newsletters/1999-Winter.pdf.

announced the forthcoming nuptials: "Drink Toast to Coming Marriage," *Evening Star* (Washington, DC), August 16, 1943.

held at the home: "Mayris Chaney Is Married," *New York Times*, August 19, 1943.

"They are wherever men": La Verne Bradley, "San Francisco: Gibraltar of the West Coast," *National Geographic* 83, no. 3 (March 1943): 296.

"are blue, with a smoky": Marjorie Wingfield, "Meeting Mrs. Roosevelt," *Australian Women's Weekly*, September 11, 1943, 9.

"I hoped in this way": *Autobiography of Eleanor Roosevelt*, 254.

"It is hard to believe": ER, "My Day," May 23, 1944.

"I would feel easier": *Autobiography of Eleanor Roosevelt*, 254.

"attacked as a political gesture": Lash, *World of Love*, 45.

"Tommy and I": *Autobiography of Eleanor Roosevelt*, 250.

"I realize that anything": Lash, *World of Love*, 55.

he perished on impact: "Final Journey," Will Rogers Memorial Museum and Birthplace Ranch, accessed April 7, 2022, https://www.willrogers.com/final-journey.

anxiously scanned newspapers: ER, "My Day," July 7, 1937.

"such a small spot": Donald M. Goldstein and Katherine V. Dillon, *Amelia: The Centennial Biography of an Aviation Pioneer* (Washington: Brassey's, 1997), 222.

"I shall be glad": Goldstein and Dillon, *Amelia: The Centennial Biography*, 223.

"Much as I hate": ER, "My Day," July 14, 1937.

"All search for Earhart": Ric Gillespie, *Finding Amelia: The True Story of the Earhart Disappearance* (Annapolis, MD: Naval Institute Press, 2006), 223.

a plane taking off: "14 Men Die in Bomber Crash," *Wilkes-Barre (PA) Record,* June 6, 1942; F. H. Oberding, *Hamilton Field Diary: The Country Club Airbase* (Bloomington, IN: Xlibris, 2011), 155–56.

same type of aircraft: Top Secret Dispatches, 1942–1945, South Pacific Area and Force, Department of the Navy, RG 313, Entry P 95, Box 14, National Archives at College Park, MD (hereafter cited as Top Secret Dispatches).

wool for uniforms: Charles E. Shelton, "Our Pacific Sky-Lane," *Air Force: Official Service Journal of the U.S. Army Air Forces* 26, no. 7 (July 1943): 10–11.

more than ninety thousand miles: "Amusements," *Rushville (IN) Republican,* June 11, 1943.

accident rate: "Calendar," *Appeal-Democrat* (Marysville, CA), November 4, 1943.

"An evil bastard contraption": Ernest K. Gann, *Fate Is the Hunter: A Pilot's Memoir* (New York: Simon & Schuster Paperbacks, 1961), 214.

"It was a ground-loving": Gann, *Fate Is the Hunter,* 215.

crashed into the ocean: Aviation Safety Network database, accessed April 7, 2022, https://aviation-safety.net/database/record.php?id=19430207-3.

Auckland, New Zealand, airport: Martin Johnston, "Secret Wartime Auckland Plane Crashes That Everyone Knew About," *New Zealand Herald,* August 1, 2017.

"by taking up": *Autobiography of Eleanor Roosevelt,* 254.

Roy Pickering: "Pilot Ends Long Career," *Salina (KS) Journal,* February 13, 1966.

Chapter 2: Rise Above These Fears

"You don't want to go": "First Lady's Plea Ignored by Youth," *New York Times,* May 27, 1940.

"Hawaii is today": U.S. Congressional Record, Proceedings and

Debates of the 77th Congress First Session, Appendix, Volume 87, Part 12, May 20, 1941, to July 14, 1941, A2586.

"a beautiful land": U.S. Congressional Record, Proceedings and Debates of the 77th Congress First Session, Appendix, Volume 87, Part 12, May 20, 1941, to July 14, 1941, A2585.

"a clutch of fear": Stephen Drury Smith, ed., *The First Lady of Radio: Eleanor Roosevelt's Historic Broadcasts* (New York: New Press, 2014), 191.

"I feel as though": Smith, *First Lady of Radio*, 192.

"Look at your map": FDR, "Fireside Chat 20: On the Progress of the War," February 23, 1942, Miller Center, University of Virginia, transcript and audio, 36:31, https://millercenter.org/the-presidency/presidential-speeches/february-23-1942-fireside-chat-20-progress-war.

some 61.3 million people: "Radio Audience Put at 61,365,000," *New York Times*, February 25, 1942.

"It is warfare": FDR, "Fireside Chat 20."

The president's suggestion: "Rush Is On to Buy Maps," *New York Times*, February 21, 1942.

Consumers turned out: "President's 'Plug' Booms Map Trade," *New York Times*, February 22, 1942.

self-imposed promise: Russell D. Buhite and David W. Levy, eds., *FDR's Fireside Chats* (Norman: University of Oklahoma Press, 1992), xvii.

"We are daily": FDR, "Fireside Chat 20."

"the worst disaster": William Bruce Johnson, *The Pacific Campaign in World War II: From Pearl Harbor to Guadalcanal* (London: Routledge, 2006), 102.

"endless battlefields": FDR, "Fireside Chat 20."

"America on the Offensive": *New York Times*, August 11, 1942.

"looked like a": Horace L. Wolf Sr., "Intro to Tooba," in *Third Marine Division's Two Score and Ten History* (Paducah, KY: Turner, 1992), 37.

"to make sure": FDR to Joint Chiefs of Staff, quoted in Paul Sparrow, "75th Anniversary of the Battle for Guadalcanal," FDRL, August 7, 2017, https://fdr.blogs.archives.gov/2017/08/07 /75th-anniversary-of-the-battle-for-guadalcanal.

"Jungle Island Becomes": *New York Times*, October 18, 1942.

"We got the news": William F. Halsey and J. Bryan III, *Admiral Halsey's Story* (New York: McGraw-Hill, 1947), 116.

"undertake some aggressive": John Wukovits, *Admiral "Bull" Halsey: The Life and Wars of the Navy's Most Controversial Commander* (New York: Palgrave Macmillan, 2010), 57.

"We had been whipped": Halsey and Bryan, *Admiral Halsey's Story*, 96.

"a rough, tough": Foster Hailey, "Halsey Is Known as a Fighting Man," *New York Times*, October 25, 1942.

"attacking and not retreating": Clark Lee, *They Call It Pacific* (The Viking Press, 1943), quoted in Wukovits, *Admiral "Bull" Halsey*, 66.

"Knock-'em Down Halsey": As he was called by the press; quoted in Wukovits, *Admiral "Bull" Halsey*, 66.

"I like your": Wukovits, *Admiral "Bull" Halsey*, xiii.

"Navy's toughest command": John G. Norris, "Admiral Halsey, Unorthodox Fighter, Takes Over Navy's Toughest Command," *Washington Post*, November 1, 1942.

"Death Island": R. L. Duffus, "With the Marines on Guadalcanal: Details of the Action on the Ground That the Japanese Call 'Death Island,'" *New York Times Book Review*, January 24, 1943.

featured on its cover: *Time*, November 2, 1942.

"Some of my men were lost": "Gen. Vandegrift Writes His Wife," *Life*, November 16, 1942, 83–90.

"Foe Quits Island": *New York Times*, February 10, 1943.

some seventy-one hundred: "The Solomon Islands Campaign: Guadalcanal," National WWII Museum, accessed April 7, 2022,

https://www.nationalww2museum.org/war/articles/solomon
-islands-campaign-guadalcanal.

front lines: ER, "My Day," September 27, 1943.

ninety-four planes: "Guadalcanal Bag Rises to 94 Planes," *New York Times*, June 20, 1943.

"when I was to be": ER, *This I Remember*, 295.

"So you too": Lash, *World of Love*, 15.

"if it did not": *Autobiography of Eleanor Roosevelt*, 253.

"super secret": Top Secret Dispatches.

"Intercept any": Top Secret Dispatches.

"My stop was": Diary of Trip to Southwest Pacific, 1943, Trip File—Pacific Area, Series 38: Miscellaneous (190), 1934–1945, ER Papers (hereafter cited as Pacific Area Trip File).

A tense day: E. B. Potter, *Nimitz* (Annapolis, MD: Naval Institute Press, 1976), 247.

"the vastest": "Pacific Battlefield: As Seen from Moon, It Covers Half the Planet," *Life*, December 22, 1941, 59.

Chapter 3: Island of Forgotten Men

"When you think": Eleanor Roosevelt, "Our Boys in the Southwest Pacific," speech, Rotary Club of New York, January 6, 1944, Speech and Article File, 1944 and undated, ER Papers.

"onlookers were": CG, "Eleanor Roosevelt Visits Island," *Pacific Times*, August 29, 1943, typed copy of article, Pacific Area Trip File.

"I wondered how": "Talk to Press," *New Zealand Herald*, August 28, 1943.

"vast distances": FDR, "Fireside Chat 20."

"There is nothing there": M. B. Gardner, quoted in Dan van der Vat, *The Pacific Campaign: World War II: The U.S.-Japanese Naval War 1941–1945* (New York: Simon & Schuster, 1991), 218.

"American fighting men": "American Fighting Men in the South Seas," *Life*, June 16, 1944, 53.

"Some things are": Special Service Division, Army Service Forces, *A Pocket Guide to New Guinea and the Solomons* (Washington: U.S. Government Printing Office, 1943), 2, https://www.history .navy.mil/research/library/online-reading-room/title-list -alphabetically/p/pocket-guide-new-guinea-solomons.html.

"Christmas is a": ER to FDR, August 29, 1943, Pacific Area Trip File.

"are beautiful": T. T. Hammond, "Forget That Dream Trip to the South Seas, Vet Says," *Atlanta Constitution*, May 25, 1944.

"Under those circumstances": Eleanor Roosevelt, "My Day," September 21, 1943.

"I think the idea": Diary of Trip to Southwest Pacific, 1943, Pacific Area Trip File.

"vastly complicated": Diary of Trip to Southwest Pacific, 1943, Pacific Area Trip File.

"taught us many": *Autobiography of Eleanor Roosevelt*, 19.

"more of an all-around": *Autobiography of Eleanor Roosevelt*, 121.

"Where are your husbands?": Elliott Roosevelt and James Brough, *An Untold Story: The Roosevelts of Hyde Park* (New York: G. P. Putnam & Sons, 1973), 193.

"by plane, boat": "Soldier Audiences in Global Hookup," *Motion Picture Daily*, April 3, 1944.

"Training films": Fred Stengel, "Films to Our Men from Leopoldville to Liberia," *Motion Picture Daily*, August 23, 1943.

"Saw a wonderful show": René Palmer Armstrong, *Wings and a Ring: Letters of War and Love from a WWII Pilot* (Mustang, OK: Tate, 2011), 282.

"Rarely is it": *War Department Field Manual FM 21–10: Military Sanitation* (Washington: U.S. Government Printing Office, 1945), 14, http://www.6thcorpscombatengineers.com/docs

/FieldManualsWWII/FM%2021–10%20(%20Military%20 Sanitation%20).pdf.

"mill about": John N. Popham, "Films Free Inhibitions of Aleutian Marines," *Motion Picture Herald*, November 6, 1943.

"Here every spectator": Popham, "Films Free Inhibitions."

"It is to the eternal": CG, "Eleanor Roosevelt Visits Island."

"I might have": Diary of Trip to Southwest Pacific, 1943, Pacific Area Trip File.

"I hope no one": Diary of Trip to Southwest Pacific, 1943, Pacific Area Trip File.

"Mrs. Roosevelt Finally": Lee McCardell, "Mrs. Roosevelt Finally Gets Tired; Shock to Reporters," *Evening Sun* (Baltimore, MD), November 12, 1942.

"It is strange": Leo H. Berman, "Where Money Has No Worth," *The American Red Cross with the Yanks Down Under: A Report by the American Red Cross on Its Activities with the U.S. Forces in the South-West and South Pacific*, February 1942 to August 1943, Pacific Area Trip File.

"It is not a glamorous": ER, "My Day," October 1, 1943.

"One of the boys": ER, "The Red Cross in the South Seas," *Ladies' Home Journal*, December 1943, 159.

"saw everything": *Autobiography of Eleanor Roosevelt*, 255.

put out a call: ER, "My Day," October 4, 1943.

"peculiar looking vehicle": "'Jeep,' Army Car, Reminiscent of Teddy Roosevelt: It's Rough Rider," *Abilene (TX) Reporter-News*, March 2, 1941.

"lonely little camps": ER, "My Day," September 21, 1943.

"knew all the boys": ER, "Red Cross," 160.

"the absence of routine": Diary of Trip to Southwest Pacific, 1943, Pacific Area Trip File.

it was discovered: Ken Bloom, *Broadway: An Encyclopedia* (New York: Routledge, 2012), 491.

The most dangerous spot: "At Cairns and Mackay," *Courier-Mail* (Brisbane), September 13, 1943.

a voracious hunger: Foster Hailey, "Yanks Live in Eden but Long for News," *New York Times*, November 22, 1942.

"A good many million": Robert L. Eichelberger, *Our Jungle Road to Tokyo*, with Milton MacKaye (New York: Viking, 1950), 84.

"Your soldier": James D. White, "X Marks Spot Where Censor Finds Self," *Richmond Times-Dispatch*, January 17, 1943.

"her presence was like": Mrs. Dwight L. Bennett to Eleanor Roosevelt, September 26, 1943, Folder: My Day Comments A–B, 1943, My Day Comments 1942N–1943D, White House Correspondence, 1933–45, ER Papers.

"She seemed to represent": Terry Flanagan, "As We See It," *Pacific Times*, August 29, 1943, typed copy of article, Pacific Area Trip File.

"She reminded one": Flanagan, "As We See It."

"agreeable or just a bore": Unspecified speech/article, Folder: Trip to the South Pacific August–September 1943, Speech and Article File, 1943, ER Papers.

"Her kindness and consideration": CG, "Eleanor Roosevelt Visits Island."

"It takes great courage": Flanagan, "As We See It."

Chapter 4: Pacific Flight 321

"The schedules are hard": Lash, *World of Love*, 64.

Pacific Flight 321: Top Secret Dispatches.

"When you did not": Raymond "Casey" Hasey, *My Bombsight View of WWII* (Bloomington, IN: AuthorHouse, 2011), 112.

"by a bunch": Carl J. Schneider and Dorothy Schneider, *World War II: Eyewitness History* (New York: Facts on File, 2003), 231.

"Cannot believe": Top Secret Dispatches.

At that time of year: ER, *This I Remember*, 276.

"From now on": ER, "My Day," August 17, 1942.

"could not catch up": "My Day by Eleanor Roosevelt Censored," *Daily Mirror* (London), October 28, 1942.

"very busy" and **"General MacArthur":** ER, "My Day," September 30, 1943.

"narrow fingers": James A. Michener, *Return to Paradise* (New York: Dial, 2015), 61.

"to have been designed": James A. Michener, *The World Is My Home: A Memoir* (New York: Random House, 1992), 42.

"Then in the dark days": Michener, *Return to Paradise*, 61.

A committee: Charles F. Barber, *History of World War II: Reminiscences of Admiral Raymond A. Spruance* (Newport, RI: Oral History Program, Naval War College, 1996), 49–50, https://archive.org/details/oralhistorytrans00barb.

tapped two sources: Barber, *History of World War II*, 49–50.

watched *Tabu*: Willard G. Triest, "Gearing up for Operation Bobcat," in *The Pacific War Remembered: An Oral History Collection*, ed. John T. Mason Jr. (Annapolis, MD: Naval Institute Press, 1986), 43.

"There was no fanfare": Jack M. Tucker, "First Lady and the Doughboys," *Democrat and Chronicle Magazine*, October 3, 1943.

"Entertainment to be restricted": Top Secret Dispatches.

"The best thing to do": "Reporter for the President," *Daily Mail* (London), October 24, 1942.

"talk among the men": ER, "My Day," October 13, 1945.

"was so quiet and civilized": Tucker, "First Lady and the Doughboys."

"We were so overtaken": Everard V. Cruca, "An El Pasoan in the South Pacific," *El Paso Herald-Post*, October 27, 1943.

"If we do our job": Eulalie McDowell, "Draft Furore Puzzles Men in Pacific," *Richmond Times-Dispatch*, September 28, 1943.

not repeat past mistakes: "First Lady Makes Plea for Soldiers," *New York Times*, April 6, 1942.

"I have always had": "Bonus Camp Viewed by Mrs. Roosevelt," *New York Times*, May 17, 1933.

"I want everyone": "Mrs. Roosevelt Makes Talk to Bonus Seekers," *Marshall News Messenger*, May 17, 1933.

"It took quite a bit": ER, *This I Remember*, 312–13.

"Many people, who": ER, "My Day," July 28, 1943.

"I hope the men": Lash, *World of Love*, 49.

"for the return": FDR, "Fireside Chat 25: On the Fall of Mussolini," July 28, 1943, Miller Center, University of Virginia, transcript and audio, 29:26, https://millercenter.org/the-presidency/presidential-speeches/july-28-1943-fireside-chat-25-fall-mussolini.

"a rusty nail": Wukovits, *Admiral "Bull" Halsey*, 99.

"know how big": Lawrence E. Davies, "First Lady Found Worries in Pacific," *New York Times*, September 24, 1943.

"send the strikers": Ray Clapper, "In Australia," *Binghamton Press*, January 7, 1944.

"The President wanted": Everett C. Watkins, "Biography of Mrs. Roosevelt Depicts Her as Part of Astute Political Team," *Indianapolis Star*, September 5, 1943.

"He said to tell you": Robert M. White to his wife, included in U.S. Congressional Record, Proceedings and Debates of the 78th Congress First Session, Appendix, Volume 89, Part 12, October 15, 1943, to December 21, 1943, A4494–A4495.

"There is something": Tucker, "First Lady and the Doughboys."

"where the enlisted man": Bill Richardson, *Yank: The Army Weekly*, November 4, 1942, 9.

"I have always been 'agin'": Alfred Steinberg, *Mrs. R: The Life of Eleanor Roosevelt* (New York: G. P. Putnam's Sons, 1958), 297.

"If they can get planes": Deborah Montgomerie, "GI Joe Down Under: American Infantrymen in New Zealand During World War II," *New Zealand Journal of History* 34, no. 2 (2000): 262–76.

"I'd rather be": Westbrook Pegler, "Mrs. Roosevelt's Trip Used Vital Materials," *Philadelphia Inquirer*, October 4, 1943.

"a Massachusetts Republican": Diary of Trip to Southwest Pacific, 1943, Pacific Area Trip File.

"I was amused": ER, "My Day," October 1, 1943.

"I have never seen": Diary of Trip to Southwest Pacific, 1943, Pacific Area Trip File.

creating a network: Harry L. Henderson and David B. Woolner, *FDR and the Environment* (New York: Palgrave Macmillan, 2005), 11.

"drove like a": "American Artifacts: Franklin D. Roosevelt's Top Cottage," CSPAN, February 23, 2018, https://archive.org/details/CSPAN3_20180224_024100_American_Artifacts_Franklin_D._Roosevelts_Top_Cottage.

"Tutuila looks like": Ridgely Cummings, "American Samoa Is Prepared; Marines Guard Vital Outpost," *Eugene (OR) Guard*, May 12, 1942.

malinga: Cummings, "American Samoa Is Prepared."

"Alcatraz in Technicolor": Cummings, "American Samoa Is Prepared."

"seemed high-spirited": Cummings, "American Samoa Is Prepared."

she reported: ER, "My Day," October 2, 1943.

"rain, wind and dust": Meta Blackwell, "Navy Nurse Finds Little Glamor on South Sea Isle," *San Bernardino (CA) County Sun*, February 20, 1944.

"Rickenbacker Missing": *New York Times*, October 24, 1942.

"I heard one thing": Diary of Trip to Southwest Pacific, 1943, Pacific Area Trip File.

"They have the most": ER to Norman Davis, September 30, 1943, Folder: Davis, Norman–Red Cross July–December, White

House Correspondence, 1933–45, Personal Letters 1943 Cr–
De, ER Papers.

"is doing a magnificent job": ER to Norman Davis, September 30,
1943.

"and get a real idea": *Autobiography of Eleanor Roosevelt*, 154.

"Did you say": ER, "Churchill at the White House," *Atlantic*, March
1965, https://www.theatlantic.com/magazine/archive/1965/03
/churchill-at-the-white-house/305459/.

"people all along": ER, "Churchill at the White House."

"was not reassuring": ER, "Churchill at the White House."

"Try to hold out": Uncensored letters to the Wehrmacht, Pacific
Area Trip File.

"cleaned out": "Island Evacuated: Aleutians Cleaned Out," *New
York Times*, August 22, 1943.

"I could find no excuse": Halsey and Bryan, *Admiral Halsey's Story*, 166.

Chapter 5: No Place for You, Ma'am

"We in America": "Day of Colour: Around Rotorua," *Auckland Star*,
September 1, 1943.

"Guadalcanal is no place": Halsey and Bryan, *Admiral Halsey's
Story*, 166–67.

"do-gooders": Halsey and Bryan, *Admiral Halsey's Story*, 166.

"play the gracious": Halsey and Bryan, *Admiral Halsey's Story*, 166.

"My son is the same": Halsey and Bryan, *Admiral Halsey's Story*,
165.

"to throw the rule book": "Halsey Promoted to Admiral's Rank:
Halsey to Rank with Nimitz," *New York Times*, November 21,
1942.

"to sail into hell": Bob Drury and Tom Clavin, *Halsey's Typhoon:
The True Story of a Fighting Admiral, an Epic Storm, and an
Untold Rescue* (New York: Atlantic Monthly, 2007), 7.

"Jesus Christ and General Jackson": Drury and Clavin, *Halsey's Typhoon*, 8.

"seafarers and adventurers": Halsey and Bryan, *Admiral Halsey's Story*, 2.

"a real old salt": Halsey and Bryan, *Admiral Halsey's Story*, 8.

"enough to make": Halsey and Bryan, *Admiral Halsey's Story*, 81.

"Boys, I've got a": Halsey and Bryan, *Admiral Halsey's Story*, 108.

"Of all the admirals": Hailey, "Halsey Is Known."

the only attire: ER to Sumner Welles, August 6, 1943, Pacific Area Trip File.

"booby traps": Eichelberger, *Our Jungle Road to Tokyo*, 78.

"I doubt if I can": Diary of Trip to Southwest Pacific, 1943, Pacific Area Trip File.

"In my capacity": ER, "My Day," May 29, 1941.

the gleam was back: Doris Kearns Goodwin, *No Ordinary Time: Franklin and Eleanor Roosevelt: The Home Front in World War II* (New York: Simon & Schuster, 2013), 280.

"that the wife": ER, "My Day," February 23, 1942.

"at not having": Lash, *World of Love*, xxiii.

"from doing any": ER, *This I Remember*, 261.

"These boys break": ER to Lorena Hickok, September 1, 1943, quoted in Lash, *World of Love*, 62.

"would have their whole": ER, "My Day," March 27, 1942.

"There seems to be no excuse": ER, "My Day," January 23, 1943.

"I simply never": Diary of Trip to Southwest Pacific, 1943, Pacific Area Trip File.

earning the admiration: Tania Long, "Mrs. Roosevelt Calmly Ignores Her First Genuine Raid Alarm," *New York Times*, October 27, 1942.

town of Canterbury: "Dean Thinks Raiders Were Seeking Mrs. F.D.R.," *Daily Herald* (London), November 2, 1942.

"I did not want": ER, *This I Remember*, 261.

"the great enemy": ER, *You Learn by Living: Eleven Keys for a More Fulfilling Life* (Louisville, KY: Westminster John Knox Press, 1983), 23.

"were one long battle": ER, *You Learn by Living*, 25.

"I am hungry": Diary of Trip to Southwest Pacific, 1943, Pacific Area Trip File.

"the one pleasant": Lash, *World of Love*, 61.

"I am sorry": Diary of Trip to Southwest Pacific, 1943, Pacific Area Trip File.

"When one isn't happy": Lash, *World of Love*, 7.

"I'm quite sure": ER, "My Day," September 2, 1943.

"I imagine every mother": *Autobiography of Eleanor Roosevelt*, 251.

assigned to an aviation unit: ER, "My Day," December 20, 1941; "Shifts Elliott Roosevelt," *New York Times*, December 17, 1941.

"Frankie is all right": Bernard Asbell, ed., *Mother & Daughter: The Letters of Eleanor and Anna Roosevelt* (New York: Coward, McCann & Geoghegan, 1982), 163.

"I know there is nothing": "Roosevelts Cheer Gold-Star Mother," *Christian Science Monitor*, August 30, 1943.

"her hardihood": Halsey and Bryan, *Admiral Halsey's Story*, 167.

Chapter 6: News to Us

"For the first time": "Visit to Dominion," *New Zealand Herald*, August 28, 1943.

"It's news to us": "Mrs. Roosevelt in New Zealand to Visit American Troops," *Washington Star*, August 27, 1943.

"had all the dramatic": "Mrs. Roosevelt Here: Surprise Visit," *Auckland Star*, August 27, 1943.

"as fresh and full": "America's First Lady," *New Zealand Herald*, August 28, 1943.

"I am very glad": "Mrs. Roosevelt Broadcasts," *Auckland Star*, August 27, 1943.

"No other President's wife": "Notable Figure," *New Zealand Herald*, August 28, 1943.

"a great fighter": "Mrs. Roosevelt's Visit," *Auckland Star*, August 28, 1943.

"It seems but yesterday": "Warm Tribute: American Forces' Aid," *New Zealand Herald*, September 2, 1943.

"topsy-turvy": ER, "My Day," August 31, 1943.

"Winter snows": Thayer Soule, *Shooting the Pacific War: Marine Corps Combat Photography in WWII* (Lexington: University Press of Kentucky, 1999), 142.

guide prepared especially: *Meet New Zealand* (Wellington: Department of Internal Affairs, 1942).

"The error lay": "Mr. Churchill's Speech," *New Zealand Herald*, January 29, 1942.

"Mr. Churchill makes": "Mr. Churchill's Speech."

"The chief fear": "New Zealand Adds Secret Defenses," *New York Times*, March 8, 1942.

"fear of our own" and "absolutely essential": Peter Fraser to Winston Churchill, February 17, 1942, New Zealand Electronic Text Collection, http://authority.nzetc.org/tm/scholarly/tei-WH2 –3Doc-c7–16.html.

would lose 25 percent: Memorandum, Pacific War Council, April 3, 1942, Naval Aide's Files A-16/3 Pacific War Council Folder 2, September 1942–April 1944, Franklin D. Roosevelt Presidential Library and Museum, http://www.fdrlibrary.marist.edu/_resources/images/mr/mr0867.pdf.

"we are straining": FDR via Walter Nash to Peter Fraser, March 24, 1942, New Zealand Electronic Text Collection, http://authority.nzetc.org/tm/scholarly/tei-WH2–3Doc-c7–32.html.

"We shall take": New Zealand Parliamentary Debates, First

Session, 27th Parliament, Legislative Council and House of Representatives, 265th Volume, July 26 to August 31, 1944 (Wellington: E. V. Paul, Government Printer, 1945), 619.

"I have had": "Talk to Press," *New Zealand Herald*, August 28, 1943.

"However, the boys": "Talk to Press."

"ink spiller": GEM, "Wife of American President Welcomed in Auckland: Friend of Journalists," *Auckland Star*, August 28, 1943.

"represented a": GEM, "Wife of American President Welcomed."

a well-kept secret: "Auckland Greets Mrs. Roosevelt: A Well Kept Secret," *New York Times*, August 28, 1943.

"KEEP HER AT HOME": *Selma (AL) Times-Journal*, September 1, 1943.

"Doing things": "Mrs. Roosevelt in New Zealand," *Morning Call* (Allentown, PA), August 28, 1943.

"not all women": "The Antipodeans Will Now See Mrs. Roosevelt," *Baltimore Sun*, August 28, 1943.

"The President is looking": Watkins, "Biography of Mrs. Roosevelt."

"I say Mrs. Roosevelt": Westbrook Pegler, "Fair Enough," *Daily Times-News* (Burlington, NC), December 8, 1943.

"a certain vitriolic columnist": Ben Hitt, "A Gracious Lady," *Pacific Times*, August 29, 1943, typed copy of article, Pacific Area Trip File.

"This last jaunt": "Suggests an Inquiry," *New York Herald Tribune*, September 5, 1943.

"She has all the qualities": "Defends Mrs. Roosevelt," *New York Herald Tribune*, September 5, 1943.

"a sailor's wife": Mrs. Dane Sylvester to FDR, September 23, 1943, PPF 2.

"to lug her all over": Fred D. Ryan to FDR, October 18, 1943, PPF 2.

"There was a very": Mrs. Bessie B. Ryan to FDR, September 25, 1943, PPF 2.

received indignant letters: "Capital Chaff," *Tucson Daily Citizen*, October 12, 1943.

"surveyed virtually": Edward H. Cavin to Dr. C. E. Price, Cecil Peterson Collection on the Tuskegee Airmen (MS 100), Box 46, Folder 4, Special Collections and University Archives, University of California, Riverside, CA.

addressed the issue: ER, "How to Take Criticism," *Ladies' Home Journal*, November 1944, 155.

Chapter 7: A Modern Crusader

"Mrs. R. literally": George Durno to Malvina Thompson, n.d., Pacific Area Trip File.

enemy submarines: Joe Parker, interview by Evelyn McAnelly, January 30, 2003, transcript, World War II Veterans Oral History Collection, National Museum of the Pacific War Digital Archive, https://digitalarchive.pacificwarmuseum.org /digital/collection/p16769coll1/id/9888/rec/1.

"Well, I'll be": "Memorable Visit: In Capital," *Auckland Star*, August 28, 1943.

"the New Zealand counterpart": "Memorable Visit: In Capital."

"the term 'American hustle'": "Busy Round: Mrs. Roosevelt: Days in Wellington," *Auckland Star*, August 30, 1943.

twenty-one shelters: "Parliament's Wartime Air Raid Shelters," New Zealand Parliament, December 12, 2019, https:// www.parliament.nz/en/get-involved/features/parliament-s -wartime-air-raid-shelters/.

"I hope when": "Working for Peace," *New Zealand Herald*, August 30, 1943.

"We're glad": "Hospital Visit," *New Zealand Herald*, August 30, 1943.

"Disease was a surer": Eichelberger, *Our Jungle Road to Tokyo*, 43.

60 to 65 percent: "Malaria in World War II," Army Heritage Center Foundation, accessed April 12, 2022, https://www .armyheritage.org/soldier-stories-information/malaria-in-world-war-ii/.

A Guadalcanal veteran: ER, "My Day," June 19, 1944.

"He said to tell you": Robert M. White to his wife.

"He can see exactly": "Mrs. F.D.R. Tells of Hope for an Early Peace," *Sun* (Sydney), September 5, 1943.

"It was done in a": Forrest C. Pogue, *George C. Marshall: Global Commander*, Harmon Memorial Lectures in Military History 10 (Colorado: U.S. Air Force Academy, 1968), 18–19.

"It was so fascinating": John Wukovits, *One Square Mile of Hell: The Battle for Tarawa* (New York: NAL Caliber, 2007), 47.

"We have found": "New Services Club," *Evening Post* (Wellington), March 5, 1943.

"back-home food": Dorothy Moses, "The Cecil—A Welcomed Retreat," in *Heritage Years: Second Marine Division Commemorative Anthology 1940–1949*, ed. William Banning (Paducah, KY: Turner, 1988), 45.

"dark State secret": "Crowded Sunday," *Evening Post* (Wellington), August 30, 1943.

"You won't find": *Meet New Zealand*, 1.

offering five hundred homes: Michael Fowler, "The U.S. Second Marine Division in New Zealand," in Banning, *Heritage Years*, 40.

invited American servicemen: Genevieve Reynolds, "Mrs. Fraser Praises Yanks 'Down Under,'" *Washington Post*, April 20, 1944.

"There are difficulties": ER, "Our Boys in the Southwest Pacific."

"News of the Day": "News of the Day: In Monetary Difficulties," *Auckland Star*, March 19, 1943.

"ought to be": ER, "Our Boys in the Southwest Pacific."

"They went from here": ER, "Our Boys in the Southwest Pacific."

A woman in Gisborne: Norman Hatch, interview, May 3, 1993, transcript, World War II Veterans Oral History Collection, National Museum of the Pacific War Digital Archive, https:// digitalarchive.pacificwarmuseum.org/digital/collection /p16769coll1/id/3688/rec/1.

"frank friendliness": ER, "My Day," October 7, 1943.

"It was just grand": ER, "My Day," October 8, 1943.

"being seen": "A Notable Visitor," *Hokitika Guardian*, September 1, 1943.

"spontaneously and lustily": "On the Run," *Auckland Star*, August 31, 1943.

"Girls who are doing": "The First Lady Visits Ford," Heritage at Hutt City Libraries, May 16, 2019, https://heritage .huttcitylibraries.co.nz/2019/05/16/the-first-lady-visits-ford/.

"dangerous work": "Women in Dangerous Work," *Auckland Star*, August 31, 1943.

"effortless, womanly talks": "Mrs. Roosevelt: Last Day in Wellington," *Evening Post* (Wellington), August 30, 1943.

"The need for women": "Women's Part in War," *The Press (Canterbury)*, December 15, 1941.

"a suggestive, thought-provoking": "People and Their Leaders," *Dominion* (Wellington), August 31, 1943.

"It may cost": ER, "Broadcast, Wellington, New Zealand," Speech and Article File, 1943, ER Papers (same as theatre address); https://ngataonga.org.nz/collections/catalogue/catalogue -item?record_id=207339.

"For too long": ER, "Broadcast, Wellington, New Zealand."

"challenging address": "Mrs. Roosevelt's Warning," *Bay of Plenty Times*, September 3, 1943.

"keenly alert": "People and Their Leaders."

"a modern Crusader": "She Came, She Smiled—and She Conquered," *New Zealand Free Lance*, September 8, 1943.

"A woman's place": *Autobiography of Eleanor Roosevelt*, 109.

"Whatever I have become": Maurine H. Beasley, Holly C. Shulman, and Henry R. Beasley, eds., *The Eleanor Roosevelt Encyclopedia* (Westport, CT: Greenwood, 2001), 594.

"Why was your mind": Lash, *Eleanor and Franklin*, 81.

"not spend another": *Autobiography of Eleanor Roosevelt*, 39.

"simply could not": Russell Freedman, *Franklin Delano Roosevelt* (New York: Clarion Books, 1990), 28.

"It would be difficult": *Autobiography of Eleanor Roosevelt*, 40–41.

"a part of the stream": *Autobiography of Eleanor Roosevelt*, 41.

"it never occurred": *Autobiography of Eleanor Roosevelt*, 63.

"For the first time": *Autobiography of Eleanor Roosevelt*, 65.

"it was a wife's duty": *Autobiography of Eleanor Roosevelt*, 66.

"I loved it": Lorena Hickok, "New First Lady Recalls Events of School Days and War Activity," *Chattanooga Daily Times*, November 11, 1932.

"I can forgive": Goodwin, *No Ordinary Time*, 377.

"All my self-confidence": Joseph P. Lash, *Love, Eleanor: Eleanor Roosevelt and Her Friends* (Garden City, NY: Doubleday, 1982), 73.

"He always loved": Lash, *Eleanor and Franklin*, 219.

noted figure: "Governor Smith's Friends," *New York Times*, May 2, 1924.

Chapter 8: More Than All the Guns, Planes and Tanks

"We call upon the president": "We Are Americans, Too!," *Pittsburgh Courier*, December 13, 1941.

"I am sorry but": Rangitīaria Dennan, *Guide Rangi of Rotorua*, with Ross Annabell (Christchurch: Whitcombe and Tombs, 1968), 141.

"see tomorrow": Dennan, *Guide Rangi of Rotorua*, 140.

"But as soon as": Dennan, *Guide Rangi of Rotorua*, 141.

"knew every nook": Dennan, *Guide Rangi of Rotorua*, 74.

"as much appeal": Dennan, *Guide Rangi of Rotorua*, 135.

"beautiful sight": ER, "My Day," *Evening Post* (Wellington), September 1, 1943.

"They feed 600": ER, "My Day," *Evening Post* (Wellington), September 1, 1943.

advised travelers: *Eleanor Roosevelt's Book of Common Sense Etiquette* (New York: Macmillan, 1962), 207.

"a wonderful woman": ER, *This I Remember*, 303.

"that would have done": "Day of Colour: Around Rotorua," *Auckland Star*, September 1, 1943.

"In America": "Day of Colour: Around Rotorua."

"very much a reality": Dennan, *Guide Rangi of Rotorua*, 122.

"The Maori have fought": *Meet New Zealand*, 14.

"the queen of a": "Hakas and Pois: Thrill for the Visitor," *New Zealand Herald*, September 1, 1943.

"We in the United States": "Hakas and Pois: Thrill for the Visitor."

"the most gallant feat": "Desert Fighters," 28th Māori Battalion, accessed April 12, 2022, https://www.28maoribattalion.org.nz/story-of-the-28th/desert-fighters.

"We think highly": "Hakas and Pois: Grateful Acknowledgment," *New Zealand Herald*, September 1, 1943.

"I am sure that this": "Hakas and Pois: Grateful Acknowledgment."

"played a prominent": "Day of Colour: Around Rotorua."

"Why can she rub noses": U.S. Congressional Record, Proceedings and Debates of the 78th Congress First Session, Volume 89, Part 6, July 7, 1943, to October 20, 1943, 8183.

published in: Mary Hornaday, "Eleanor Roosevelt: The Woman Nobody Understands," *Look*, December 28, 1943, 40.

"cause a good bit of": Peter Edson, "Washington Column," *Denton (TX) Record-Chronicle*, December 29, 1943.

"Nothing Like Good Nose Rub": *Times-Gazette* (Union City, IN), December 17, 1943.

"First Lady and Maori 'Kiss'": *Bradford (PA) Evening Star*, December 22, 1943.

"Maori squaw": Louis Sobol, "New York Broadway Cavalcade: Snapshots at Random!," *Press Democrat* (Santa Rosa, CA), December 30, 1943.

"I hear the picture": Sobol, "New York Broadway Cavalcade."

"simple hongi": Dennan, *Guide Rangi of Rotorua*, 141.

"plenty of pakehas": Dennan, *Guide Rangi of Rotorua*, 142.

"I am in complete": "February 26, 1939—Eleanor Roosevelt Resigns from the Daughters of the American Revolution," FDRL, accessed April 12, 2022, http://docs.fdrlibrary.marist.edu/tmirhfee.html.

"This is democracy": Nancy J. Weiss, *Farewell to the Party of Lincoln: Black Politics in the Age of FDR* (Princeton, NJ: Princeton University Press, 1983), 255.

"You would have to have": Weiss, *Farewell to the Party*, 256.

Eleanor was the first: National First Ladies' Library, First Lady Biography: Eleanor Roosevelt, http://www.firstladies.org/biographies/firstladies.aspx?biography=33.

"not only for the": "First Lady Makes Poll Tax Appeal," *People's Voice*, May 29, 1943, clipping in FBI file on Eleanor Roosevelt, https://archive.org/details/EleanorRooseveltFBIFiles/erosevlt12a/page/n19/mode/2up.

planning to denounce: Drew Pearson, "The Washington Merry-Go-Round: Alabama Governor to Seek Anti New Deal Delegation to Convention," *Suffolk (VA) News-Herald*, August 30, 1943.

"the black pot": "National Affairs: Black on Blacks," *Time*, April 27, 1936, 11.

"I am a southerner": *Investigation of Lobbying Activities: Hearings*

Before a Special Committee to Investigate Lobbying Activities (Washington, DC: U.S. Government Printing Office, 1936), 1972–73.

"Why curse Hitler": "War!: ER and Wartime Social Changes," FDRL, accessed April 12, 2022, http://www .fdrlibraryvirtualtour.org/page07–21.asp.

"This seems to me": Goodwin, *No Ordinary Time*, 423.

"Uncle Sam's": "How Nazi Germany Weaponized the Race Card againsttheUSArmy,"U.S.HolocaustMuseum,February13,2017, https://us-holocaust-museum.medium.com/the-nazi-plan-to -divide-and-conquer-the-us-army-296a3c97fb54.

"some innocently": Carroll Kilpatrick, "Malicious Rumor," *News & Observer* (Raleigh, NC), December 22, 1942, attached to a letter sent to Eleanor Roosevelt from Josephus Daniels, File Josephus Daniels (2), 1934–1945, Selected Digitized Correspondence of Eleanor Roosevelt, 1933–1945, FDRL, http://www.fdrlibrary.marist.edu/_resources/images/ersel /ersel023.pdf.

"whispering campaign": Ann Cottrell, "Mrs. Roosevelt Assails Stories About Waacs," *New York Herald Tribune*, June 9, 1943.

"When you realize": ER, "If You Ask Me," *Ladies' Home Journal*, August 1943, 39.

"playing Hitler's game": ER, "If You Ask Me."

"falling for such": Cottrell, "Mrs. Roosevelt Assails Stories."

"leave politics alone": "Nazis Ask Mrs. Roosevelt to End Political Comment," *New York Times*, February 5, 1939.

wrote in "My Day": ER, "My Day," February 3, 1939.

"One should ask her": "Nazis Ask Mrs. Roosevelt."

"This nation is": "First Lady Warns on a Hitler Peace," *New York Times*, November 27, 1941.

"Mrs. Roosevelt is shooting": Goodwin, *No Ordinary Time*, 215.

"The hullabaloo": Willi A. Boelcke, ed., *The Secret Conferences of*

Dr. Goebbels: The Nazi Propaganda War, 1939–43 (New York: E. P. Dutton, 1970), 291.

"and their toadies": N. F. Newsome, "Man in the Street," October 28, 1942, Scrapbook, Eleanor Roosevelt's Visit to Great Britain, October–November 1942, Series 63: Oversized Topical File Materials, ER Papers.

Chapter 9: Like Mushrooms in the Jungle

"So many rumors": Lash, *World of Love*, 52.

"I [have] a son": *Autobiography of Eleanor Roosevelt*, 257.

"I have never made": ER, "My Day," *New Zealand Herald*, September 6, 1943.

"out-and-out": "Barnum Was Wrong," *Yank: The Army Weekly*, October 22, 1943, 15.

"since the individual": Samuel E. Stavisky, *Marine Combat Correspondent: World War II in the Pacific* (New York: Ivy Books, 1999), 203.

"Again and again": Stavisky, *Marine Combat Correspondent*, 204.

by their voices: Arnold S. Lott, *Brave Ship, Brave Men* (Indianapolis and New York: Bobbs-Merrill Co., 1964), 65.

"Hi GIs": Chris Bourke, *Blue Smoke: The Lost Dawn of New Zealand Popular Music 1918–1964* (Auckland: Auckland University Press, 2013), 145.

"are evidently": ER, "My Day," September 26, 1944.

"Last Sunday Mrs. Roosevelt": "Two Postville Boys Serving in Australia Meet in Movie House," *Postville (IA) Herald*, September 29, 1943.

"as far as our bunch": Lash, *Eleanor and Franklin*, 688.

"I want to give you": "Mrs. F.D.R. Lunched with Wounded Men," *Daily Mirror* (Sydney), September 8, 1943.

"You could see": ER, "My Day," September 21, 1943.

the popular practice: "Baby Pictures Vital," *Oakland (CA) Tribune*, September 24, 1943.

"I'm speaking on": "Our Buddy," *Auckland Star*, September 2, 1943.

"It is one of the reasons": "City's Warmth to Mrs. Roosevelt," *Auckland Star*, September 3, 1943.

"It is not pleasant work": "Huge Audience: Talk to Women," *Auckland Star*, September 3, 1943.

"As you may know": George Durno to Malvina Thompson, n.d., Pacific Area Trip File.

"I used to think": "Mrs. Roosevelt & The V Sign," *The Age* (Melbourne), September 2, 1943.

"would still further": "Auckland's Day," *Auckland Star*, September 1, 1943.

"bright and cheerful": "Mrs. Roosevelt & The V Sign."

"All the men ask": Lash, *World of Love*, 63.

what the president wanted: ER to Lorena Hickok, August 25, 1943, quoted in Lash, *World of Love*, 61.

"I dread Australia": Diary of Trip to Southwest Pacific, 1943, Pacific Area Trip File.

Chapter 10: No Frail Flower

"Her visit here": Jay Luvaas, ed., *Dear Miss Em: General Eichelberger's War in the Pacific, 1942–1945* (Westport, CT: Greenwood, 1972), 73.

"They had come": Eichelberger, *Our Jungle Road to Tokyo*, 81.

"Please, Mrs. Roosevelt": "Orchids and Violets to Welcome Mrs. F.D.R.," *Daily Mirror* (Sydney), September 3, 1943.

"with all the simplicity": "Mrs. Roosevelt's Visit," *Armidale Express*, September 6, 1943.

"official pooh-bahs": "Let's Leave the Red Carpet in the Cellar," *Sunday Telegraph* (Sydney), August 29, 1943.

"Any fussy stooges": "Let's Leave the Red Carpet."

"The success of your visit": Nelson Johnson to ER, September 7, 1943, Pacific Area Trip File.

"Good-o": Pain, "Mrs. Roosevelt Finds Our Slang 'Good-o.'"

"You must have a spirit": "Fifty Reporters at Interview," *Sydney Morning Herald*, September 4, 1943.

"She won't be satisfied": "Brought Soldier's Comforts," *Daily Telegraph* (Sydney), September 4, 1943.

"like a frail flower": Diary of Trip to Southwest Pacific, 1943, Pacific Area Trip File.

"I've never been so": Diary of Trip to Southwest Pacific, 1943, Pacific Area Trip File.

"I have an M.P.": Lash, *World of Love*, 66.

Eleanor's itinerary: "Mrs. Roosevelt Arrives; Welcome at Canberra," *Sun* (Sydney), September 3, 1943.

"Australia is now inside": John Curtin, "The Task Ahead," *Herald* (Melbourne), December 27, 1941.

"After all the assurances": John Curtin to Winston Churchill, January 23, 1942, Australian Government Department of Foreign Affairs and Trade, Historical Documents, https://www .dfat.gov.au/about-us/publications/historical-documents /Pages/volume-05/294-mr-john-curtin-prime-minister-to -mr-winston-churchill-uk-prime-minister.

Darwin was bombed: David Watt, "The 75th Anniversary of the Bombing of Darwin,"Parliament of Australia,February 15,2017, https://www.aph.gov.au/About_Parliament/Parliamentary _Departments/Parliamentary_Library/FlagPost/2017 /February/Bombing_of_Darwin.

as though fifty thousand men: "Visit by Mrs. Roosevelt to Hawaii Completes Her Tour of War Zones in the Pacific," *Honolulu Star-Bulletin*, September 21, 1943.

"If Germany were defeated": Memorandum, Pacific War Council, April 10, 1942, Naval Aide's Files A-16/3 Warfare-Pacific War

Council Folder 2, September 1942–April 1944, FDRL, http://
www.fdrlibrary.marist.edu/_resources/images/mr/mr0867.pdf.

"two men": "Wartime Friction 1942–44," The Prime Minister
and the President: John Curtin and Franklin D. Roosevelt in
World War II, accessed April 12, 2022, http://john.curtin.edu.au
/roosevelt/friction.html.

received a summary (all Cuhel quotes): Lester Gottlieb (Mutual
Broadcasting System) to Eleanor Roosevelt, January 16,
1943, with statements from Cuhel's speech attached, Folder:
Roosevelt, Franklin D., White House Correspondence, 1933–
45, Personal Letters 1943 Roosevelt, Eleanor—Sc, ER Papers.

"I think it would": Pain, "Mrs. Roosevelt Finds Our Slang 'Good-o.'"

"Valuable Ambassadress": *Dubbo Liberal*, September 7, 1943.

"not only in": Visit to Australia of Mrs. Franklin D. Roosevelt,
official lunch program, September 4, 1943, Curtin University,
https://ap01-a.alma.exlibrisgroup.com/view/delivery
/61CUR_INST/12191672200001951.

"I like Mr. Curtin": Lash, *World of Love*, 65.

another invitation: FDR to John Curtin, January 3, 1944,
Australian Government Department of Foreign Affairs and
Trade, Historical Documents, https://www.dfat.gov.au/about
-us/publications/historical-documents/Pages/volume-07/3
-roosevelt-to-curtin-letter.

"I don't care how": *Autobiography of Eleanor Roosevelt*, 246.

"Truth to tell": Lash, *World of Love*, 66.

"America's Public Energy No. 1": "Mrs. Roosevelt Lives Up to
Reputation," *Argus* (Melbourne), September 6, 1943.

"a wonderful impression": Lash, *World of Love*, 65.

"[He] was too busy": ER to Doris Fleeson, October 4, 1943, File
Fleeson, Doris, 1937–1945, Selected Digitized Correspondence
of Eleanor Roosevelt, 1933–1945, FDRL, http://www
.fdrlibrary.marist.edu/_resources/images/ersel/ersel044.pdf.

politically motivated: "Congressmen Study Outlook for Presidential Campaign," *Marysville (OH) Journal-Tribune*, September 16, 1943.

"This is the kind of thing": Lash, *World of Love*, 66.

"I kept everything": *Japan and America, c1930–1955, The Pacific War and the Occupation of Japan*, series 1, Papers of General Robert L. Eichelberger (1886–1961), Part 3: Correspondence, Reel 44, Box 8, Folder 3 October 1943–December 1943, William R. Perkins Library, Duke University, Durham, NC.

"It would have pleased": Lash, *World of Love*, 70.

"America's First Lady": "White House Lady Has Human Touch," *Sunday Telegraph* (Sydney), September 5, 1943.

"Jeepers": "Democratic Women's Day in Washington," *Democratic Digest*, December 1943, 9.

"to keep them close": ER, "Our Fighting Men," War Bonds Speech, Treasury Department, September 1943, Speech and Article File, 1943, ER Papers.

"a brace of generals" and subsequent quotes: Cover note, Harry Hopkins to ER, October 19, 1943, with a copy of a letter sent to Florence Kerr by a sailor attached, Folder: Roosevelt, Eleanor, White House Correspondence, 1933–45, Personal Letters 1943 Roosevelt, Eleanor—Sc, ER Papers.

Chapter 11: Womanpower

"Women in the United States": "Meeting Mrs. Roosevelt," *Australian Women's Weekly* (Sydney), September 11, 1943.

"The whole world": "Women's Worth," *West Australian* (Perth), September 7, 1943.

"a hurricane rush": "Women Workers Visited," *Sun* (Sydney), September 7, 1943.

met with women: ER, "My Day," September 9, 1943.

"the intense physical": "War and the Woman," *Argus* (Melbourne), January 13, 1940.

"ridiculous": "Rural Recruiting," *Argus* (Melbourne), May 16, 1941.

"In England and France": "Women Workers in Military Camps Proposed," *Mercury* (Hobart), December 15, 1939.

Women's Land Service: Nancy M. Taylor, *The Home Front Volume II: The Official History of New Zealand in the Second World War* (Wellington: Historical Publications Branch, 1986), 1053, New Zealand Electronic Text Collection, https:// nzetc.victoria.ac.nz/tm/scholarly/tei-WH2–2Hom-c21.html; "Honouring New Zealand's Wartime 'Land Girls,'" *New Zealand Herald*, October 15, 2020, https://www.nzherald .co.nz/the-country/news/honouring-new-zealands-wartime -land-girls/XKRKL6U6KILLNNLAKBS6FGGU3I/; Deborah Montgomerie, "Men's Jobs and Women's Work: The New Zealand Women's Land Service in World War II," *Agricultural History* 63, no. 3 (Summer 1989): 1–13, https:// www.jstor.org/stable/3743731.

ice vendors: Elise Weightman, "Australian Women at Work in WWII: Keep Cool and Carry On," State Library of Queensland, August 13, 2020, https://www.slq.qld.gov.au /blog/australian-women-work-wwii-keep-cool-and-carry.

"The U.S. manpower problem": "Women & Machines," *Time*, May 11, 1942, 64.

wrote to the First Lady: Donald E. Blount to ER, February 1, 1943, Folder: Letters from Servicemen Bi to Bo, 1943, Letters from Servicemen 1943 Bi-E, White House Correspondence, 1933–45, ER Papers.

sent this reply: ER to Donald E. Blount, February 6, 1943, Folder: Letters from Servicemen Bi to Bo, 1943, White House Correspondence, 1933–45, ER Papers.

"I want a women's corps": Melissa Ziobro, "'Skirted Soldiers': The Women's Army Corps and Gender Integration of the U.S. Army during World War II," Army Historical Foundation, accessed April 13, 2022, https://armyhistory.org/skirted-soldiers-the-womens-army -corps-and-gender-integration-of-the-u-s-army-during-world -war-ii/.

"Who will then do": Judith A. Bellafaire, "The Women's Army Corps: A Commemoration of World War II Service," U.S. Army Center of Military History, accessed April 13, 2022, https://history.army.mil/brochures/WAC/WAC.HTM.

"This is the army": ER, "My Day," February 16, 1943.

"Mrs. Roosevelt proposed": Westbrook Pegler, "Fair Enough: Mrs. Roosevelt's PMA," *Pittsburgh Press*, December 6, 1943.

"women's work": Goodwin, *No Ordinary Time*, 414.

"The political candidate": "Meeting Mrs. Roosevelt," *Australian Women's Weekly*, September 11, 1943.

"took it for granted": *Autobiography of Eleanor Roosevelt*, 68.

"I had learned": *Autobiography of Eleanor Roosevelt*, 103.

"Let us be": "'End All War,' Mrs. Catt Begs League Women," *New York Tribune*, April 14, 1921.

"No men allowed": "10,000 See Guest Enter Crowded Town Hall," *Melbourne Herald*, September 6, 1943.

fifty thousand people: "50,000 Line Melbourne Streets," *Sydney Morning Herald*, September 7, 1943.

"Being a housewife": "More Women's Work Than in U.S.," *Daily Telegraph* (Sydney), September 7, 1943.

"Their only thought": "Mrs. Roosevelt in Melbourne: Tribute to Women," *Advocate* (Burnie), September 7, 1943.

"Was your husband": "Mrs. Roosevelt Lives Up to Reputation."

"Mrs. Roosevelt Meets Heroines": *Courier-Mail* (Brisbane), September 9, 1943.

Sister Ellen Savage: Story covered in several articles: "Hospital

Ship Sank with 299 Lives Lost," *Goulburn Evening Post*, May 18, 1943; "Loss of Centaur: Woman Survivor's Story," *West Australian* (Perth), May 24, 1943; "Hospital Ship Sunk: Inspiring Bravery," *Telegraph* (Brisbane), May 18, 1943.

"We had no first aid": "Loss of Centaur."

"She never told me": "Hospital Ship Sunk: Inspiring Bravery."

"for they are allowed": ER, "My Day," October 15, 1943.

"They are not living": ER, "My Day," August 30, 1943.

"a very happy": ER, "Red Cross," 158.

other challenges: "Sydney Greets Mrs. Roosevelt: Nurses From New Guinea," *Sydney Morning Herald*, September 8, 1943.

"Oh, the blessed relief": ER, "Red Cross," 158.

"Add to all this": ER, "American Women in the War," *Reader's Digest*, January 1944.

debt of gratitude: ER, "My Day," August 30, 1943.

officers' rest home: Helen Hall, "Red Cross Under the Southern Cross," *Survey Graphic*, January 1944, 29.

"most tragic": Mary Ferebee Howard, *No Drums, No Trumpets: Red Cross Adventure* (Rocky Mount: North Carolina Wesleyan College Press, 1992), 18.

"My hat is off": ER, "My Day," August 30, 1943.

"ridiculous": ER, "American Women in the War."

"It seems to me": Ruth Millett, "War Changes Women, Too," *Anniston (AL) Star*, December 15, 1943.

"I don't think I'm fit": "Fighters Change, Mrs. F.D.R. Warns," *Chattanooga Times*, October 15, 1943.

"We at home": "Fighters Change, Mrs. F.D.R. Warns."

Chapter 12: The Heroism and the Horror

"Let us hear": "Mrs. Roosevelt Abroad," *Gazette*, Charleston, West Virginia, September 18, 1943.

all its lights: "Mrs. Roosevelt Near New Guinea," *Christian Science Monitor*, September 10, 1943.

In "My Day": ER, "My Day," September 17, 1943.

"My first impression": ER, "My Day," September 13, 1943.

"savagery and anarchy": Eichelberger, *Our Jungle Road to Tokyo*, 65.

"is immense": James M. Mead, *Tell the Folks Back Home* (New York: D. Appleton-Century, 1944), 149–50.

"It is perhaps": Eichelberger, *Our Jungle Road to Tokyo*, 20.

"Such enemy concealment": Eichelberger, *Our Jungle Road to Tokyo*, 30.

"It was easy for": Eichelberger, *Our Jungle Road to Tokyo*, 41.

"Bob," he said: Eichelberger, *Our Jungle Road to Tokyo*, 21.

"To evacuate all": Eichelberger, *Our Jungle Road to Tokyo*, 23.

"inclined to believe": Eichelberger, *Our Jungle Road to Tokyo*, 26–27.

"The commanding general": F. Tillman Durdin, "Buna Beach Fight Led by Sergeant," *New York Times*, December 11, 1942.

on Christmas morning: Eichelberger, *Our Jungle Road to Tokyo*, 50–51.

ancient military maxim: Eichelberger, *Our Jungle Road to Tokyo*, 28.

"I was glad on": Eichelberger, *Our Jungle Road to Tokyo*, 28–29.

"The breakthrough was": Eichelberger, *Our Jungle Road to Tokyo*, 31.

"bearded, grimy crew": Durdin, "Buna Beach Fight."

at the ice cream counter: "Capt. Bottcher, Hero of Buna, Killed on Leyte," *New York Herald Tribune*, January 17, 1945.

"was only the beginning": Eichelberger, *Our Jungle Road to Tokyo*, 32.

"all the jungle": Eichelberger, *Our Jungle Road to Tokyo*, 37.

"In battle the margin": Eichelberger, *Our Jungle Road to Tokyo*, 48–49.

"I am so glad": Eichelberger, *Our Jungle Road to Tokyo*, 49.

"could see the sea": Eichelberger, *Our Jungle Road to Tokyo*, 49.

told the audience: "Democratic Women's Day in Washington," *Democratic Digest*, December 1943, 10.

tank battalions: Eichelberger, *Our Jungle Road to Tokyo*, 33–34.

"No war is a": Eichelberger, *Our Jungle Road to Tokyo*, 34.

"a sly and sneaky": Eichelberger, *Our Jungle Road to Tokyo*, 33.

"grim hide-and-seek": F. Tillman Durdin, "Hide and Seek of Jungle War," *New York Times*, March 7, 1943.

"The invisibility": Eichelberger, *Our Jungle Road to Tokyo*, 52.

"The first boys": "Democratic Women's Day in Washington," 10.

"Someone making a new": ER, "Red Cross," 30.

"I didn't understand": "First Lady Leaves Oakland for Home; Lauds U.S. Troops," *Oakland Tribune*, September 24, 1943.

"But even so": "Democratic Women's Day in Washington," 10.

"I might have": ER, *This I Remember*, 305.

"It hurt like hell": "7-Hour Tour for Mrs. Roosevelt," *Courier-Mail* (Brisbane), September 11, 1943.

a tank destroyer: Wisconsin National Guard, *654: The Red Arrow in WWII* (Madison: Wisconsin National Guard Public Affairs Office, 2020), 31, https://media-cdn.dvidshub.net/pubs/pdf _56303.pdf.

One of the most interesting: ER, "My Day," September 20, 1943.

army engineer unit: "Outline of Program. Unit: 592nd Engineer Boat & Shore Regiment/Place: Yorkeys Beach," Pacific Area Trip File.

"It seemed to me": ER, "My Day," September 20, 1943.

"ended a campaign": "The Battle of Buna," *Life*, February 15, 1943, 17.

"His pictures": "Battle of Buna," 17.

"Studying them": "Life on the Newsfronts of the World: How the Heroic Boys of Buna Drove the Japs into the Sea," *Life*, February 22, 1943, 24.

second of its issues: "Life on the Newsfronts," 24.

"The job of men": "Life on the Newsfronts," 24.

"The reason we print it": "Three Americans," *Life*, September 20, 1943, 34.

"I wonder if you": ER, "Our Boys in the Southwest Pacific."

"Without exception": George Korson, *At His Side: The American Red Cross Overseas in World War II* (New York: Coward-McCann, 1945), 51.

"I traded a carton": "Mrs. Roosevelt Sees Men on Way to Battle," *Courier-Mail* (Brisbane), September 13, 1943.

"Well, this is": "Mrs. Roosevelt Sees Men."

"This is what": "Mrs. Roosevelt Sees Men."

"Don't worry about me": "Mrs. Roosevelt Sees Men."

"took their first": "Air Raid on Townsville," *Western Star and Roma Advertiser*, July 31, 1942.

For the first time: "Australia's First Air Raid Baby," *Daily News* (Perth), July 27, 1942.

"air raid baby": "Australia's First Air Raid Baby."

"Gosh": "Australia's First Air Raid Baby."

"poured lead": L. J. Fitz-Henry, "Air Battle Ends Third Townsville Raid; Pilots' Stories," *Courier-Mail* (Brisbane), July 30, 1942.

"under the most unusual": "Mrs. Roosevelt's Tribute to Women of the North," *Townsville Daily Bulletin*, September 13, 1943.

"took pride": Mary Ellen Condon-Rall and Albert E. Cowdrey, *The Medical Department: Medical Service in the War Against Japan* (Washington, DC: U.S. Army Center of Military History, 1998), 64, https://history.army.mil/html/books/010/10–24/CMH_Pub _10-24-1.pdf.

handed his write-up: Ray E. Boomhower, *Dispatches from the Pacific: The World War II Reporting of Robert L. Sherrod* (Bloomington: Indiana University Press, 2017), 16.

suppressed the report: Ray Holyoak of James Cook University uncovered evidence of the mutiny while researching Lyndon B. Johnson's visit to Townsville in 1942. "Historian Uncovers Townsville Mutiny," *New Zealand Herald*, February 10, 2012, https://www.nzherald.co.nz/world/historian-uncovers-townsville -mutiny/HB2AO2APNDQPR2Y5JABXDS75EY/.

White Australia policy: "White Australia Policy," National Museum of Australia, accessed April 13, 2022, https://www. nma.gov.au/defining-moments/resources/white-australia -policy.

"a white man's" and **"We were allowed":** Sean Brawley and Chris Dixon, "Jim Crow Downunder? African American Encounters with White Australia, 1942–1945," *Pacific Historical Review* 71, no. 4 (2002): 607.

"they were treated": "Facts and Nonsense," *New York Amsterdam News*, June 12, 1943.

"in the Jim Crow section": "Jim Crow Soldiers in Australian City," *Chicago Defender*, November 13, 1943.

Stories circulated: Brawley and Dixon, "Jim Crow Downunder?," 607.

visited local schools: Brawley and Dixon, "Jim Crow Downunder?," 620.

cursed them out: "Facts and Nonsense."

failed to reach: Brawley and Dixon, "Jim Crow Downunder?," 608.

"We were greeted": "Seamen Welcomed by Australian Populace," *Baltimore Afro-American*, April 18, 1942.

"were very indignant": Blanche Wiesen Cook, *Eleanor Roosevelt*, vol. 3, *The War Years and After 1939–1962* (New York: Penguin Books, 2017), 440.

"I think we will": Steven White, *World War II and American Racial Politics: Public Opinion, the Presidency, and Civil Rights Advocacy* (Cambridge, UK: Cambridge University Press, 2019), 118.

"the differential treatment": White, *World War II*, 118.

"our attitude": Cook, *Eleanor Roosevelt*, 3:440.

asked to visit: Enoc P. Waters Jr., "First Lady Visits Our Troops," *Chicago Defender*, September 18, 1943.

"an eloquent plea": Waters, "First Lady Visits Our Troops."

"We need a changed": "Changes Inevitable After War to Ensure Peace," *Courier-Mail* (Brisbane), September 14, 1943.

"I must be off": Diary of Trip to Southwest Pacific, 1943, Pacific Area Trip File.

Flight 246: Top Secret Dispatches.

"somewhere in Australia": "President's Wife Ends Trip and Starts Home," *Christian Science Monitor*, September 15, 1943.

"It's a hell of a way" and subsequent quotes: Robert M. White to his wife.

Chapter 13: Morale Wins Wars

"Well, we saw": Rochelle Chadakoff, ed., *Eleanor Roosevelt's My Day: Her Acclaimed Columns 1936–1945* (New York: Pharos Books, 1989), 274.

solely out of concern: William F. Halsey, "Life of Admiral W. F. Halsey," unpublished manuscript, 1946, MSS 5:9 H1654:1; Virginia Historical Society, Richmond, VA.

"When I say": Halsey and Bryan, *Admiral Halsey's Story*, 167.

"I wish to God": Foster Hailey, "Halsey Defends Battleship Role," *New York Times*, November 19, 1942.

"marveled most": Halsey and Bryan, *Admiral Halsey's Story*, 167.

to do the same: Wukovits, *Admiral "Bull" Halsey*, 107.

"My situation looked": Frank Tremaine, "The Battle of Arundel Island," *Life*, November 8, 1943, 57.

"palm-frond lean-to": Tremaine, "Battle of Arundel Island," 58.

"like hell": Dan McGuire, "Navy Officer Says Will-To-Win Pays Off," *Piqua (OH) Daily Call*, November 17, 1943.

"red beard": Tremaine, "Battle of Arundel Island," 64.

"gallant and courageous": Stephen Harding, *The Castaway's War: One Man's Battle Against Imperial Japan* (Boston: Da Capo, 2016), 203.

"I was ashamed": Halsey and Bryan, *Admiral Halsey's Story*, 167–68.

outpaced her escorts: ER, "My Day," September 22, 1943.

"Do you think it's": Lash, *Eleanor and Franklin*, 688.

not inclined to change: Joseph Driscoll, *Pacific Victory: 1945* (Philadelphia: J. B. Lippincott, 1944), 94.

"She alone": Halsey and Bryan, *Admiral Halsey's Story*, 168.

two most strenuous: ER, "Our Boys in the Southwest Pacific."

"We couldn't start": William Bradford Huie, *Can Do! The Story of the Seabees* (Los Angeles: P-47 Press, 2018), 52.

"Colorful as": Mack Morriss, *South Pacific Diary 1942–1943*, ed. Ronnie Day (Lexington: University Press of Kentucky, 1996), 117.

"I was told": Morriss, *South Pacific Diary*, 120.

"One saw the results": *Autobiography of Eleanor Roosevelt*, 261.

"I did my best": Lash, *World of Love*, 41.

never forgot the smell: Edna P. Gurewitsch, *Kindred Souls: The Friendship of Eleanor Roosevelt and David Gurewitsch* (New York: St. Martin's, 2002), 188.

video tutorial: ER, "My Day," October 5, 1942.

"the horrible consciousness": *Autobiography of Eleanor Roosevelt*, 261.

"the subject of": Elliott Roosevelt, ed., *F.D.R.: His Personal Letters 1928–1945* (New York: Duell, Sloan and Pearce, 1950), 1443.

"I knew that that": *Autobiography of Eleanor Roosevelt*, 261.

about three weeks: Lash, *World of Love*, 42.

"quite a collection": ER, *This I Remember*, 269.

"2nd Lt. LeRoy D. Mitchell": List of Patients Seen by Mrs. Franklin D. Roosevelt While Visiting the 42nd General Hospital A.P.O. 923, Pacific Area Trip File.

"No bombs are": ER, "War Bonds Radio Broadcast," September 27, 1943, Speech and Article File, 1943, Papers of Eleanor Roosevelt, Franklin D. Roosevelt Presidential Library and Museum, Hyde Park, NY.

"the American sense": ER, "War Bonds Radio Broadcast."

Disney cartoonist: "On the Run," *Auckland Star*, August 31, 1943.

"Pants": Eichelberger, *Our Jungle Road to Tokyo*, 32.

13th Troop Carrier Squadron: Thirsty 13th (website), https://www.thirsty13th.com; Seth Washburne, *The Thirsty 13th: The U.S. Army Air Forces 13th Troop Carrier Squadron 1940–1945* (Dallas, TX: Thirsty 13th, 2011).

"It gave them": ER, "War Bonds Radio Broadcast."

"I also knew": James A. Michener, *Tales of the South Pacific* (Boston: G.K. Hall & Co., 1981), 4.

twenty hours straight: Wesley Frank Craven and James Lea Cate, eds., *The Army Air Forces in World War II*, vol. 4, *The Pacific, Guadalcanal to Saipan, August 1942 to July 1944* (Washington, DC: Office of Air Force History, 1983), 38.

accompanying the announcement: "New Hebrides Air Base on Espiritu Santo Island," *New York Times*, October 14, 1942.

dropped numerous bombs: "Mrs. Roosevelt a Day Behind Jap Bombers," *The Long Beach (CA) Sun*, September 24, 1943; Peter Stone, *The Lady and the President: the Life and Loss of the S.S. President Coolidge* (Yarram, Australia: 1999), 68.

"lit only by": Mead, *Tell the Folks Back Home*, 208.

"bounding in a jeep": Mead, *Tell the Folks Back Home*, 209.

Chapter 14: Rest in Peace

"On Guadalcanal, as in many other places": Diary of Trip to Southwest Pacific, 1943, Pacific Area Trip File.

six fighter planes: Third Marine Division's Two Score and Ten page 37; Duane T. Hove, *American Warriors: Five Presidents in the Pacific Theater of World War II* (Shippensburg, PA: Burd Street Press, 2003), 111.

Guadalcanal was bombed: "Navy Department Communiques," *Bureau of Naval Personnel Information Bulletin,* October 1943, 45, https://media.defense.gov/2019/Apr/10/2002112293/-1/-1 /0/AH194310.pdf; "Navy Department Communiques," *Bureau of Naval Personnel Information Bulleting,* November 1943, 46, https://media.defense.gov/2019/Apr/10/2002112294/-1/-1 /1/AH194311.pdf.

"if our team": Halsey and Bryan, *Admiral Halsey's Story,* 168.

"Hi, babe!": "First Lady Reveals: Soldiers Shouted, 'Hi, Babe,' Then Gasped, 'It's Eleanor,'" *Troy (NY) Record,* November 13, 1943.

"Gosh, there's Eleanor" and **"They were so evidently":** Diary of Trip to Southwest Pacific, 1943, Pacific Area Trip File.

"However, it didn't have": ER, "Our Boys in the Southwest Pacific."

Improvised urinals: John Berglund, interview by G. Kurt Piehler and Scott Carroll, April 9, 1988, transcript, Rutgers Oral History Archives, New Brunswick, NJ, https://oralhistory .rutgers.edu/alphabetical-index/interviewees/30-interview -html-text/720-berglund-john.

was taken down: "Society: Jachris," *Bulletin* (Sydney), October 20, 1943.

"Marine, you die!": Richard Wheeler, *A Special Valor: The U.S. Marines and the Pacific War* (Edison, NJ: Castle Books, 1996), 104.

"This is going to be": Richard Tregaskis, *Guadalcanal Diary* (New York: Modern Library, 2000), 19.

predicted by: Linda Kush, *The Rice Paddy Navy: U.S. Sailors Undercover in China: Espionage and Sabotage Behind Japanese Lines During World War II* (Oxford, UK: Osprey, 2012), 139.

"Unless the Japs": Tregaskis, *Guadalcanal Diary*, 28.

"I walked among": Tregaskis, *Guadalcanal Diary*, 36.

"prize of the": Tregaskis, *Guadalcanal Diary*, 44.

"God knows": Halsey and Bryan, *Admiral Halsey's Story*, 113.

used ruses: "Marines in Solomons Reveal Tricks of Foe," *New York Times*, September 12, 1942.

"a typical night": F. Tillman Durdin, "It's Never Dull on Guadalcanal," *New York Times*, September 18, 1942.

"Life is reduced": Durdin, "It's Never Dull on Guadalcanal."

"We were told": "Guadalcanal Foes Quitting in Disgust," *New York Times*, February 4, 1943.

"were not worth": Johnson, *Pacific Campaign in World War II*, 288.

"But then the fight": ER, "My Day," September 23, 1943.

"As you look at the crosses": ER, "My Day," September 23, 1943.

"a stinking, muddy" and subsequent quotes: "Guadalcanal Is Transformed, With Stores, Roads, Food Replacing Mud and Misery," *New York Times*, June 24, 1943.

"The chance of that": Lash, *World of Love*, 31.

"For me it was": Lash, *Eleanor and Franklin*, 689.

"She kissed": U.S. Congressional Record, Proceedings and Debates of the 78th Congress First Session, Volume 89, Part 6, July 7, 1943, to October 20, 1943, 8183.

"kissed her radical": "First Lady's Pacific Tour Burned Up Much Precious Gasoline—and Pegler," *Burlington (VT) Daily News*, October 20, 1943.

"Mrs. Roosevelt and the Reds": *Richmond Times-Dispatch*, July 25, 1941.

"Eleanor's tax-the-rich pals": Warren Hall, "Eleanor's Tax-the-Rich Pals May Wed," *Daily News* (New York), August 2, 1943.

"The poor General": Lash, *Eleanor and Franklin*, 689.

"a legendary figure": Lash, *Eleanor and Franklin*, 689.

"I gulped and said": Lash, *Eleanor and Franklin*, 690.

"I don't get any mail": ER, "My Day," May 11, 1942.

Morale Corps: Marguerite Higgins, "Women at Home Keep Up Morale of Reform-School Boys in Army," *New York Herald Tribune*, November 28, 1943.

her invitation: Cecil Peterson's account of the visit is from the Cecil Peterson collection on the Tuskegee Airmen (MS 100), Box 9, Folder 11, Special Collections and University Archives, University of California, Riverside, CA.

"simply couldn't get": Higgins, "Women at Home."

"take a peek": Lash, *Eleanor and Franklin*, 689.

"Between them they": F. Barrows Colton, "Weather Fights and Works for Man," *National Geographic* 84, no. 6 (December 1943): 641.

"Lucky that": Lash, *Eleanor and Franklin*, 690.

"disregarding the speed limit": Lash, *Eleanor and Franklin*, 690.

"Air raid!": ER, "My Day," September 24, 1943.

"rather tense": ER, *This I Remember*, 308.

"to change the": Diary of Trip to Southwest Pacific, 1943, Pacific Area Trip File.

"Hospitals and cemeteries": Diary of Trip to Southwest Pacific, 1943, Pacific Area Trip File.

"She must have": Lash, *Eleanor and Franklin*, 690.

Chapter 15: The Real Tragedy

"This visit to the Pacific": "Report to the Nation," *Honolulu Star-Bulletin*, September 21, 1943.

received a Navy Cross: "James Roosevelt Gets Navy Cross; 15 Other Marines Honored for Raid," *New York Times*, January 14, 1943.

special forces unit: U.S. Marine Raider Association (website), accessed April 14, 2022, https://www.marineraiderassociation .org.

"How I wish": ER, "My Day," September 27, 1943.

"Out here with": Diary of Trip to Southwest Pacific, 1943, Pacific Area Trip File.

the planned route: "Top Secret Dispatches."

"Yes, Ma'am" and subsequent quotes: The description of this encounter is compiled from numerous sources, including ER's Pacific trip diary; *Autobiography of Eleanor Roosevelt*; newspaper accounts; and the typed copy of an article ER wrote for *This Week* magazine in January 1944 titled "Our Wounded Boys," Speech and Article File, 1944 and undated, ER Papers.

"Science has": ER, "Our Boys in the Southwest Pacific."

"after the war": "First Lady Urges Help for Maimed," *New York Times*, September 22, 1943.

"Next to our ammunition": "Blood Plasma Is Like Gift from Heaven," *Barre (VT) Daily Times*, March 30, 1943.

"the easiest service": ER, "My Day," September 26, 1951.

"I would like": ER, "My Day," September 28, 1943.

"to have the dust": ER, "My Day," September 28, 1943.

"for those who have": Gene Ward, "Luxurious Royal Hawaiian Hotel Becomes Navy Rest Resort—at Only 25 Cents Per Week," *Daily Herald* (Provo, UT), June 16, 1943.

"We think of it": Ward, "Luxurious Royal Hawaiian Hotel."

"The boys were": Mead, *Tell the Folks Back Home*, 234–35.

submarines: "Experiencing War: Stories from the Veterans History Project," Library of Congress, accessed April 14, 2022, https://www.loc.gov/vets/stories/ex-war-submarines.html; "Submarines before Nuclear Power: Submarines in World War II," National Museum of American History, accessed April 14, 2022, https://americanhistory.si.edu/subs/history/subsbeforenuc/ww2/.

"I have watched": Ward, "Luxurious Royal Hawaiian Hotel."

"not even": Mead, *Tell the Folks Back Home*, 235.

"wholly inaccurate": William Ewing, "Mrs. Roosevelt Pays Tribute to Work of Youths in This War," *Honolulu Star-Bulletin*, September 21, 1943.

"she seemed to": "Mrs. Roosevelt First President's Wife to Visit This Territory," *Honolulu Star-Bulletin*, September 21, 1943.

"meant men only": Virginia Bennett Hill and Gwenfread E. Allen, "Girl Reporters of Star-Bulletin Have Their Day with First Lady," *Honolulu Star-Bulletin*, September 21, 1943.

Honolulu Academy of Arts: Now called the Honolulu Museum of Arts.

"something was brewing": Hill and Allen, "Girl Reporters."

one hundred men waited: ER, "My Day," July 7, 1944.

a predetermined plan: Lesa Griffith, "Remembering Dec 7: The Museum's Ultimate Disaster Plan," Honolulu Museum of Art, December 5, 2016, http://blog.honoluluacademy.org /remembering-dec-7-the-museums-ultimate-disaster-plan/.

topped one hundred thousand: Lincoln Leung, "The Wide Horizon: Hawaii and Defense," *Christian Science Monitor*, November 19, 1941.

"The Army and Navy": Bob Dye, ed., *Hawaii Chronicles III: World War Two in Hawaii, from the pages of* Paradise of the Pacific (Honolulu: University of Hawaii Press, 2000), 13.

third annual drill: "Flares Instead of Explosives Drop as Hawaii Tests Blackout," *Christian Science Monitor*, May 22, 1941.

"JAPANESE MAY": Dye, *Hawaii Chronicles III*, 14.

"Japan Gives": W. J. Holmes, *Double-Edged Secrets: U.S. Naval Intelligence Operations in the Pacific During World War II* (Annapolis, MD: Bluejacket Books, 2012), 27.

"in either Siberia": *Pearl Harbor Attack: Hearings before the Joint Committee on the Investigation of the Pearl Harbor Attack* (Washington, DC: U.S. Government Printing Office, 1946), 560.

Hitler's tactic: "Japan Opens War on U.S.; Hawaii Is Attacked, Bombed," *Washington C.H. (OH) Record-Herald*, December 7, 1941.

Battleship Row: "Battleship Row," Pearl Harbor National Memorial, National Park Service, accessed April 14, 2022, https://www.nps.gov/perl/learn/historyculture/battleship-row.htm.

"I was numbed": Edward C. Raymer, *Descent into Darkness: Pearl Harbor, 1941: A Navy Diver's Memoir* (Annapolis, MD: Naval Institute Press, 2012), 15.

Forty-nine civilians: "Civilian Casualties," Pearl Harbor National Memorial, National Park Service, accessed April 14, 2022, https://www.nps.gov/perl/learn/historyculture/civilian-casualties.htm.

Margaret Lutz quotes: Korson, *At His Side*, 8.

"like any European": Joseph C. Harsch, "Blackouts Find Honolulu Ready for Any Challenge," *Christian Science Monitor*, December 15, 1941.

February 1942 and **120,000:** "Executive Order 9066," FDRL, https://www.fdrlibrary.org/executive-order-9066.

practices and restrictions: Schneider and Schneider, *World War II: An Eyewitness History*, 242.

"making a great hit": ER, "My Day," September 25, 1943.

"about the powers": Maurice Evans, *All This—And Evans Too: A Memoir* (Columbia: University of South Carolina Press, 1987), 163.

Judith Anderson quotes: Tamara Andreeva, "Miss Anderson Cheers Boys in Hawaii," *Christian Science Monitor*, January 4, 1944.

"I found out": Andreeva, "Miss Anderson Cheers Boys."

"It turned out": Desley Deacon, *Judith Anderson: Australian Star: First Lady of the American Stage* (Melbourne: Kerr, 2019), 260.

"more overwhelming": Deacon, *Judith Anderson*, 262.

"the blow had fallen": ER, "My Day," December 8, 1941.

between the ship: The *Oklahoma* was turned over and secured by mid-June and came afloat in November 1943; "Salvage of USS Oklahoma, 1942–1944," Naval History and Heritage Command, accessed April 14, 2022, https://www.history. navy.mil/our-collections/photography/wars-and-events/world -war-ii/pearl-harbor-raid/post-attack-ship-salvage/salvage -of-uss-oklahoma—1942–1944.html.

a memorial overlooking: Location of memorial and text confirmed via email with staff at Pearl Harbor National Memorial.

Epilogue

"The Pacific trip": ER, *This I Remember*, 313.

as exhausted as: Diary of Trip to Southwest Pacific, 1943, Pacific Area Trip File.

"As long as she": Lash, *World of Love*, 81.

"soul-stirring": ER, *This I Remember*, 313.

"tremendous obligation": Roosevelt, "War Bonds Radio Broadcast."

"If we do not": *Autobiography of Eleanor Roosevelt*, 261–62.

"There is one great": ER, "My Day," June 26, 1944.

"Through the years": ER, "Women at the Peace Conference," *Reader's Digest*, April 1944, 48–49.

"How Women May": "Women Ask Place in Peace Councils," *New York Times*, June 15, 1944.

"A United Nations organization": Bess Furman, "Mrs. Roosevelt Urges Waiting for All Facts Before Forming Opinion on Reich's Future," *New York Times*, April 13, 1945.

"The story is over": "Says 'Story Is Over,'" *Knoxville News-Sentinel*, April 21, 1945.

"would like to see": "Mrs. Roosevelt in Rockhampton," *Central Queensland Herald*, September 16, 1943.

"Recognition of the": "Universal Declaration of Human Rights," United Nations, accessed April 14, 2022, https://www.un.org /en/about-us/universal-declaration-of-human-rights.

"You have rendered": Steve Neal, ed., *Eleanor and Harry: The Correspondence of Eleanor Roosevelt and Harry S. Truman* (New York: Citadel, 2004), 161.

"a woman who has": Ewing, "Mrs. Roosevelt Pays Tribute."

Photo Insert

News reports estimated and **staking out:** "Sydney Welcomes Mrs. Roosevelt: 20,000 Acclaim President's Wife," *The Daily Telegraph*, September 8, 1943.

"I have the greatest": ER, "American Women in the War."

from Fort Worth: ER, "The Red Cross in the South Seas," 30.

INDEX

A

Air Force Victorettes, 179
airplane nose art, 199, 204
air raids, 77–78, 181–182, 215–216
Air Transport Command, 14, 93
air travel, 3–16
    Eleanor's embrace of, 3, 4–7
    Pacific trip and, 13–15, 93,
        203–204
    risks of, 12–15, 46
Aitutaki, 57, 58–59
Aleutians, 64
Allen, Gwenfread E., 222–224
Allenswood Academy, 109–110
Allied Services Club, 104
American Red Cross
    in Australia, 38, 179–180,
        185–186
    clubs run by, 103–104, 185–186

Eleanor and, 9–11, 37–39, 62,
    96, 112–113
founding, 10
in Honolulu, Hawaii, 222–223,
    224, 225
in New Zealand, 38, 103–104
services for troops, 38–39
in South Pacific, 38–39, 62,
    162–164, 220
American Samoa, 59–63
American servicemen. *See also*
    hospital visits; South Pacific
in Australia, 105, 128, 141,
    147–149, 182–186
Black soldiers, 57, 123, 182–
    186, 213–214
cultural clashes and, 105
eagerness for news from home,
    41–42

Eleanor's interactions with, 50–54, 147–149

favorable effect of Eleanor's visits on, 43, 56, 94–96, 130–131, 192

jungle warfare and, 174–177, 179–180

malicious rumors about Eleanor among, 127–129

in New Zealand, 86, 88, 90–91, 99–100, 101–106, 117–118, 127–128

postwar support for, 52–55, 219–220, 235–237

reality of conditions for, 31–33, 42, 177–179

recreation/entertainment for, 35–36, 38, 39, 62, 103–104, 229–232

Red Cross services for, 38–39

sacrifices of, 76–77

World War I and, 52–53, 112, 113

American servicewomen, 60–61, 124, 154–157, 161–162

American Youth Congress, 212

Anderson, Judith, 229–232

Anderson, Margaret, 160

Anderson, Marian, 121

Arizona, USS, 226, 227

Army Air Forces, U.S., 123, 199, 214–215

Army, U.S., 156–157, 161–162, 167–168, 182–184

Arundel Island, 193–194

Auckland, New Zealand, 15, 85–97, 127–132

Australia, 87

American Red Cross in, 38, 179–180, 185–186

American servicemen in, 105, 128, 141, 147–149, 182–186

Brisbane, 177, 185–186

Cairns, 177

Canberra, 133–147

diplomatic fracas before Eleanor's visit to, 72–73

Mackay, 14–15, 179–180

Melbourne, 147–152, 159–160, 183

Rockhampton, 167–168, 177

Sydney, 133–134, 160–161, 162, 184

threats to security of, 21, 88, 89, 139–142, 169, 181

Townsville, 180–183, 185

women's war efforts in, 136, 151–153, 160–161, 181

Australian Army Nursing Service, 160–161

Australian Red Cross, 152

Australian War Memorial, 139

Australian Women's Army Service, 152–153

Axis Sally, 129

B

B-24 bomber-to-transport planes, 13–15

Barton, Clara, 10

Berle, Milton, 120

Bethune, Mary McLeod, 121

"Bill" (soldier killed at Buna), 178–179

Black Americans
  civil rights advocacy, xiv, 186, 120–123
  soldiers, 57, 123, 182–186, 213–214
  women, 154–155

blood donation program, 220

bonus army veterans, 52–53

Bora Bora, 45, 48–55

Bottcher, Herman, 173, 199

Brisbane, Australia, 177, 185–186

Buna, 169–179, 199

C

Cairns, Australia, 177

California, USS, 227

Canberra, Australia, 133–147

Canton Island, 14, 61, 218

cartoons, 79, 100

Carver, George Washington, 185–186

casualties, 25, 61–62, 103, 178–179, 209–210

Catholic Church, 157

Catt, Carrie Chapman, 158

Cecil Red Cross Club, 103–104

censorship, 42–43, 46–48, 178–179, 182–183, 184, 195

Centaur (hospital ship), 160–161

Chaney, Mayris, 8

Chiang Kai-shek, Madame, 11–12

Christmas Island, 29–43, 57, 94, 218–219

Chung, Margaret "Mom Chung," 8–9

Churchill, Winston, xii–xiii, 2–3, 63–64, 89–90, 132, 139–141, 142, 159

Civilian Conservation Corps, 53

civil rights advocacy, xiv, 120–123, 186

clubs, service, 104, 185–186

coal mine visit, xi, 100

Coney Island (film), 35

Cook Islands, 47–48, 57

Coral Sea, 142, 169

"Cousin Susie," 111

Coyne, Bill, 214

C. S. Hammond & Co., 20

Cuhel, Frank J., 143

Cummings, Ridgely, 59

Cunningham, Arthur, 39, 41

Curtin, John, 139–145

D

Daughters of the American Revolution, 120–121

Davis, Norman, 10, 62
deaths, 25, 61–62, 103, 178–179,
    209–210
Dennan, Rangitīaria, 115–116, 120
disabilities, soldiers with, 219–220
Dixon, Travis, 184
Doolittle, James, 71
"Doolittle raid," 71
Dr. Carver Club, 185–186
Durno, George, 131–132

E

Earhart, Amelia, 3, 5, 6, 12–13
Efate, 192–193, 195–196
Eichelberger, Emmeline, 172
Eichelberger, Robert, 42, 72–73,
    146, 168, 171–174
Eisenhower, Dwight D., 53
Elizabeth, Queen of England, xii,
    58–59, 135
England. *See* Great Britain
Enterprise, USS, 70
entertainment for troops, 35–36,
    38, 39, 62, 103–104, 229–232
Espiritu Santo, 200–202, 217–218
Europe-first strategy, 142
Evans, Maurice, 230

F

FBI, 212, 228–229
Fiji archipelago, 60, 63–64
First Lady role, x–xiii
Flight 246, 186

"Flying Senators," 7
Flying Tigers, 8
Fraser, Janet, 105, 107–108
Fraser, Peter, 89–90, 100, 105, 120

G

gender equality, 157–158
George VI, King of England, xii,
    135
German prisoners of war, letters
    of, 64
Germany, 74, 77–78, 87, 88. *See
    also* Nazis
"Germany First" policy, 142
GI Bill of Rights, 236
GIs. *See* American servicemen
Goebbels, Joseph, 125
Grable, Betty, 35
Great Britain, xii–xiii, 21, 46, 56,
    76, 77–78, 96, 139, 185. *See also*
    Churchill, Winston
Grew, Joseph, 225
Guadalcanal, 106
    battle for, 22–25, 72, 200–201,
        205–210
    "Cactus" code name, 207
    Eleanor's arrival and tour of,
        ix–x, 203–216
    Eleanor's determination to
        visit, xiii, 25–26, 67–68,
        74–79, 132
    Halsey's decision to let
        Eleanor visit, 191–195

Red Cross in, 38, 162–163,
        220
Guadalcanal Diary (Tregaskis),
        24
Guess Where 2 (transport plane), 7

H

Hall, Mary, 109
Halsey, William F. "Bull"
    battle for Guadalcanal and,
        23–24, 69, 72
    Eleanor's visit to Guadalcanal
        and, 67–68, 74, 191–195,
        203, 212–213
    Eleanor's visit to New
        Caledonia and, 65, 191–195
    family background and career,
        69–72
    personal woes, 68–69
    provisions for Eleanor's
        Pacific trip, 26–27, 46, 50
    tapped as commander of the
        South Pacific forces, 23–24,
        69, 72
Hamilton Army Airfield, 9, 13
Harlem Week, 121–122
Hawaii. *See* Honolulu, Hawaii
Hickam Field, 27
Hill, Virginia Bennett, 222–224
Hirohito, Emperor of Japan, 18
Hitler, Adolf, 87, 125
hongi greeting, 115–116, 120
Hong Kong, 140

Honolulu Academy of Arts,
        222–223
Honolulu, Hawaii
    Eleanor's trip from San
        Francisco to, 13, 17–28
    final stop on Eleanor's Pacific
        trip, 220–233
    Pearl Harbor, 17–19, 27, 49,
        70, 89, 224–233
    Red Cross in, 222–223, 224,
        225
Hoover, J. Edgar, 212
hospital ships, 160–161
hospital visits, 37, 61, 101–102,
        112, 113, 195–199
Hotel Cecil, 103–104
Howard, Archie, 212, 213
Howard, Mary Ferebee, 163–164
Howe, Louis, 114
Human Rights Commission, 238
humor, 198–199
Hyde Park, 58–59

I

Ilma, Viola, 213, 214

J

Japan, 20–21, 64, 160, 193–194.
    See also Pearl Harbor
    battle for Guadalcanal and,
        22–25, 72, 200–201, 205–
        210
    Efate and, 195–196

Halsey's bombing raid on, 71
New Guinea campaign and,
    140, 169–183
plan to seize South Pacific
    islands, 60
radio propaganda and, 129
threat to New Zealand and
    Australia and, 21, 89–91,
    139–142, 169, 181
Japanese Americans, detention of,
    228–229
jeeps, 40
Johnson, Lyndon B., 183
journalists. *See* media
jungle warfare, 174–177, 179–180

L
Lamour, Dorothy, 32
Lash, Joseph "Joe," 26, 79, 93,
    210–215, 216
LB-30s, 13–15
League of Nations, 158
League of Women Voters, 114,
    158
Life magazine, 177–179
Lindbergh, Charles, 3
Lutz, Margaret, 228

M
MacArthur, Douglas, 61, 72–73,
    141–142, 146–147, 170–171,
    174, 183
Macbeth (play), 229–230, 231

Mackay, Australia, 14–15, 179–
    180
Madame Chiang Kai-shek, 11–12
Majestic Theatre, speech at, 107–
    109
Makin Island, 218
malaria, 101–102
malingas, 59
Manahi, Haane Te Rauawa, 119
Māori, 115–120
Map Room, 102–103
Marines, U.S., 22–25, 59–60,
    99–100, 106, 123, 127–129,
    155–156, 205–210
Marshall, George, 54, 103, 156
Martin, Hershey, 8
Maugham, W. Somerset, 60
McCormick, Robert R., 148–149
Mead, James, 7, 201–202, 221, 222
media
    coverage of Eleanor's trip, 92–
        95, 120, 211, 222–224
    Eleanor's press conferences
        for, 91–92, 136–137
    interest in Eleanor's personal
        life, 1–3
    war front, reporting on, 24–
        25, 177–179
    wartime secrecy and
        censorship, 46–48, 178–
        179, 182–183
Melbourne, Australia, 147–152,
    159–160, 183

Mercer, Lucy, 113
Michener, James, 48–49, 200
Midway Island, 71, 142, 209
"Milk Run, the," 45–46
Miller, Hugh Barr, 193–194
Millett, Ruth, 164
Mitchell, H. Tai, 119–120
Montgomery, Thomas S., 38
movies and movie theaters, 35–36
Mussolini, Benito, 54
"My Day" (newspaper column), 1,
    2–3, 47–48

N

National Association for the
    Advancement of Colored
    People (NAACP), 121
National Consumers League, 111
National Geographic, 50
National Urban League, 121
Naval Construction Battalion
    ("Seabees"), 163, 200
Naval Hospital, 112, 113
Navy Cross, 193–194, 218
Navy Hydrographic Office, 49–50
Navy Nurse Corps, 60–61
Navy, U.S., 22–23, 123
Navy Women's Reserve, U.S.
    (WAVES), 8
Nazis, 20, 21, 49, 64, 123–126,
    129. See also Germany
Nevada, USS, 226
New Britain, 140

New Caledonia, 46, 67–81, 163–
    164, 191–195, 199
New Georgia, 64, 67–68, 191, 193
New Guinea, 140, 146–147, 162,
    168–169, 231
news reporting. See media
New York to San Francisco trip,
    1–16
New Zealand
    American servicemen in, 86,
        88, 90–91, 99–100, 101–
        106, 117–118, 127–128
    Auckland, 15, 85–97, 127–
        132
    Red Cross in, 38, 103–104
    Rotorua, 115–126
    threats to security of, 21,
        87–91
    Wellington, 99–114
    women's war efforts in, 88,
        107–108, 131, 153
Ngārimu, Te Moana-nui-a-Kiwi,
    118–119
Nimitz, Chester W., 69, 71, 72
99th Pursuit Squadron, 123

O

Office of Censorship, 42, 47, 179
Office of Civilian Defense, 75,
    224
Oklahoma, USS, 226, 227, 232–
    233
One World (Willkie), 29

Operation FS, 60
Operation Watchtower, 22–25
Over Our Coffee Cups (radio
    show), 19

P

Pacific Flight 321, 46
Pacific Times (magazine), 94
Pago Pago, 59–60
Papua New Guinea, 168, 169–
    179
Paris (rest camp), 41
Patrol Bombing Squadron 104
    ("The Buccaneers"), 204
peace, 101, 108–109, 158–159,
    237–239
Pearl Harbor, 17–19, 27, 49, 70,
    89, 224–233
Pegler, Westbrook, 93–94, 157,
    211
Penrhyn Island, 47–48, 57
Peterson, Cecil, 26, 213–214
Philippines, 30–31, 76–77, 141–
    142
Pickering, Roy, 15
Port Moresby, 146–147, 169
post-traumatic stress disorder
    (PTSD), 197
Post, Wiley, 12
Pratt, Trude, 79, 211, 212
Prayer Book for Soldiers and
    Sailors, A, 102
President Johnson, SS, 31

propaganda, 123–126, 128, 129
PTSD (post-traumatic stress
    disorder), 197

R

Rabaul, 140
racism/racial tensions, xiv, 57,
    120–123, 154–155, 182–186
Raymer, Edward C., 227, 232
recreation/entertainment for
    troops, 35–36, 38, 39, 62, 103–
    104, 229–232
Red Cross. *See* American Red
    Cross
religious services, 102
Return to Paradise (Michener),
    48
Rickenbacker, Eddie, 61
Rockhampton, Australia, 167–
    168, 177
Rogers, Edith Nourse, 156
Rogers, Will, 6–7, 12
Roosevelt, Eleanor
    childhood and youth, 109–
        111
    civil rights advocacy, xiv, 120–
        123, 186
    communications with
        Franklin during trip, 145
    courage of, 77–78
    criticism of, xii, xiii–xiv, 75,
        92–94, 95, 96–97, 148–149,
        157

depicted on nose art of plane, 199

desire to contribute to war effort, 74–76

embrace of air travel by, 3, 4–7

First Lady role and travels, x–xiii, xiv, 6–7

Franklin's approval of Pacific trip by, xiii, 25–26, 143–144

goals, following Pacific trip, 235–239

Halsey's change of heart about, 191–195

hospital visits by, 37, 61, 101–102, 112, 113, 195–199

independence of, x, 34–35, 63–64

interactions with enlisted men, 50–54, 147–149

island commanders' responses to presence of, 50–51, 57–59

as "listening post" for Franklin, x–xi

MacArthur's brush-off of, 146–147

malicious rumors among troops about, 127–129

marriage to Franklin, 111–114

military service of sons and, 79–80

Nazi animosity toward, 124–126

personal costs of journey, xiii, xv, 235

planes used for travel during Pacific trip, 13–15, 93, 203–204

postwar peace and, 101, 108–109, 237–239

press conferences held by, 91–92, 136–137, 222

public/media reactions to Pacific trip, 92–97

reasons for taking Pacific trip, xiv–xv

recognition of troops' sacrifices, 76–77

Red Cross and, 9–11, 37–39, 62, 96, 112–113

as seasoned traveler, 11–12

secrecy surrounding travel of, xii, 1–3, 26–28, 42–43, 46–48, 186

soldiers' favorable responses to, 43, 56, 94–96, 130–131, 192

uniform worn by, 9–11

veterans, support for, 52–55, 219–220, 235–237

women's suffrage and, 158

women's war work, support for, 124, 131, 151–165

World War I and, 112–113

Roosevelt, Elliott, 78, 80
Roosevelt, Franklin D., 3, 58–59,
    62–63, 76, 87
    airplane designated for, 7
    Black Americans and, 121,
        122, 185
    death of, 237
    Eleanor as "listening post"
        for, x–xi
    Eleanor's Pacific trip and, xiii,
        25–26, 143–145
    marriage to Eleanor, 111–114
    plane travel by, 4
    polio and, 4, 34, 114
    preparations before entry into
        war, 17–18, 74–75
    soldiers' welfare, concern for,
        197
    use of women in war effort
        and, 154
    veterans and, 52–53, 54–55
    wartime leadership of, 17–20,
        22, 89–90, 102–103, 142,
        229
    women's suffrage, support for,
        158
    World War I and, 112, 113
Roosevelt, Franklin, Jr., 80
Roosevelt, James, 25–26, 64, 80,
    218
Roosevelt, John, 80
Roosevelt, Theodore, 34
Rotorua, New Zealand, 115–126

Royal Hawaiian, 221–222
rumors, false, 123–124, 127–129
Ryan, Coletta, 137, 162–163, 204

S
San Francisco
    Eleanor's trip from New York
        to, 1–16
    Eleanor's trip to Honolulu
        from, 13, 17–28
Saratoga, USS, 68–69
Savage, Ellen, 160–161
Schenck, Edgar C., 223
Seabees, 163, 200
Sears, Harry, 204
2nd Marine Raider Battalion, 79,
    218
secrecy, xii, 1–3, 26–28, 42–43,
    46–48, 186
Secret Service, 138
service clubs, 104, 185–186
servicemen. *See* American
    servicemen
Servicemen's Readjustment Act,
    236
servicewomen, 60–61, 124, 154–
    157, 160–165
Sherrod, Robert, 183
"short snorters," 27
Silverstream, 101–102
Singapore, 21, 89–90, 99, 140–
    141
soldiers. *See* American servicemen

Solomon Islands campaign, 22–25

South Pacific. *See also* Guadalcanal; Honolulu, Hawaii

Aitutaki, 57, 58–59

Bora Bora, 45, 48–55

Christmas Island, 29–43, 57, 94, 218–219

Efate, 192–193, 195–196

Espiritu Santo, 200–202, 217–218

Halsey's provisions for Eleanor's trip to, 26–27, 46, 50

Halsey tapped as commander of forces in, 23–24, 69, 72

island commanders' responses to Eleanor's visits, 50–51, 57–59

jungle warfare and, 174–177, 179–180

"Milk Run" route, 45–46

New Caledonia, 46, 67–81, 163–164, 191–195, 199

New York to San Francisco leg of trip, 1–16

Penrhyn Island, 47–48, 57

Red Cross in, 38–39, 62, 162–164, 220

San Francisco to Honolulu leg of trip, 13, 17–28

secrecy surrounding Eleanor's trip to, 1–3, 26–28, 46–48

Tutuila, 59–63

Viti Levu, 63–64

Wallis Island, 218

Souvestre, Marie, 110

Sparks, Chauncey, 122

Stavisky, Samuel E., 128–129

Stimson, Henry, 54, 61, 123, 185

Strock, George, 178

Strong, USS, 193

submariners, 221–222

Sweet Rosie O'Grady (film), 35

Sydney, Australia, 133–134, 160–161, 162, 184

T

Tabu (film), 50

Tales of the South Pacific (Michener), 200

Tennessee, USS, 227

They Were Expendable (White), 76–77

13th Troop Carrier Squadron ("Thirsty 13th"), 199

Thompson, Jimmy, 116, 120

Thompson, Malvina "Tommy," 11–12, 15, 78

Tilden, Edna R., 60–61

Tokyo Rose, 129

Townsville, Australia, 180–183, 185

Tregaskis, Richard, 24, 205–207

Truman, Harry S., 238

Tuskegee Army Flying School,
    123, 213
Tutuila, 59–63

U
United Kingdom. *See* Great
    Britain
United Nations, 237–239
United States, xiv–xv, 22–25, 120–
    123, 153–158. *See also* Pearl
    Harbor
Universal Declaration of Human
    Rights, 238
Utah, USS, 70

V
Vandegrift, Alexander, 24–25
veterans, support for, 52–55, 219–
    220, 235–237
Viti Levu, 63–64

W
WAAC (Women's Army
    Auxiliary Corps), 124, 156–157
Wakefield, USS, 99–100
Wallis Island, 218
War Department, 14, 30–31, 40, 73
WAVES (U.S. Navy Women's
    Reserve), 8
weather forecasting, 214–215
Wellington, New Zealand, 99–114
West Virginia, USS, 226, 227
White, Robert, 186–187

White, Walter, 121
Willkie, Wendell, 29
women-only press conferences,
    91–92
Women's Army Auxiliary Corps
    (WAAC), 124, 156–157
Women's Army Corps, 156
Women's Land Army, 136, 152–
    153
Women's Land Service, 153
women's role in world peace, 158–
    159, 237
women's suffrage, 158
Women's War Service Auxiliary,
    88, 108
women, war work of, 151–165.
    See also American Red Cross
    Australia and, 136, 151–153,
        160–161, 181
    Eleanor's support for, 124,
        131, 151–165
    military, roles in, 60–61, 154–
        157, 160–165, 181
    New Zealand and, 88, 107–
        108, 131, 153
    United States and, 153–157
World War I, 52–53, 70, 108,
    112–113, 139, 158
World War II, xiv–xv, 22–25. *See
    also* Pearl Harbor

Y
Youth Morale Corps, 213–214

ABOUT THE AUTHOR

Shannon McKenna Schmidt is the coauthor of *Novel Destinations: A Travel Guide to Literary Landmarks from Jane Austen's Bath to Ernest Hemingway's Key West* and *Writers Between the Covers: The Scandalous Romantic Lives of Legendary Literary Casanovas, Coquettes, and Cads.* In addition, she has written for *National Geographic Traveler, Shelf Awareness,* NPR.org, and other websites and publications.

From 2010 through 2017, Shannon traveled full-time—first in the United States by RV and then backpacking around the globe. She now lives in Hoboken, New Jersey.

www.shannonmckennaschmidt.com